Working Free

Working Free

The Origins and Impact of New Zealand's Employment Contracts Act

ELLEN J. DANNIN

AUCKLAND UNIVERSITY PRESS

To Emma Simone

First published 1997
Auckland University Press
University of Auckland
Private Bag 92019
Auckland

© Ellen J. Dannin 1997

This book is copyright. Apart from fair dealing for the purpose of private study, research, criticism, or review, as permitted under the Copyright Act, no part may be reproduced by any process without the prior permission of Auckland University Press.

ISBN 1 86940 174 3

Front cover photographs: New Zealand Engineering and Godfrey Boehnke

Typeset by Auckland University Press
Printed by GP Print, Wellington

Contents

Abbreviations		vi
Acknowledgements		vii
1.	Introduction: The Present . . . The Future	1

Part I: How the Employment Contracts Act Came to Be

2.	The Past: A Sketch of New Zealand Labour Law up to 1987	13
3.	The Campaign for Freedom	26
4.	The Campaign to Eliminate the LRA, 1987–1990	39
5.	The 1990 Election Campaign—Unions Prepare for Change	62
6.	Drafting and Introducing the Employment Contracts Bill	88
7.	In the Shadow of the ECA	115
8.	The General Strike That Never Was	136
9.	The Debate in Parliament	152

Part II: Life Under the Employment Contracts Act

10.	The ECA and Its Economic and Social Impacts	167
11.	An Introduction to ECA Bargaining	186
12.	Bargaining and Bargaining Representatives	194
13.	Party status and Workplace Access	214
14.	Contracting and Duress	230
15.	Impasse and Partial Lockouts	252
16.	Collectivity, Free Choice, and Schism	267
17.	Multi-Employer Bargaining	287
18.	Who Owns the Job? Work, Unions, Society, Law, and Justice	304

Statutory Citations	316
Cases Cited	317
Index	319

Abbreviations

CECs	collective employment contracts
CEWU	Communication and Energy Workers Union
CTU	New Zealand Council of Trade Unions
IC & A Act	Industrial Conciliation and Arbitration Act, 1894
IECs	individual employment contracts
IMF	International Monetary Fund
LRA	Labour Relations Act, 1987
NLRA	National Labor Relations Act
NUPE	National Union of Public Employees
NZBR	New Zealand Business Roundtable
NZEF	New Zealand Employers Federation
NZEI	New Zealand Educational Institute
OECD	Organisation for Economic Cooperation & Development
PSA	Public Service Association
SWF	Service Workers Federation of Aotearoa
SWU	Service Workers Union of Aorearoa
TUF	New Zealand Trade Union Federation

Acknowledgements

PRODUCING A BOOK DEMONSTRATES THAT ANY ENTERPRISE IS A GROUP effort no matter whose name appears as author. I owe thanks to a number of people and institutions for their support during the years of writing and researching this book. Doing research in a distant country means that the researcher needs financial support to make periodic visits, buy materials, and post materials. The Fund for Labor Relations Studies has made it possible for me to make several return visits to keep abreast of events in New Zealand and to amass what must have become the largest Northern Hemisphere collection of materials on New Zealand labour relations. My school, California Western School of Law, has willingly provided the support that has made the book possible. The Victoria University of Wellington Law Faculty and Industrial Relations Centre and the University of Waikato School of Strategic Management and Leadership also provided office space and other support.

Thanks go to the many individuals and institutions by whose assistance I was able to obtain the materials I used in writing the book. Amongst them are Brian Easton, Raymond Harbridge, John Hughes, the Dan Long Library, Ian McAndrew, the Manufacturing & Construction Workers Union, the New Zealand Business Roundtable, the New Zealand Employers Federation, the New Zealand Engineering Union, the Alexander Turnbull Library, and Richard Whatman.

I would like to thank those who read drafts and made helpful comments, including comments on very early drafts and articles that were eventually incorporated into the final product. Thanks go to Mark Broida, Marion Crain, John Deeks, Brian Easton, Jack Getman, Barrie Gordon, Paul Gudel, George Hagglund, Ali Hebshi, Greg Higgins, John Hughes, Kenneth Klein, Richard Lempert, Diane Nichols, Theodore St. Antoine, and Jackie Slotkin. It is a privilege to have had input from all of you.

In my opinion, the book would not be what it is without its interviews with union officials and others active in the events described here. Not only did the interviewees produce important documents, they also gave me invaluable insights into the events they discussed. I am happy to share their words and their ideas with those who read this book. Those interviewed include Rick Barker, Graeme Clarke, Joris de Bres, Murray French, Maxine Gay, Robyn Haultain, Paul Kimble, Anne Knowles, Hel Loader, Dave Morgan, Rosslyn Noonan, Donna Payne, Francis Wevers, Suze Wilson. I must also mention here the painstaking work by the California Western School of Law faculty support staff who transcribed the tapes—no easy job in the best of circumstances, but especially when one has to grapple with an unfamiliar accent.

A special appreciation is owed to Ali Hebshi for his unfailing support and enthusiasm.

Finally, thanks to Elizabeth Caffin of Auckland University Press and to Simon Cauchi for their efforts in producing this book.

Thank you for all your support along the way.

1

Introduction: The Present... The Future

WHETHER WE REALISE IT OR NOT, THE 1990s ARE THE AGE OF WORK and the worker. It is hard to pick up a newspaper or magazine without seeing the subject of work. We read about the "globalisation" of work or about the impact of technology on work—how work is done, how it will be done, who does it, who will do it, who is hurt and who is helped by these changes.

Work affects our environment in every sense of the word. Having a goal of rising productivity and consumption may mean destroying the environment. Occasionally we read about worldwide unemployment and the end of work. If there is not enough work for the workers available, how will society change in the face of enforced leisure?

We are all desperately dependent on work. Our own jobs—or lack of them—give us our status, our world-view, our friends, our enemies, our opportunities, and our children's opportunities—or lack of them. Adding or subtracting jobs can make communities grow or decline. We care very much about all of this.

When we start to talk about work, the subject soon turns to unions. Many say unions are now dinosaurs, once useful but no longer relevant. Union density rates have declined around the world—more quickly in some countries than in others, but with almost no country immune to the trend. What impact, if any, does this have on us personally?

A fair reading of history shows that it is unions around the world which waged the fights for improved working, social, and living conditions. What would a world without unions be like?

What is the cause and significance of this worldwide decline? What are the value and role of unions? Should we try to reverse their decline, or should we regard their disappearance as an unavoidable artefact of modern society?[1]

Amidst this discussion is a debate about work, unions, society, and law. Does law help or hinder the processes of production? Should laws be enacted to help unions survive? Some ask: Don't unions belong to the old confrontational way of doing things? Aren't we better off with the tools of labour–management cooperation as a way to build a more productive, conflict-free workplace? Should laws place more restrictions on corporations and what they can do to and with jobs? If law is about property, then who owns the job?

The debate in the United States is an example of the range of reform proposals in most developed countries. Some say that employer–union power has swung out of balance because of the way labour laws are applied and enforced.[2] Some propose moving to a system based on individual contracting.[3] Others promote labour reform "based on direct governmental intervention guaranteeing individual rights to employees and substantive protections to unions under labor law, that are designed to alter the power imbalance between employees and employers."[4] Some argue that labour problems are rooted in patriarchal conceptions of power and that only fundamental change based on feminism can empower workers and revitalise labour unions.[5] Suggestions have ranged from major legislative supports for unions[6] to more subtle legislative or regulatory tinkering.[7] Others contend that unions themselves are to blame because they have been "complacent, have lost their sense of mission, have assigned incompetent people to organising, and have failed to adopt organising tactics in response to changing conditions"—problems which cannot be solved by legislative action.[8]

All these proposals assume that there is a connection between outcomes—such as union representation or increased productivity or justice—and law. Some view law as the enemy at the same time as they turn to law for their salvation. The difficulty in untangling these complex social and legal issues is that the social sciences have trouble being scientific in the way the physical sciences are. There are no social science experiments, with control groups and replicability, that can answer these important questions. As a result, discussions about work, unions, and law reform are as passionate as they are speculative.

In the absence of a social science laboratory in which to run experiments testing these contesting theories, New Zealand's Employment Contracts Act has been advanced as offering a model for successful labour law reform based on freedom of the market. When the ECA became law on May 15, 1991, it replaced nearly a century of legalised collective bargaining with a radically new way to set workplace terms.

The ECA was based on neo-liberal ideas that came mainly from the United States and from the University of Chicago School of Law in particular. Under the ECA employment contracts can be individual or collective. A contract is collective if two employees sign it. Unions are not outlawed; they are treated as agents. A union must have current individual authorisations from each employee it claims to represent. Nothing supports union existence or collective action; rather, the system relies on market forces. To the extent possible, the ECA is based on the common law of contracts. In other words, the ECA is a direct repudiation of those labour law systems which support collective action and bargaining, as well as unions, as a means to control workplace relations.

Since becoming law, the ECA has been the focus of widespread global attention. Commonwealth countries, such as Canada, Australia, and the United Kingdom, have enthusiastically watched events in New Zealand. The Canadian media praise New Zealand's liberalisation of its economy as an example Canadians must follow.[9] In early 1994, W5, a Canadian news show, featured New Zealand government and public figures enthusiastic about their path to economic success. Roger Douglas, proponent of the liberal reforms, makes regular speaking tours of Canada and the world. His *Unfinished Business* was at the top of Canadian best-seller lists for weeks.[10] Other Canadians question these optimistic reports and the wisdom of such a course.[11]

The Australian states of Victoria and Western Australia now have their own versions of the ECA: the Employee Relations Act 1992 (Victoria) and the Minimum Conditions of Employment

Act 1993 and the Workplace Agreements Act 1993 (Western Australia). During the 1996 Commonwealth elections an important issue was whether and how much of the ECA would be imported to Australia.

The British papers argue back and forth over New Zealand. On March 13, 1994, for example, the (London) *Observer* expressed confidence that New Zealand's laws would or should be imported to other countries.[12] On the same day, *The Independent* carried a story about New Zealand's rising violent crime, food banks, hunger, and despair.[13] Britain has played host to Roger Douglas numerous times. In March 1996, he and Labour MPs participated in a private policy conference sponsored by the Adam Smith Institute, a free-market think-tank.[14]

Other countries appear on the verge of enacting ECA-inspired laws, including Finland, the Netherlands, Germany, and Sweden.[15] As the Japanese economy has stalled, it too has begun looking at New Zealand and the ECA. In late 1995, Isamu Miyazaki, director general of the Economic Planning Agency, announced his interest in studying New Zealand's reforms and considering adopting them.[16] Interest in the ECA at the highest levels has spread before most of the world even knew it existed. *Unfinished Business* says: "Roger Douglas has travelled as an international consultant advising on privatisation and structural reform in countries as diverse as Russia, Brazil, Mexico, Pakistan, Canada, Peru, Vietnam, China, Australia, South Africa and Singapore."

In the United States proposals have been made for labour law reform similar to the ECA. In 1994, amidst the early fervour for the Contract With America, the Employment Policy Foundation urged labour law reform in terms that recall the campaign waged in New Zealand for the ECA. It called for more flexibility in the workplace to enhance productivity and competitiveness.[17] In April 1996, House Majority Leader Newt Gingrich sent a congressional delegation to study New Zealand.

What can we—New Zealanders and others—gain by studying the ECA now? First, there is an important story to be told about the way the ECA became law. The way it was discussed and the missed opportunities for discussion, the human reactions, the failures and successes, the struggle to do the right and moral thing for society, the struggle to find truth and to act on one's beliefs—all these are part of the ECA story and the story of democracy in the late twentieth century. The enactment of the ECA has as much to do with our support for or opposition to democratic processes and values as about labour law itself.

There is also the central question of the ECA's performance as labour law. Most people—even in New Zealand—know only part of the story. They may have seen reports about economic improvements or the economic crisis in New Zealand and know that these have some relationship to labour law reform. ECA supporters say they are solidly pleased with the law and readily cite statistics and anecdotes to show improved figures for productivity, unemployment, the balance of trade, and the easing of workplace tensions. An opinion poll commissioned by the New Zealand Employers Federation (one of the key supporters of the ECA) sparked off glossy brochures, press conferences, and news stories in February 1996—five years after it became law—because approval for the ECA had risen to 41%.[18]

The ECA's supporters include the International Monetary Fund, the World Bank, and the Organization for Economic Cooperation and Development (OECD)—certainly groups with influence and power in the world. The IMF, for example, credits the ECA with lowering New Zealand unemployment rates.[19]

ECA critics remain strongly opposed to the legislation. They argue that it has created an unequal and unjust society. Even ECA supporters quietly admit to concerns about troubling, less discussed changes in New Zealand and the workplace. In 1993, a parliamentary committee appointed to study the impact of the ECA found the following about how workplace conditions were set:

> [E]vidence received has also shown that some employers are using the removal of compulsory unionism as a way to tell employees less than before about their rights. Witnesses said that, especially in companies where the employer has actively encouraged staff to resign from a union, employers often impose contracts without negotiations. Sometimes these contracts contain scant information about employment conditions. Many witnesses, particularly from service and retail industries, said employers

do not communicate with them about their contracts and frequently intimidate employees into signing contracts with the message that they will be dismissed if they do not.[20]

Other reports suggest that productivity is lagging, that quit rates are very high, that training and skills are inadequate.

Which is it? Is the ECA a good system for labour law—the new, modern way to run a workplace? Is it evil or the product of greedy and powerful forces? Is it more complex than that or somewhere in the middle?

The ECA tells us about the interaction of law and society. New Zealand has made itself into an "experiment" that can give us insights into the impact of law on unions. From 1894 to 1991, New Zealand labour law was one of the most protective of unions and unionisation in the world. Union density was measured at between 60% and 70%. Within the ECA's first year, New Zealand unions lost approximately 50% of their members. Several unions disappeared. As of December 1994, New Zealand's union density was 23%, a drop of 38–47% in three and a half years.[21]

How can freedom do this? Does this mean that, if unions can't exist without props from the state, they are illegitimate institutions, as many have argued? Or is the ECA profoundly anti-union legislation, as others have claimed?

The enactment of the ECA—legislation which transformed a highly protective industrial relations system into one founded on the principles of freedom of contract and unrestrained market forces—is a story of high drama. The ECA was enacted in the face of popular opposition; 500,000 people out of a population of 3.2 million—nearly one-sixth of the inhabitants—demonstrated against it or went on strike against it. Were they right or misguided to have opposed the legislation?

Certainly, the ECA has transformed New Zealand society. The story of the ECA is not all about winners. Union density does not fall so far so quickly with no negative social consequences. There are reports that some wages are very low.[22] Newspapers carry advertisements for jobs at no pay, and hundreds of job seekers have lined up, hoping that eventually the employer will take them on or hoping to gain experience so that a paying job can be found somewhere else. Although it is a food-exporting country, food banks now are a common resource for many newly impoverished New Zealanders. At Christmas 1993, three church officials announced that they did not consider it a sin to steal to feed one's family, the need was so dire. In April 1994, the International Labour Organisation (ILO) found that the ECA violated important labour conventions.

On the other hand, some segments of New Zealand society and even some unions have prospered under the legislation. In addition, some who supported the ECA have actually suffered from its enactment. In short, the ECA's impact is about more than economic figures and theory. It has a human side. Today that is a vitally important story, especially with groups such as the IMF, OECD, and World Bank focusing world attention on the ECA. Roger Douglas and others circle the globe telling the world that they once were socialists but have become converts to a new way of ordering society. No matter where one lives, events in New Zealand are not distant or peripheral.

The story to be told here starts with the efforts of those who advocated transforming New Zealand from a country with socialist leanings to the most unprotected or deregulated country in the world. Slowly they gained converts, including the Labour Party, which began to enact this program in 1984. Many, especially among the unions, failed to notice the changes or did not believe they would come to be. Others saw the danger to themselves and their way of life and tried to prepare and to rally their allies.

So much was claimed for the ECA—good and bad. It has fulfilled these predictions but has also operated in unanticipated ways. Put together, these help us understand the processes of fundamental law reform as they are shaped by and themselves shape society.

Confronting the phenomenon of the ECA means asking difficult questions about the nature of the society we wish to have. In the face of the profound moral and ideological change wrought in New Zealand it means asking questions based not only on economic theory but about issues of morality and justice.

8 WORKING FREE

This, then, is the story of the ECA's intellectual origins; the social and economic exigencies which led to its enactment; how it has functioned; and its economic, social, and legal impact.

Notes
1. See, e.g., Michael Gottesman, "Wither Goest Labor Law: Law and Economics in the Workplace," 100 Yale L.J. 2767 (1991); Werner Sengenberger, "Intensified Competition, Industrial Restructuring and Industrial Relations," 131 Int'l Lab. Rev. 139 (1992).
2. William Cooke, *Union Organizing and Public Policy: Failure to Secure First Contracts*, 144 (1985); Paul Weiler, *Governing the Workplace: The Future of Labor and Employment Law* (1990).
3. See Marion Crain, "Images of Power in Labor Law: A Feminist Deconstruction," 33 Bost. Coll. L. Rev., 481, 525 (1992) for sources.
4. *Id.*, 525–26 (views of Critical Legal Studies theorists).
5. Marion Crain, "Feminism, Labor and Power," 65 S. Cal. L. Rev., 1819 (1992).
6. Katherine Van Wezel Stone, "The Legacy of Industrial Pluralism: The Tension Between Individual Employment Rights and the New Deal Collective Bargaining System," 59 U. Chi. L. Rev., 575, 578–84 (1992).
7. Charles Morris, "Renaissance at the NLRB—Opportunity and Prospect for Non-Legislative Procedural Reform at the Labor Board," 23 Stetson L. Rev. 101 (1993); Thomas Kochan, Harry Katz and Robert McKersie, "The Transformation of American Industrial Relations" (1994); Ellen Dannin, "Labor Law Reform— Is There a Baby in the Bathwater?" 44 Lab. L.J., 626 (1993).
8. Julius Getman, "Ruminations on Union Organizing in the Private Sector," 53 U. Chi. L. Rev., 45 (1986); *Let's Get Moving! Organizing for the '90's* (Lab. Res. Rev. 1991).
9. Rafe Mair, "We Will Be Hearing More of Sir Roger and ACT New Zealand: Let's Hope Canadian Leaders Listen," *Financial Post*, Mar. 10, 1995, at 11; John Schreiner, "Industry Has Thrived in New Zealand's 'Revolution'," *Financial Post*, Aug. 30, 1994, at 11.
10. Jim Levi, "Rogernomics Returns," *Observer*, Mar. 13, 1994, at 6; Murray Dobbin, "Remaking of New Zealand, Part I," *CBC Ideas*, Oct. 12, 1994.
11. Chris Bradshaw, "Ignore the Right! Don't Look to New Zealand for Debt Ideas," *Vancouver Sun*, Feb. 6, 1995, at A8; Roman Cooney, "Contrived Crisis? Debt Load May Have Had Little to Do with New Zealand's Alberta-like Cuts," *Calgary Herald*, May 12, 1994, at A5; Patricia Finn, "New Zealand 'Model' Really a

Mirage," *Ottawa Citizen*, May 19, 1995, at A11; "G-7 Message: Let World's Unemployed Fend for Selves, Chamber Says," *Vancouver Sun*, June 6, 1995; Michael Kane, "Bearing Fruit in Land of Kiwis: New Zealand's Example Could Be Good for Canada," *Vancouver Sun*, May 30, 1994, at D10; Ted White, "New Zealand's Miracle: Labor Law Changes Brought Workers More Freedom, Income and Job Opportunities," *Ottawa Citizen*, May 26, 1995, at A13.

12. Jim Levi, 6; see also David McKie, "And Now for Next Week's News," *Guardian*, Feb. 24, 1995, at T5.
13. Peter Walker, "What Happens When You Scrap the Welfare State?" *Independent*, Mar. 13, 1994, at 17.
14. David Rennie, "Is Labour Falling for Rogernomics?" *Daily Telegraph*, Mar. 18, 1996, at 21.
15. Murray Dobbin, Pt. I; Murray Dobbin, "Remaking of New Zealand, Part II," *CBC Ideas*, Oct. 19, 1994; "New Zealand Now the Model," *Employer*, 2 (Mar. 1994).
16. "EPA Chief Hopes to Learn from N.Z., Australia Deregulation," Kyodo News Service, Japan Economic Newswire, Aug. 22, 1995.
17. "Reassessment of U.S. Employment Law Called for in New Book on Competitiveness," 222 *Daily Lab. Rep.*, Nov. 21, 1994, at D-15.
18. Graeme Hunt, "New Zealand: New Zealanders Back Labour Reforms," *National Business Review*, Feb. 16, 1996.
19. Peter Norman, "IMF Seeks Labour Reform to Cut Europe's Jobless," *Financial Times*, Apr. 21, 1994, at 30.
20. Report of the Labour Committee on the Inquiry into the Effects of the Employment Contracts Act 1991 on the New Zealand Market, 20 (1993).
21. Raymond Harbridge & Anthony Honeybone, *Employment Contracts: Bargaining Trends & Employment Law Update: 1993/1994*, 3 (1994).
22. "NZ Manufacturing Workers Least Paid in West," *Xinhua News Agency*, Aug. 30, 1994.

Part One

How the Employment Contracts Act Came to Be

2

The Past: A Sketch of New Zealand Labour Law up to 1987

NEW ZEALAND BECAME THE FIRST COUNTRY IN THE WORLD TO LEGALISE collective bargaining when it enacted the Industrial Conciliation and Arbitration Act 1894, popularly referred to as the IC & A Act. The IC & A Act's basic framework was retained in numerous revisions for most of the next century.[1] The last of these was the Labour Relations Act 1987 (LRA), which was replaced by the ECA in 1991.[2]

The IC & A Act was born in a tumultuous period for New Zealand. The disastrous impact of economic depression on fledgling industries led to wage undercutting. This in turn led to union militancy and then to such harsh repression that from 1890 to 1894 unions in New Zealand nearly ceased to exist. This changed quickly and dramatically. In 1889, universal male suffrage was enacted, leading to the election of the progressive 1891 Parliament, which enacted woman suffrage in 1893 and the IC & A Act the next year. The IC & A Act removed New Zealand industrial relations from the common law system which was imperilling unions in the United States and Britain.

These events heartened labour reformers for decades after the enactment of the IC & A Act. The IC & A Act inspired at least nine states in the United States to introduce similar legislation.[3]

Not all was positive, however. New Zealand labour law was constricted and controlled unions, as Alan Geare points out:

> There was a desire to foster unions as unions were seen as the best protection for workers. While collective bargaining was

seen as desirable if peaceful solutions could be reached, the state provided conciliators to chair the bargaining sessions. Strikes and lockouts were illegal and, if negotiation failed, arbitration was provided to achieve a settlement. . . . [S]ome issues were deemed non-negotiable as they were deemed management prerogatives.[4]

Under the last of the IC & A Act's descendants, the LRA, registered unions represented all persons falling within the occupations described as within the union's jurisdiction. For example, a union registered to represent clerical workers would represent all persons performing that work in workplaces throughout the geographic area in the registration, whether nationwide or regional.[5] Unions' members had paid time to attend two two-hour union "stopwork" meetings a year,[6] and unions had a legal right to enter a workplace.[7]

Registration gave a workers' union the right to negotiate an award with designated employer representatives. Some revisions of the IC & A Act provided for interest arbitration. Under the LRA, awards were arbitrated only if both employers and union agreed.[8] The "blanket clause" bound the union and all employers in the designated industry to the award.[9] This system also existed and still exists in much of Australia.[10]

Although New Zealand's law seems wholly different from the Wagner Act model, by the 1980s the two operated in ways that were remarkably similar, though with important exceptions.[11] One important difference is that almost all collective bargaining in New Zealand from 1894 to early 1991 took place on a multi-employer basis, whereas this was not so widespread in the United States. In addition, awards usually prescribed only minimum terms.[12] Second-tier bargaining topped up the conditions set out in awards.[13] It was also not illegal and not unusual for an employer unilaterally to set pay by deciding to pay above-award rates.[14]

When the LRA was enacted in 1987, there were 383 awards and approximately 200 unions. A workplace could have as many awards as there were different occupational groups.[15] This emphasis on occupations as the basis for initial union organisation, as opposed to the single worksite as in the United States, reflects the conditions and views prevalent when each country's laws were enacted. New Zealand has and had a sparse, dispersed population and a large number of small worksites. This continues to be the case. In 1994, approximately 9% of worksites had fewer than four employees.[16]

Without awards, multi-employer bargaining, and blanket coverage unionisation would have been difficult, if not impossible. The IC & A Act system made collective bargaining and worker representation cost-effective.[17] In fact, it was so cost-effective that even very small unions could survive. In 1983, 67.3% of unions had total memberships of fewer than 1000 members.[18] If small unions are weak unions, then New Zealand was in danger of being a country filled with weak unions. The LRA tried to remedy this by requiring that unions have more than 1000 members.[19]

One consequence of the award system was that terms of employment for each job classification were substantially uniform across workplaces. This largely took wages and working conditions out of competition and put employers on a level playing field. Within the workplace, it meant that workers had little reason to be competitive with one another, for good or ill. Unions also had little opportunity or need to compete for members, since registration defined representation.

The collective bargaining laws in effect from 1894 until 1991 had negative impacts on unions as well as positive ones. In many ways, the laws did not empower but controlled unions.[20] Registered unions had little ambit for operation. Until 1987 and the LRA, unions could not bargain about subjects other than "industrial matters," as opposed to political, social or management issues.[21]

A hidden but highly pernicious negative impact came from the high level of support law gave unions. Unions had no need to seek out or work for members when registering created representative status and preserved it in virtual perpetuity. Law compelled union membership and payment of dues, although there were many exceptions.[22] This was a system so stable that, by the 1980s, many workers were covered by documents created nearly a century earlier.[23] As a consequence, union boundaries, the mix of persons and jobs represented, and award terms might no longer be a good fit by the late twentieth century.

The system also experienced an innate tension. As Nigel Haworth puts it:

> Once enmeshed in the compulsory arbitration process, the majority of unions came to accept the legitimacy of the system and the bargaining status it conferred. Consequently, they defended a system that was patently an enduring contradiction in that it tied the unions into an economistic bargaining framework that undermined the political sophistication and independence of the union movement, decreed the organisational structure of union activity, determined the internal processes of union life, and determined many membership attitudes toward the union, all in ways likely to undermine union movement autonomy and innovation.[24]

It is not surprising, given the longevity of the award system and its protections, that New Zealand unions of the 1980s tended to take a conservative view of how they should or could operate. The LRA tried to change attitudes and opportunities by providing more variety in the way collective bargaining could take place. Section 132(a) allowed unions to "cite out," that is, to remove an employer from award coverage so they could engage in individual or enterprise bargaining.[25]

However, unions did not cite out very many employers. Two years after the LRA's enactment, during the 1989/1990 wage round, some, but not much, citing out had occurred.[26] This can be explained in part by the unions' conservative approach, but there were other important factors that made unions unwilling to experiment. The 1980s were a time of massive industrial restruct-uring, privatisation, and corporatisation. Many of these changes weakened unions and left them with little bargaining strength.[27]

Massive unemployment meant a drop in dues-paying members, and this in turn left unions with fewer financial resources to risk. Citing out an employer meant losing award coverage, because the law provided no way to reverse the process, even if negotiations went badly. In addition, some of the positive effects of enterprise bargaining could be achieved through other, less drastic means, such as composite awards. Given this, unions took a sensible wait-and-see approach.

Events showed that unions who refused to cite out were making a rational choice. Thirty-six percent of employers cited out failed to enter into any succeeding agreement.[28] Letting the more powerful employers out of the award would depress award wages.[29] Finally, unions had fundamental philosophical reasons to oppose bargaining on an enterprise basis. Taking wages out of competition is done through award negotiations.

On the other hand, groups such as the New Zealand Employers Federation (NZEF) wanted to eliminate awards. Their campaign against the award system will be explored in the next chapters, but some mention of them needs to be made here. Murray French of the Wellington Employers Association observed:

> It was quite apparent those companies covered by awards simply got a mediocre result from a mediocre environment of negotiating. Those companies I represented that had been cited out of the award were able to move ahead quite significantly with the support of the union representing them at that time. And I think it was a useful example of ownership, of documents.
>
> And let's get it straight. I don't see documents determining people's thinking. I think the documents only reflect a culture of an organisation. Obviously there needs to be a lot of work and communication and a foundation of support and trust in an organisation which subsequently is reflected in written contracts.[30]

By remaining staunchly with awards when employers took this position, unions either failed to understand valid employer frustration with an inferior system of bargaining or they failed to defuse propaganda against unions. No matter how it was characterised, the fact that the collective bargaining landscape was not radically and quickly altered under the LRA provided fuel for those who argued that the current system had failed business by providing no way for their needs to be met.

The truth is that changes were occurring in the bargaining system under the LRA. During the parliamentary debates on the ECA, example after example of restructuring was presented. However, this change was invisible in the period preceding the introduction of the ECA. As a result, pressure to accelerate change meant that, in 1990, the Labour government amended the LRA to permit employers to initiate a workers' ballot to determine whether bargaining would be based on awards or enterprise agreements.[31]

The truth is also that, in many ways, the award system hurt unions. On the one hand, it left them with very little bargaining experience. Even though New Zealand had one of the most highly organised workforces in the world, at about 50%–65%,[32] unions were, in many important ways, irrelevant. Many employers liked awards because they kept unions away from their workplaces and less able to limit managerial prerogative.[33] As long as awards were minimum condition documents, they allowed employers to set virtually all terms and conditions of employment.[34] This trained employers to engage in an autocratic style of management.

> One of those who preferred award coverage said that his firm had an informal, house agreement which was determined by senior management. This was flexible because the firm had the discretion to adjust the above-award margins according to the success of the business. It did not have to negotiate with staff.[35]

In 1990 85% of employers paid at least some above-award rates and most set wages unilaterally.[36] Employers could control their price increases through awards yet assure themselves of a good workforce with above-award payments.[37] Only 15% of employers discussed above-award payments with either the union or employees concerned.[38] In fact, most employers acted unilaterally on all important workplace issues, such as safety, overtime, and new technology.[39]

This culture of workplace management was not used to forecast how the ECA would operate. Employers who ran their businesses unilaterally with, at best, sporadic consultation would lack both the experience and the inclination to negotiate when no law required negotiating. Many employers under the LRA already behaved as ECA opponents feared employers under the ECA would. Logic should have suggested that the new law would not alter these attitudes or lead employers to embrace a world of joint partners in the enterprise.

Once this is known, New Zealand's high union density figures take on a new significance. New Zealand had the trappings of an active labor movement but mostly allowed employers to conduct their businesses without interference. Paul Kimble of the Distribution Workers Federation described award bargaining as a sort of sport.

> The industry traditionally, under the award structure, once every year with those companies we would have a big punch up and all be out. There would be a song and dance, and then everyone would go back to work and there would be a wage increase. It was all very 'matey.' It was all very 'boys' own stuff', and they were always pretty friendly. It was a bit like a rugby game, really. . . . Everyone seemed to enjoy this. It was something that was expected really, every couple of years. It was great to do—yelling and screaming and the cities would be cut off and there would be huge trucks and there would be a settlement in the end. It was sort of like a game to people in the industry.[40]

Francis Wevers, a management consultant who was once a union official, had a slightly different perspective:

> You see what used to happen is that in this ritual abuse session that we used to have—every 12 months there was the annual bargaining round. It was like the duck-shooting season. Or the deer-hunting season, or whatever you like. But people did nothing for nine months and then for three months there was this intense period of frenetic activity and strikes and all those sorts of things, to try to establish the relationship for the next year.
>
> What used to happen is that a small group of people used to get in a smoke-filled room in Wellington, thump the table, reach an agreement and then impose it around the country on people who had never been party to it. People had never heard the discussion, never heard the debate, never valued the outcome which just appeared in the letter box one day and said, "Thou

shalt now do this." Neither employees nor employers felt particularly committed to those outcomes.[41]

The advantages of this system were strikingly similar to that in the United States during this period.

> For management, the traditional model also had various advantages. It helped ensure a stable, skilled workforce. It provided a system for resolving disputes, unquestioned control over key decisions and an efficient way of dealing with many employees simultaneously through their representatives.[42]

In *James v. James*, the New Zealand court mentioned, with no apparent surprise, that the employer had to ask the butchers in his shop what the going rate was for butchers, because he was not aware of the award's terms.[43]

How was it that one of the most highly unionised countries had no meaningful collective bargaining? The answer seems to be that the system was so efficient at protecting unions and unionisation that it ultimately acted to their detriment. Unions had little need to communicate with members, since the legislation delivered them permanently to the union and mandated dues through compulsory unionism based, however, on membership balloting.[44] As a result, union representatives made little effort to learn organising or servicing skills.[45] "The delegate structure in New Zealand has never been particularly strong, and people tended to view unions as the organiser that came in from outside."[46] In the year preceding one study, most employers had either no contact or only one to two contacts with the union which represented their employees. Most employers were even unaware whether they had a shop floor delegate/steward.[47]

This distance might have been forgiven if it had resulted in good representation. However, New Zealand unions did not do particularly well for their members. In January 1991, the Minister of Employment issued a list of twenty-nine awards with a base pay rate lower than the unemployment benefit of $223.22 for a married couple without children.[48] Fifty percent of registered awards in the late 1980s provided a weekly adult pay rate of $295 when the minimum wage was $235.[49] After nearly a century

THE PAST 21

of legalised collective bargaining, unions either had actually lost or believed they had lost the ability to function without an extremely supportive legislative environment.

New Zealand unions, before the enactment of the ECA, could be seen as external to employees, as "a large, bureaucratic organisation whose full-term officials periodically negotiate a long-term contract behind closed doors with the employer, and then represent a fairly small number of employees who are aggrieved by the way management administers the contract during its lifetime."[50] This creates a situation in which, rather than being a collective of employees, unions may be seen as professional organisations on a par with an employer's personnel department.

Much of this malaise was disguised because for decades the economy provided well for the people of New Zealand. The system in place when they fared well was the award system. Professor Margaret Wilson points out:

> Whether the law is seen to be to your advantage or detriment will largely depend on your economic bargaining power. Thus for many years, although the law made strikes illegal, when unions struck, employers did not enforce their legal rights because it was not in their best interests to do so. Skilled labour was scarce and it was easy to pass on to the consumer any extra costs incurred.
>
> ... [I]t was a characteristic of our social system that most people expect improvement in their working conditions will be gained primarily through legislation, and not through industrial bargaining. Governments, not trade unions, have been expected to deliver social justice.[51]

It was natural for unions to ascribe all things good to the award system, just as, when the economy began to deteriorate in the mid-1970s, it became easy for those who advocated change—primarily the New Zealand Employers Federation (NZEF) and New Zealand Business Roundtable (NZBR)—to attribute all things bad to it.

What view did employers have of unions and their roles in the period just prior to the enactment of the ECA? Many employers were content with the system because it delivered low-cost, low-wage settlements. But while one-fourth of employers believed unions did a good job, most had a predominantly, if mildly, negative view, that unions did too little, too timidly, rather than too much, too aggressively. Close to one-third felt that unions simply did nothing. Employers saw unions as not responsive to their members, as do-nothing organisations of officials who seldom or never visited the job-site, and as not sufficiently aggressive in representing their own members. Paradoxically, those employers who dealt with unions more frequently tended to have more positive evaluations of unions, even though their dealings involved the strife of resolving disputes over award interpretation, discharges, or other conflicts.[52]

Considering the absence of unions from the workplace and the employer's role in determining employment conditions, it was hard for workers to feel much connection with their unions. There was unquestionably a price to pay for the high levels of unionisation achieved under this system. This would become devastatingly visible in the way unions responded in 1990 and 1991 when fundamental legislative change was imminent and in the way their former members behaved under the ECA. The union members of 1990 would take actions in 1991 that revealed that "without the props of compulsory membership and monopoly coverage rights, union solidarity is in many instances a pretence."[53]

By at least 1990, it was hard to avoid believing that the National Party would win the next election and that it intended to implement massive legislative change in industrial relations. National made no secret that it intended to implement the policies which had been forcefully advocated by the NZBR and the NZEF throughout the 1980s.[54]

This then was the state of New Zealand unions when the National Party regained office on October 27, 1990, after two terms out of power. Within two months, on December 1990, National introduced the Employment Contracts Bill as part of a package of social legislation. The ECA was rapidly enacted and became effective May 15, 1991, as the Employment Contracts Act 1991.

THE PAST 23

This speed is deceptive. Years of unceasing pressure applied in campaigns by some of the most powerful forces in New Zealand were necessary to prepare the way.

Notes

1. Alan Geare, "The Proposed Employment Relations Act," 18 N.Z. J. Ind. Rel., 194, 194 (1993); John Deeks, "New Tracks, Old Maps: Continuity and Change in New Zealand Labour Relations, 1984–1990," 15 N.Z. J. Ind. Rel., 99, 102 (1990); "The Employment Contracts Act 1991: Introduction," 16 N.Z. J. Ind. Rel., 105, 105 (1991).
2. Gordon Anderson, "A Summary of Industrial Law Research in New Zealand: 1970–1986" in *Contemporary Industrial Relations in Australia and New Zealand: Literature Surveys*, 101, 102 (Kevin Hince & Alan Williams, eds., 1987); *Labour and Industrial Relations in New Zealand* (John Howells, et al., eds. 1974).
3. Peter Coleman, *Progressivism and the World of Reform: New Zealand and the Origins of the American Welfare State*, 132 (1987).
4. Alan Geare, "Proposed Act," 194.
5. Cf. LRA 1987 ss 3–7, 132–34.
6. LRA 1987 s 57.
7. LRA s 196. Such a right of access could give unions powerful assistance in maintaining and establishing their representational status.
8. LRA s 147.
9. LRA s 160(2).
10. Steve O'Neill, "Labour Market Deregulation: The New Zealand Experience," 4 (Parl. Res. Serv. Background Paper No.5 1993).
11. Ellen Dannin, "Labor Law Reform in New Zealand," 13 N.Y.L. Sch. J. Int'l & Comp. L., 1 (1992).
12. See "ECA: Introduction," 105.
13. Raymond Harbridge, "The Impact of Economic Liberalisation on Labour Relations in New Zealand 1984–1990," *British Review of New Zealand Studies*, 4, 69, 71 (1991).
14. Raymond Harbridge & Stuart McCaw, "Award, Agreement or Nothing? A Review of the Impact of S132(a) of the Labour Relations Act 1987 on Collective Bargaining," 17 N.Z. J. Ind. Rel., 175, 176 (1992).
15. Minister of Labour, *Industrial Relations: A Framework for Review*, 1, 22 (1985) [Green Paper]; O'Neill, 4.
16. Richard Whatman et al., "Labour Market Adjustment Under the Employment Contracts Act," 19 N.Z. J. Ind. Rel. 53, 54 n.2 (1994).
17. Dannin, 43.
18. Nigel Haworth, "Unions in Crisis: Deregulation and Reform of

the New Zealand Union Movement" in *Organized Labor in the Asia-Pacific Region: A Comparative Study of Trade Unionism in Nine Countries*, 282, 284–85 (Stephen Frenkel, ed. 1993).
19. LRA s 6(2).
20. Haworth, 283.
21. Alan Geare, *The System of Industrial Relations in New Zealand*, 189–90 (1988); cf. LRA s 170.
22. Dannin, 42–43.
23. Interview with Rick Barker, National Secretary, Service Workers Federation of Aotearoa, in Wellington (May 14, 1992).
24. Haworth, 284.
25. New Zealand Amalgamated Engineering and Related Trades Industrial Union of Workers, *Strategies for Change: Representing Workers in a New Environment*, 3 (1987).
26. Harbridge & McCaw, 178.
27. Harbridge, "The Impact of Economic Liberalisation," 77.
28. Harbridge & McCaw, 178.
29. *Id.*, 180.
30. Interview with Murray French, Manager of Labour Relations Services, Wellington Employers Association, in Wellington (May 14, 1992).
31. O'Neill, 12.
32. Richard Freeman & Joel Rogers, "Who Speaks for Us? Employee Representation in a Nonunion Labor Market" in *Employee Representation: Alternatives and Future Directions*, 13, 16 (Bruce Kaufman & Morris Kleiner, eds. 1993); Raymond Harbridge & Kevin Hince, "Organising Workers: The Effects of the Act on Union Membership and Organisation" in *Employment Contracts: New Zealand Experiences*, 224, 226, 228 (Raymond Harbridge, ed. 1993).
33. Peter Franks, "Report on Employers' Views on Industrial Relations Reform," 4, 6 (Jan. 1991); Ian McAndrew & Paul Hursthouse, "Southern Employers on Enterprise Bargaining," 15 N.Z. J. Ind. Rel., 117, 126 (1990).
34. "ECA: Introduction," 105.
35. Franks, 6.
36. McAndrew & Hursthouse, "Southern Employers on Enterprise Bargaining," 119; Ian McAndrew & Paul Hursthouse, "Reforming Labour Relations: What Southern Employers Say," 16 N.Z. J. Ind. Rel., 1, 5 (1991).
37. Harbridge & McCaw, 176.
38. McAndrew & Hursthouse, "Reforming Labour Relations," 5.
39. *Id.*, 6–7.
40. Interview with Paul Kimble, Organiser, Distribution Workers Federation, in Wellington (May 12, 1992).
41. Interview with Francis Wevers, Principal, Francis Wevers and Associates, in Wellington (May 20, 1992).

42. Julius Getman & F. Ray Marshall, "Industrial Relations in Transition: The Paper Industry Example," 102 Tex. L. Rev., 1804, 1807–08 (1993).
43. [1991] 3 ERNZ 547, 549 (Empl. Trib.).
44. The LRA allowed a union membership clause to be inserted in any award or agreement if agreed the employer and union agreed or by ballot of the members held every third award or agreement —LRA ss 61–66. Where a union membership clause existed, employees who failed to join within fourteen days of request could be justifiably dismissed—s 71.
45. Owen Harvey, "The Unions and the Government: The Rise and Fall of the Compact" in *Controlling Interests: Business, the State and Society in New Zealand*, 59, 64 (John Deeks & Nick Perry eds., 1992); Barker.
46. Interview with Hel Loader, Research Advocate, New Zealand Engineering Union, in Wellington (May 13, 1992).
47. See McAndrew & Hursthouse, "Southern Employers on Enterprise Bargaining," 119; Janet Hector, Jan Henning & Mary Hubble, "Industrial Relations Bargaining in the Retail Non-food Sector: 1991–1992," 18 N.Z. J. Ind. Rel., 326, 337 (1993).
48. Herbert Roth, "Chronicle," 16 N.Z. J. Ind. Rel., 100 (1991).
49. Harbridge, "The Impact of Economic Liberalisation," 77.
50. Paul Weiler, *Governing the Workplace: The Future of Labor and Employment Law*, 11–12 (1990).
51. Margaret Wilson, "The Next Phase for New Zealand Industrial Relations: The Employment Contracts Bill," 7–8 (Longman Professional Conference, Auckland, May 7–8, 1991).
52. McAndrew & Hursthouse, "Reforming Labour Relations," 7–8; Ian McAndrew, "Southern Employers on Labour Market Reform" in *Researching Management Strategies and Bargaining: Papers Presented at the Union/Tertiary Research Conference, Victoria University, Wellington*, 19, 22 (Linda Sissons, ed., 1991); McAndrew & Hursthouse, "Southern Employers on Enterprise Bargaining," 119.
53. Rebecca Macfie, "An End to Equity," *Political Review*, 20 (June 1992).
54. Service Workers Federation of Aotearoa, "The Employment Contracts Bill: Submissions of the Service Workers Federation of Aotearoa," 2 (n.d.).

3

The Campaign for Freedom

THE EMPLOYMENT CONTRACTS ACT WAS THE CULMINATION OF A LONG campaign spearheaded by the New Zealand Employers Federation (NZEF) and New Zealand Business Roundtable (NZBR). For more than a decade they argued that New Zealand's labour relations system needed radical change if the country was not to sink to third-world status. The NZEF and NZBR's campaign focused on a few simple points and promoted and publicised them, with but small variations, through the years.

Examining their campaign provides an opportunity to reconstruct the inner logic of what the NZEF and NZBR wanted and to uncover the moral and political vision embedded in the values and images of justice and workplace rights they advocated. They advanced a vision of a reformed New Zealand which was attractive and seductive to many New Zealanders in the 1990s. As seductive as this vision was, the specific proposals suggest that their inner moral and political vision was quite different.[1]

By the 1980s, New Zealanders seemed to have forgotten their labour history. Embarrassment replaced pride in having progressive legislation and an egalitarian system. These were ineffective at holding economic and political turmoil at bay. Fundamental changes beginning in 1984 were both a response to economic problems and, in turn, created new problems which became a basis for instituting even greater change.[2]

The industrial relations system was the last of the major changes to be made, but the campaign for it began as early as 1983. That year, Max Bradford, who became an important force in enacting the ECA, advanced what were to be the main themes of the NZEF-NZBR campaign.³ The enactment of the Labour Relations Act (LRA) was a response to this and other concerns, but instead of quelling discontent, the campaign only gathered force after the LRA was enacted.

Advocates for labour law reform were raising fundamental questions about what sort of society New Zealand was and would be, but few responded to the NZEF and NZBR. The NZEF and NZBR often acted in a coordinated way and had many overlapping members; however, there were important differences between the two, mainly growing out of the differences in their constituencies. Richard Mulgan comments: "Not having to consult a large and diverse membership means that the [NZBR] can support much more clear-cut and intellectually coherent policies. This was noticeable, for instance, in the early 1980s when the Business Roundtable was able to take the lead in supporting a much more radical industrial relations strategy than the more broadly representative Employers' Federation could at the time."[4]

1 The New Zealand Employers Federation: The NZEF is the national umbrella association of employers. At the time of the campaign for the ECA, it was composed of four regional employers' associations and 65 national trades associations.[5] It had between 12,000 and 13,000 direct member employers, as well as 70 affiliates which represented other employer organisations from 150,120 enterprises as well as the self-employed.[6] The NZEF provides its members with negotiating expertise, information of interest to employers, and lobbying. The NZEF has been partly funded by the government. In fiscal year 1990-1991, it received $67,000.[7]

Regional associations such as the Wellington Employers Association provide advocates to represent employers in negotiations or legal matters. Under the award system the employer associations affiliated with the NZEF played a key role in setting award terms.

2 The New Zealand Business Roundtable: The NZBR was formed by Auckland industrialists in 1976 as a forum for chief executives of major New Zealand corporations. By the late 1980s, NZBR members were either chief executives of major corporations or of state-owned enterprises. NZBR member companies were worth $18 billion or 77% of the New Zealand sharemarket in the late 1980s. Prominent NZBR members included Douglas Myers (the largest shareholder of Lion Nathan), Ronald Trotter (chair of state-owned enterprise Telecom and of Fletcher Challenge), Alan Gibbs (chairperson of state-owned enterprise Forestry Corporation and of Gibbs Security), Lindsay Fergusson (board member of state-owned enterprise the Reserve Bank and of Magnum Corporation), and Rod Deane (former deputy governor of the Reserve Bank and chief executive of Electricorp).[8]

The NZBR says it takes "an objective, non-partisan and longer term view, rather than to operate for the benefit of any one group at the expense of others."[9] NZBR executive director, Roger Kerr, says that it attempts "to look at issues from a national perspective not a business perspective."[10] Given its membership, its positions, and the sources it relies on, these statements are open to question. It cites only New Right sources and espouses only a New Right philosophy. Typical was a 1993 speech in Australia by Roger Kerr. He referred liberally to United States Judge Richard Posner and law professor Richard Epstein—advocates of neo-liberal economics—and to "Rush Limbaugh, the American radio talk show phenomenon."[11]

The NZBR believes in both the instrumental and absolute value of the market, the need to limit the role of government in society and reduce government expenditure, and the need to weaken the power of unions. According to Roger Kerr:

> A World Bank Study in the 1980s found that the difference between growth rates of countries which distorted their labour markets—for example by regulations to protect trade unions and enforce minimum wages—and those that kept their labour markets relatively free of distortions was of the order of 1.4 percentage points per annum. Over a working career (say 40 years) a differential growth rate of 1.4 percentage points per annum adds up to a 74 percent difference in attainable standards

of living. The evidence is crystal clear that, far from protecting wages and advancing worker's interests, the ideology of trade unionism as we have known it has massively retarded the increase in workers' standards in recent decades.[12]

Within New Zealand, the NZBR has created and maintained ties to the NZEF and the National Party by opening its meetings to them. The NZEF's officers and "National's entire front bench" regularly attend NZBR meetings.[13] In addition, NZBR members' size and wealth can make them particularly powerful and influential as members of other organisations, as when NZBR members join the NZEF or NZEF constituent organisations.[14]

3 *The NZBR and its relationships:* One of the more interesting examples of the NZBR's connections can be found in its ties to the Labour Party during its 1984 and 1987 terms in office. Normally Labour ideology would find no common ground with the New Right. However, individual members of the NZBR became major Labour Party contributors during the 1987 elections and enabled Labour to amass an enormous war chest. Their donations of approximately $3 million were made to promote the economic policies of Labour Minister of Finance, Roger Douglas, the minister who oversaw the Department of the Treasury.[15]

Treasury's views and NZBR members found a warm reception from Roger Douglas.[16] Labour soon set about the process of implementing the NZBR/Treasury program as it began moving to a more market-driven economy. An important part of this process was privatising state services which had for decades been state-owned and controlled.[17] This formed part of the program popularly referred to as "Rogernomics."[18]

After the Labour Government enacted legislation in 1986 transforming state agencies and assets into "state-owned enterprises" (SOEs), it placed NZBR members on many important SOE boards, including the Reserve Bank, Railways Corporation, Post Office Bank, Electricity Corporation, and Telecom. NZBR member Rod Deane became the Commissioner of State Services, the representative of government agencies charged with negotiating with public sector unions, while others were appointed to key government task forces.[19] These appointments further introduced NZBR ideas into government circles.

Throughout the Labour Government, Treasury and the NZBR engaged in a symbiotic relationship cross-fertilised through exchanges of personnel. In 1986, the NZBR hired Roger Kerr as its executive director. Before this, Kerr had headed Treasury's think-tank, Economics II.[20] ECA supporters, including Treasury, based their economic argument for labour change, in part, on OECD reports. In doing so, Treasury was indirectly quoting itself, since OECD reports were based on reports made by Treasury to the OECD.[21]

Treasury promoted "a rigid ideological line based on a near-religious belief in the theories of Hayek, Friedman and other gurus of the so-called New Right, rather than impartially advising the government of the day on the financial implications of alternative policies."[22] The NZBR, Treasury, the Reserve Bank, the Centre for Independent Studies (CIS), and Rogernomics have been closely allied in terms of the sources they rely on. The connections were not merely ideological. NZBR members David Richwhite, Ron Trotter, Rod Deane, and Douglas Myers were members of the Centre for Independent Studies' board of directors. Alan Gibbs was a NZBR member and chair of CIS.[23] So close are the ties among and within these groups, that the business editor of the *Dominion* characterised the NZBR as the "public relations branch of Treasury."[24]

In practice, Rogernomics included restrictive monetary policy to engender recession and restore profitability; dismantling social services; high unemployment; tax reductions as part of supply-side economics; privatisation; deregulation; and limiting state responsibilities.[25] Rogernomics policies—such as higher exchange rates; high interest rates; lower tariffs for imported goods; increased foreign competition; removing government incentives for research and development and investment in infrastructure; deregulating financial markets, export and import trade, banking, and other industries—placed pressures on the economy that forced New Zealand companies to look "more critically at their labour costs, at their labour management practices and at the institutional constraints incorporated in the country's system of labour relations."²⁶

Rick Barker, General Secretary of the Service Workers Union of Aotearoa, observed:

> But people are trimming costs everywhere. In the past, factories, for example, used to offer cafeteria services to their staff and expect to subsidise it. Now they don't. They have cut the service or cut the subsidy or both.
>
> That's had an effect on us and an obvious effect on the contract caterers. And it is all part of the trimming. Employers that used to fly first or business class, I now see down at the back of the plane when I'm flying, flying economy class on discount tickets.²⁷

4 *The NZBR and NZEF as spokespersons for employers:* By late 1989, the NZEF's labour philosophy had begun to resemble the NZBR's in advocating employee and employer freedom to contract on an individual basis.²⁸ Some claimed this resulted from a coup by the NZBR within the Auckland Employers Association, the largest constituent organisation in the NZEF.²⁹ NZBR Executive Director Roger Kerr, however, denied this, though such a coup was feasible. NZBR members could use their weighted votes—one vote for each 75 employees—to elect themselves to the AEA's ruling council and executive committee.³⁰ "[W]hoever controls Auckland commands huge sway—if not control—over the Employers Federation as a whole."³¹

The New Zealand Council of Trade Unions (CTU) feared the election would "serve as a Trojan horse in importing the Roundtable's radical philosophy into the traditionally more pragmatic Employers Federation, [where the] main employer concern [was] that it would convert the federation into just another mouthpiece of big business."³² Many employer members of the NZEF saw NZBR members as predatory towards their smaller competitors.³³ Smaller employers viewed the NZBR as a "self-appointed group which was not representative of employers but which carried an awful lot of weight"³⁴ and "as foreign to the run of the mill NZ company, 'which has a level of social conscience', and as being ideologues—not really practical and asking for what was beyond possibility."[35]

Small employers saw NZBR members as large companies with resources not available to them and thus not qualified to impose their views on others. They believed the NZBR espoused a philosophy based on "a world of perfect employers and perfect workers" which was as out of touch with business realities for the average New Zealand business as "the secretary of the CTU."[36] One employer stated:

> [I]n his dealings with the [NZBR] companies he had seen some of the most appalling management he had ever come across. This was because they were too big and because they worked on the principle that everything had to be sacrificed for short-term profit. This principle was a phenomenon of modern big business.
>
> Big companies were also characterized by great remoteness from top to bottom. This meant that the top executives could dream up policies that they wouldn't dare carry out themselves. Essentially, big companies were as bureaucratic as government departments, a great irony considering the philosophy behind privatisation.[37]

In the early 1990s, most New Zealand employers did not share the NZBR's enthusiasm for radical change. When asked about issues central to the NZBR's campaign in August 1991, most northern employers felt no urgent need to increase workplace flexibility. Two-thirds saw no need to increase hours or the use of part-time or temporary workers. Employers' views split according to numbers of workers employed. While 82% of employers of over 500 workers supported change, only 23.1% of employers of workforces smaller than 5 persons did.[38]

South Island employers presented a similar picture. Indeed, 95% expressed satisfaction with the existing system, and 81 of 92 employers surveyed were satisfied with wages negotiated over the last five years.[39] Another study found that only 33% of southern employers had a strong preference for the award system.

Employers split 48 to 44 for enterprise bargaining.[40] The NZBR, however, argued that an NZEF survey showed 80% of employers wanted enterprise bargaining.[41]

It was easy to understand why smaller employers with fewer personnel resources preferred awards. Awards were an efficient way to set workplace terms. They provided stability in labour costs, wage rises lower than inflation, and no personal need to bargain to gain these benefits. Some employers liked awards because they kept unions farther from the workplace and thus less able to limit managerial prerogative.[42]

Labour Law Reform in 1987
The NZEF/NZBR vision began to take form in the enactment of the Labour Relations Act (LRA) in 1987. The LRA emerged from a two-year consultative and drafting process. On December 17, 1985, the Department of Labour had issued the Green Paper, a report that analysed existing legislation, identified areas for reform, and asked for responses to specific questions.[43] In September 1986, after responses were submitted by government, unions, and employer organisations, the Minister of Labour issued the White Paper, which outlined the Labour Relations Bill.[44] The Bill was introduced a year after the process had begun in December 1986,[45] and the LRA was enacted May 27, 1987, and effective August 1, 1987.[46] This deliberative and inclusive process contrasts with the ECA, which was introduced as a bill on December 19, 1990, two months after National won its election, and became law May 15, 1991.

The LRA was compromise legislation based mainly on the existing system but with new forms of enterprise bargaining available.[47] This compromise displeased supporters of Rogernomics. They argued that the economy had to be consistent: deregulation of one part required deregulation of the whole.[48] "[L]abour-market deregulation was the final necessary step that would somehow unleash new productive forces leading to the long-awaited economic recovery."[49]

When the New Zealand sharemarket crashed in the wake of the global 1987 crash and New Zealand's economy plunged into recession, the NZEF blamed New Zealand's crash and decline on an unsuitable labour market: "The distortions occurring previously where a company was expected to be locally and internationally competitive in a fully deregulated environment—with the exception of the labour market—played a major part in New Zealand's steady economic decline."[50]

The NZEF and NZBR blamed New Zealand's economic woes on its labour laws and used this to advance a program that broke with a long-standing national consensus that workers were liable to be exploited unless the state intervened and that the public supported intervention.[51] They denied that individual workers could be exploited[52] and advocated "a system focusing on the rights and responsibilities of individuals in deciding upon the contractual arrangements best suiting their particular enterprise."[53] This was part of a New Right philosophy that tells "workers that isolation from one another enhances their dignity as individual human beings."[54] The vehemence of NZEF-NZBR arguments "divert[ed] attention from the more fundamental failures in which their own sector played such a significant part."[55]

One would think from the NZEF-NZBR criticism that the LRA was wholly pro-union. The reality was different. The Minister of Labour berated unions for being overly dependent on legislative support, offering a limited range of services to members, not being sufficiently accountable to their membership, resisting organisational change, and showing reluctance to coordinate their activities at the level of the workplace.[56] He also chided employers for important failings: not recognising the importance of wage fixing and industrial relations to their economic performance; not putting forward a case to support their objectives; blaming unions for problems actually caused by poor management; and seeing unions as having no right to play a role in decisions affecting their members' lives.[57]

The NZEF-NZBR reaction to the passage of the LRA was strange. It would be fair to say that the employers won more through the LRA and other legislation of this period than did unions or workers.[58] Not only had the debate taken place on their terms, the LRA also set up a system that encouraged exit from the award system to enterprise agreements. Interest arbitration was so limited it was unlikely to occur.[59] Compulsory payment of union dues could only occur if employers agreed to it or workers voted for it.[60]

However, the NZEF and NZBR complained that the new legislation failed to rectify a situation that left them powerless before the unreasonable demands of overly powerful unions. The LRA did not have a sufficiently long life to reveal what its impact on industrial relations would have been, but even by 1989 studies refuted NZEF-NZBR claims about wage rises, the balance of power, and bargaining structures. Studies showed that awards were actually responsive to industrial needs.[61] Furthermore, employers had demonstrated a high degree of power even before the LRA could have had much impact, as even the NZEF admitted in 1987.[62] Greater flexibility was beginning to take place in work hours, as a trade-off for higher rates of pay.[63]

These findings suggest one reason why the employer associations continued to advocate abolishing the system. Under the award system, employers had to concede higher wages to get the terms employers wanted as to hours and job demarcations. Under the system they advocated, they thought they could get these results without having to give up higher pay as a quid pro quo. The NZBR ignored the data about what was occurring and complained about the pace of change from awards.[64] The LRA was an important victory for the NZEF-NZBR. They not only framed the discussion, the legislation demonstrated an acceptance of their views. Despite this, they reacted as though they had achieved nothing and had even been betrayed by the LRA.

They girded their loins anew for battle. Minister for Labour Helen Clark said of the amendments: "I had hoped that opening up some possibility of enterprise bargaining would have been regarded more positively—and I suppose it would have been had there not been waiting in the wings an alternative government with proposals not to amend the Labour Relations Act, but to dump it entirely."[65]

Notes

1. On the value of critical legal analysis in reconstructing the moral and political vision embedded in labour law, see especially Karl Klare, "Critical Theory and Labor Relations Law" in *The Politics of*

Law: A Progressive Critique, 65, 73 (David Kairys, ed., 1982).
2. Steve Britton et al., *Changing Places in New Zealand: A Geography of Restructuring* (1992); Ian Duncan & Alan Bollard, *Corporatization & Privatization: Lessons from New Zealand* (1992); *The Fourth Labour Government: Politics and Policy in New Zealand* (Martin Holland & Jonathan Boston eds., 1990); Bruce Jesson, *Fragments of Labour: The Story Behind the Labour Government* (1989).
3. Max Bradford, "Issues of Concern to Employers in Industrial Relations: Issues of Concern," 14, 20–22 (Raymond Harbridge, ed. 1983).
4. Richard Mulgan, *Politics in New Zealand*, 206 (1994).
5. Ian McAndrew & Paul Hursthouse, "Reforming Labour Relations: What Southern Employers Say," 16 N.Z. J. Ind. Rel., 1, 2 (1991).
6. John Deeks et al., *Labour and Employment Relations in New Zealand*, 245–49 (2d ed. 1994); Dept. of Labour, Ministerial Brief, October 1990 123 (1990); Nicola Natusch, *An Analysis of the Influence of the New Zealand Business Roundtable Since Its Inception*, 59 (1990).
7. Dept. of Labour, Ministerial Brief, 120; Rebecca Macfie, "Employers Do the Decent Thing," *National Business Review*, Apr. 9, 1991, at 1.
8. David Steele, *The Business Roundtable*, 2–7 (1989); Jane Kelsey, *Rolling Back the State: Privatisation of Power in Aotearoa/New Zealand*, 41, 135–36 (1994); Georgina Murray & Grant Fleming, *The Organisation of Economic Advice in New Zealand: Some Evidence Towards a Marxist Analysis*, 12–36 (1990); Natusch, 2, 27–28, 33, 70, 81; "Nation's Most Exclusive Club," *PSA Journal*, Sept. 1992, at 7; "The New Right," *PSA Journal*, Mar. 15–Apr. 11, 1990, at 14; Dept. of Labour, Ministerial Brief, 123; Chris Trotter, "New Industrial Relations Era Frogmarching History to the Door," *Examiner*, Feb. 28, 1991, at 7.
9. Natusch, 1.
10. Roger Kerr, *The New Zealand Business Roundtable: Roles and Goals in Building a Competitive Economy*, 275 (NZBR ed., 1991); Peter Franks, "Report on Employers' Views on Industrial Relations Reform," 12 (Jan. 1991).
11. Roger Kerr, "The Challenge for the '90's: Labour Reform in Australasia," Speech to the Australasian Institute of Company Directors Western Australia Division, Perth 8 (Feb. 19, 1993).
12. *Id.*, 6.
13. Natusch, 38.
14. *Id.*, 2.
15. *Id.*, 67–68; Allan Hawkins, *The Hawk: Allan Hawkins Tells the Equiticorp Story* 126 (1989); Brian Easton, "From Rogernomics to Ruthanasia: New Right Economics in New Zealand," 5–6 (Aug. 7, 1992).
16. Jane Kelsey, *The New Zealand Experiment: A World Model for Structural Adjustment?*, 29–39 (1995).
17. Mark Bray & David Nielsen, "Industrial Relations Reform and the

Relative Autonomy of the State" in *The Great Experiment: Labour Parties and Public Policy Transformation in Australia and New Zealand*, 68, 75–78 (Francis Castles et al., eds., 1996); Dept. of Labour, Ministerial Brief, 125; Margaret Wilson, "The Next Phase for New Zealand Industrial Relations: The Employment Contract Bill," 12 (Longman Professional Conference, Auckland, May 7–8, 1991).
18. Colin James, "Overview" in *Rogernomics: Reshaping New Zealand's Economy*, 1, 8 (Simon Walker, ed., 1989); *The Making of Rogernomics* (Brian Easton, ed., 1989); Roger Douglas, *There's Got to Be a Better Way! A Practical ABC to Solving New Zealand's Problems* (1980).
19. Steele, 35–36; Kelsey, *Rolling Back the State*, 41, 135–36; Natusch, 69–70.
20. Kelsey, *Rolling Back the State*, 76–79.
21. Gordon Campbell, "Bill's Act of Faith," *Listener & TV Times*, May 27, 1991, at 15, 16.
22. David McLoughlin, "Don't Write Off Ruth," *North & South*, 36 (June 1992)
23. Kelsey, *Rolling Back the State*, 136–38; "New Right," 12.
24. Natusch, 63; "New Right," 11–14.
25. Kelsey, *Experiment*; Ian Shirley, "Unemployment—Its Realities and Human Costs" in *Towards a Just Economy*, 21, 23–24 (Pelly, ed. 1991); Roger Douglas, *Unfinished Business* (1993); Douglas, *Better Way*; *Rogernomics: Reshaping New Zealand's Economy* (Simon Walker, ed., 1989); Holland & Boston.
26. John Deeks, "New Tracks, Old Maps: Continuity and Change in New Zealand Labour Relations, 1984–1990," 15 N.Z. J. Ind. Rel., 99, 99–100 (1990); Allen Taylor, "Implications for Private Sector Bargaining," 4 (Longman Professional Conference, Auckland May 7–8, 1991).
27. Interview with Rick Barker, National Secretary, Service Workers Federation of Aotearoa, in Wellington (May 14, 1992).
28. McAndrew & Hursthouse, "Reforming Labour Relations," 2.
29. Patricia Herbert, "Auckland Coup Shifts Employers to Right," *Evening Post*, Mar. 30, 1990, at 7.
30. Franks, 12.
31. Herbert, "Auckland Coup."
32. Owen Harvey, "The Unions and the Government: The Rise and Fall of the Compact" in *Controlling Interests: Business, The State and Society in New Zealand*, 59, 64 (John Deeks et al., eds., 1992).
33. Steele, 24.
34. Franks, 13.
35. Natusch, 54.
36. Franks, 13.
37. *Id.*, 13.
38. Rose Ryan, "Flexibility in New Zealand Workplaces: A Study of Northern Employers," 17 N.Z. J. Ind. Rel., 129, 142–43 (1992).
39. McAndrew & Hursthouse, "Reforming Labour Relations," 4–5.

40. *Id.*, 121–22.
41. Douglas Myers, "Where To Now in Labour Relations?" Address to the Managing Change in Industrial Relations Conference Institute for International Research 7 (July 31, 1990).
42. Franks, 4, 6; Ian McAndrew & Paul Hursthouse, "Southern Employers on Enterprise Bargaining," 15 N.Z. J. Ind. Rel., 117, 126 (1990).
43. Minister of Labour, *Industrial Relations: A Framework for Review*, Vol. I (1985) (Green Paper).
44. Minister of Labour, *Government Statement on Labour Relations II* (1986) (White Paper).
45. Martin Vranken & Kevin Hince, "The Labour Court and Private Sector Industrial Relations," 18 Vic. U. Well. L. Rev., 105, 115 (88).
46. LRA 1987 s 1.
47. Margaret Wilson, 13.
48. Anne Knowles, "Four Months Down the Track: Is the Employment Contracts Act Working?" *Examiner*, Sept. 5, 1991, at 19.
49. Roger Kerr, "The Challenge for the '90's," 2; "Leading From the Rear," *Listener & TV Times*, June 3, 1991, at 30, 33; Myers, "Where To Now," 1; *N.Z.P.D.*, 1448 (Apr. 23, 1991); *N.Z.P.D.*, 1680 (Apr. 30, 1991); Harvey, 63.
50. Knowles, 19.
51. Patricia Herbert, "Battle for Power in the Workplace," *Evening Post*, July 2, 1990, at 7.
52. Herbert, "Battle."
53. Knowles, 19.
54. Edmund Byrne, *Work, Inc.: A Philosophical Inquiry*, 132 (1990).
55. Brian Easton, "Reforming the Labour Market—Again," 1 (Dec. 13, 1990).
56. White Paper, at v.
57. *Id.*, 1–2.
58. Peter Brosnan & Frank Wilkinson, *Low Pay and the Minimum Wage*, 40–43 (1989).
59. LRA s 147(2).
60. LRA s 61.
61. Raymond Harbridge, "The Way We Were—A Survey of the Last Wage Round Negotiated Under the Industrial Relations Act 1973," 10 N.Z. J. Bus., 49, 55 (1988).
62. NZEF, 1987 Annual Report 3; Mike Clark, "Award Renewals," *Employer*, Apr. 1989, at 5.
63. Raymond Harbridge & Michael Dreaver, "Changing Patterns of Working Time Arrangements in Registered Collective Agreements in New Zealand," 14 N.Z. J. Ind. Rel., 251, 253, 257 (1989).
64. NZBR, *Review of the Operation of the Labour Relations Act in the 1988/89 Wage Round*, 8 (1989).
65. Helen Clark, Address to the New Zealand Employers Federation 1 (May 13, 1992).

4

The Campaign to Eliminate the LRA, 1987–1990

AFTER THE LABOUR RELATIONS ACT (LRA) WAS ENACTED, THE NZEF-NZBR campaigned even more vigorously to abolish the existing award system. The campaign focused on outlawing compulsory unionism, eliminating unions' rights to exclusive representation, abolishing the Labour Court, and obliterating structures based on a belief that the interests of employers and the employed were not identical.

The NZEF and NZBR claimed that these features made New Zealand's labour relations system unique and thus had caused the country's recent economic troubles.[1] They claimed that replacing these unique features with a flexible, decentralised bargaining would enhance, "through productivity, the returns for both investment of labour and investment capital."[2] Of countries New Zealand should emulate, the United States, Japan, and Switzerland were the most frequently mentioned. These themes were repeated after the election of the National Party on October 27, 1990, through to the enactment of the Employment Contracts Act.[3]

In addition to their arguments, the tone and style of the NZEF-NZBR campaign deserves some brief comment. What first strikes the reader is how remarkably repetitious are their proposals, speeches, and position papers. Even the same anecdotes and phrasings appear in document after document, year after year. Occasionally there is a change in geography or company name in an anecdote to match the audience or speaker. The tone is strident, hostile and sneering to those who oppose them. There is limitless enthusiasm for their program and confidence in the broad range of good it will achieve.

Second, it is striking how lightweight their arguments are and how poor their research was. This campaign was conducted by the most powerful, moneyed and well-connected groups in New Zealand, so lack of resources cannot explain the poor quality of what they advanced. Some claims simply defy experience and could not be accepted by any person who gave even the slightest thought to what was being said. The earlier statements, in particular, provide no support for assertions and no citations to facts, studies, or explanations. Unexplained and unattributed statistics are given, and claims about other countries are made, all without crucial information such as the names of the countries or years, data bases, methodology, or any of the normal information that makes it possible to check reliability. Often when claims involve other countries, a reader aware of foreign events could have known that the claims were either untrue or omitted crucial factors so that the claim as made was misleading. The NZBR also made an odd choice of experts. It tended to based its economic analyses, not on studies by economists, but on articles by attorneys.[4]

It should have been easy to confront the campaign during these early stages. Yet little was done to refute them. Their opponents merely dismissed them as ideologues. There was a price for ignoring what the NZEF and NZBR were saying. Over time, the public and even students of the NZBR came to accept their pronouncements on labour issues. For example, in his careful 1989 study of NZBR power, David Steele noted that the NZBR wanted "to move us towards a de-regulated United States or Japanese-style system in which there are no national awards, no compulsory unionism and no minimum wage law."[5] It is true that the NZBR made this claim, but the content of the statement about other countries is untrue in important ways. If the core of the campaign was to move New Zealand to the system other countries had, then it was important to keep them honest about how those systems operated. In part, the NZEF and NZBR were helped by a willingness on the part of New Zealanders to believe the worst of other countries, particularly about the United States.

Despite their inaccuracy, the NZBR gained a reputation for injecting a higher quality of research and discussion into the public arena. Yet there should have been warnings that prompted deeper investigation. For example, there was the problem of their relying only on limited theories as the basis for all their proposals:

> Their power comes from the simplistic consistency of the position from which they argue—accept the premise and the rest falls into place—and the dearth of similarly resourced pressure groups able to test the arguments and respond tract for tract.[6]

It was not until just before the 1990 election that the NZEF-NZBR began to produce what had the appearance, if not the substance, of respectable scholarly research. The major piece designed to give intellectual respectability to their labour views was *Freedom at Work*,[7] by NZBR policy analyst and economist Penelope Brook. "Brook's proposals for labour law reform match[ed] almost exactly the legislative program of the National party. A conspiracy theorist might even assert that the publication of *Freedom at Work* was perfectly timed to provide a veneer of intellectual respectability to the actions of the National government."[8] Brook gives strong credit to United States tort and contracts law professor Richard Epstein for her ideas. Comparing her book and his writings shows a very close tracking.

Delving into the arguments the NZEF and NZBR were making about labour relations law provides frustrating insights into lost opportunities to have confronted their program with the truth. Careful analysis and strong opposition beginning in the mid-1980s could have changed the way the next decade unfolded. In countries where similar groups and arguments are still centre-stage, these lost opportunities and their consequences should provide a lesson and a spur to action.

Specific NZEF–NZBR Arguments
1 *Voluntary versus compulsory unionism:* The NZEF-NZBR strongly objected to compulsory unionism or dues payment,[9] although many New Zealand employers worried that opposing systematic payment of union dues might damage harmonious workplace

relations and waste time and production to sort matters out.[10] Despite this employer concern, the NZEF-NZBR objected to it on four main grounds. First, New Zealand was unique as "one of a very few OECD countries that now insists on this outdated practice."[11] Second, workers were harmed by it.[12] Third, voluntary unionism would force unions to improve services for members.[13] Finally, voluntary unionism was part of a program of reforms "aimed at establishing a free and decentralised system of contracting" and would facilitate "individualised forms of contracting which suit workers whose needs vary from the norm."[14]

Robert Dahl asks: "But why should happiness, justice, personal freedom, equality, security and all other values yield to the supreme value of autonomy? Is autonomy good in itself, or is it good at least in some measure to the extent that it is exercised in a responsible choice of good ends?"[15] The NZBR and NZEF position was that autonomy was good in and of itself and even if it led to bad ends.

The NZBR and NZEF often linked voluntary unionism to eliminating unions: "Experience in [other countries] also demonstrates the fallacy of the claims in the New Zealand debate that compulsory unionism is needed to protect workers and defend wages. Unionism is voluntary and rates of unionization in Japan and the United States are below 30 and 20 percent respectively."[16] Workers, they said, could do better on their own:

> In logic, the starting point for a worker should be the decision whether or not to join a union for the purpose of collective representation (or other benefits), or whether to negotiate acceptable arrangements on an individual basis. . . . Unionization makes little sense where work patterns and preferences are diverse, individual incentives matter and few economies are obtained from collective negotiation, monitoring and enforcement of bargains.[17]

The NZBR and NZEF said they were motivated by altruism and concern for workers and unions and a system that would best provide for each worker's uniqueness. They mixed contempt for unions with arguments that unions should be exposed to market forces and competition.

> In no way can our proposals be construed as anti-union. Trade unions reflect the need to have associations in many circumstances, not least to minimise the costs of negotiating and enforcing agreements. They can also provide valued services to members. What is at issue is the form of many unions, which is often divorced from the common interests of a workplace, and the lack of effectiveness stemming from protected positions. Unionization should not be forced on groups in the economy where such arrangements are not relevant. But in an environment where unions were free to adapt their structures and compete for the provision of services, their vitality, responsiveness and democratic accountability to members could only be enhanced.[18]

Unions were portrayed as tyrannical[19] and collective bargaining as irrelevant or even harmful to workers.[20] They suggested that unions were an impediment to important economic objectives.

> The central issues in any labour relations regime are its rules governing the way employees represent themselves individually or collectively in contracting with employers, and the rules governing the way contracts are struck. The issue for public policy is to determine a regulatory environment which facilitates job creation and higher living standards by allowing workers to compete for jobs and employers to compete for workers, with the lowest possible costs of contracting.[21]

NZEF-NZBR statements suggest that, although they claimed to be concerned for workers' rights to liberty and freedom of association, the debate was actually about economic power.

Brook also argued that employees' interests were different from and not represented by their unions: "Claims by employers for cost-reducing measures have tended to be resisted by union officials rather more than by workers themselves. . . ."[22] Brook did not consider the possibility that workers might not oppose employer cost-cutting as vigorously as unions, not because they agreed with it, but because individual workers can only achieve their goals collectively.

The NZEF said unions were "superfluous",[23] unnecessary or impediments in the workplace. Anne Knowles, NZEF Labour

Market Manager, wrote: "[I]t is the equally firmly held view of proponents of the [ECA] bill that . . . divisions that have been created in the workplace by outside constraints imposed by current legislation will be removed, allowing the employer and employees at an enterprise to have full and open communication."[24]

Was there evidence that could have been marshalled to cast light on the claims made about unions, dues, and union membership? In fact, there was not only theoretical but also empirical evidence that when they had been given a chance to eliminate compulsory payment of union dues, New Zealand workers had voted to keep them. This had occurred after National Government legislation in the late 1970s required votes on compulsory unionism. Not one clause was eliminated as a result, and the overall vote was over 89% in favour.[25] Workers "went to the polls" seven years later in 1984, when National simply outlawed compulsory unionism. Most unions lost only 1–5% of members during that period, with some losses resulting from lay-offs or redundancies rather than refusals to join unions and pay dues.[26] Unions which lost the most members were those made up mostly of women and part-time workers,[27] an experience that would predict life under the ECA.

Even the LRA provided evidence that workers were not eager to leave unions or cease paying dues. The LRA allowed individuals to opt out of union membership.[28] Furthermore, if employers refused to agree to a union membership provision, employees could vote on compulsory unionism. These ballots supported compulsory unionism.[29]

There was also readily available evidence that could have countered the argument that all but New Zealand workers had complete freedom whether to join a union or pay dues. The United States was a favourite exemplar of a country with no compulsion; however, simply reading the National Labour Relations Act would have dispelled that claim. It states that workers can be terminated for refusing to pay dues.[30] Compulsory unionism was also common in other countries at the time, including payment of dues even by non-members—something not provided for in New Zealand.[31]

Considering all this—that New Zealand workers had greater ability to opt out of union membership and dues, that they had repeatedly voted on the issue, that other countries had similar systems—the NZEF-NZBR managed to overlook clear and easily accessible evidence to the contrary of their positions. Many NZBR members had overseas holdings and first-hand experience with foreign systems. How did they get it so wrong when it should have been easy to locate accurate information?

In the ultimate test, however, accuracy did not count, for ECA ss 6–8 eliminated compulsory unionism and membership.

2 Voluntary representation: The NZEF and NZBR argued that unions should only have the right to represent a worker who had personally recently chosen the union.[32] They argued that competing for members would make unions more responsive.[33] Ron Trotter urged that active competition between unions to provide services to workers would not be disruptive and that workers should be able to determine their own best interests in deciding on union services, just as they freely choose to engage other professional services.[34]

The NZEF and NZBR also proposed that, when an award expired, employers could offer individual contracts to workers in competition with the union.[35] Eventually individual employment contracts would be the norm in smaller workplaces.[36] They claimed "that the overwhelming majority of the OECD countries have labour relations systems based on collective bargaining in the unionised sector coupled with voluntary unionism and individual contracting."[37] The NZBR further claimed that "the development of non-unionised arrangements" was permitted elsewhere,[38] without specifying where or in what context.

Competition would also benefit unions: "The standing of trade unions in the community would be enhanced if the monopoly privilege they enjoy were withdrawn, and the allegiance and loyalty of their members were attracted on a voluntary basis."[39] This would not weaken worker representation and welfare, they argued,[40] but other statements suggested that they had a special definition of worker welfare:

> Union representatives argued against the formation of enterprise unions and "contestability" on the grounds that "sweetheart"

unions would develop and disruptive inter-union rivalry would occur. The self-interested and empty nature of these claims is illustrated by the following observations on the harmonious and highly productive Japanese industrial relations system from a member of the United States Council of Economic Advisers:

> Why do Japanese unions allow a degree of flexibility that would be an anathema to American unions? The reason: they are organised companywide rather than industrywide. Because national unions in Japan rarely control locals' policies, a single industry contains several different "enterprise unions" as they are called, and these unions compete with one another. Workers will moderate wage demands rather than jeopardise their firm's market share.[41]

The proposals on representation were confusing and inconsistent. Some favoured having one union for each workplace, while others wanted each employee to exercise full and frequent freedom of association even if this resulted in multiple representatives within each workplace. Worker self-determination and freedom of choice were not compatible with the goal of having only one workplace representative. Freedom of choice does not exist if there is only one choice.

Freedom to choose a representative also did not mean freedom to choose an effective representative. Employees could choose union membership; however, "membership of a particular union by a majority of workers in a particular workplace would [not] confer on a union an automatic right to bargain."[42]

Permitting employers to offer individual contracts in competition with unions would create chaos and undercut the unions' ability to resolve workplace problems and co-determine workplace terms. Employers who wished to throw off unions would first undermine the union by refusing to resolve grievances. The employer could then capitalise on employee dissatisfaction, by holding a one-time "fire sale"—offering bonuses and other incentives if workers would repudiate the union. This would lead to weeks and months of uncertainty as an employer waged negotiations on several fronts. Bitterness and uncertainty, the seeds of industrial unrest, would be likely to linger whatever the outcome.

No structure was proposed to promote stability. This was such an enormous change that the practical effect was unclear. One model was the British system in which many unions represented an employer's workforce, based on their extent of organisation. This had tended to lead to greater workplace strife and militancy, with competing unions waging jurisdictional or demarcation disputes, creating the need for frequent negotiation, and wasting time and production.[43] Despite all these problems, this proposal became the core of the ECA.[44]

The NZEF and NZBR championed more than competition among unions for members. They advocated having non-employees compete for the jobs of those currently employed. They complained about the problem of "current registration rules [which] put obstacles in the way of people from outside unions, such as the unemployed, offering to provide work at a lower price."[45] Douglas Myers asked: "Why can't a young unemployed kid in Gisborne go to an employer and say: 'Give me a chance, take me on for six months at half the going rate, let me learn and see what I am worth at the end of that time?'"[46] Another NZBR member asked: "Another symptom—Why can't an unemployed kid in this region [Nelson] go to an employer and ask for a chance of taking him or her on the payroll at a special rate to learn something and establish a relationship with the employer, which may lead to a permanent job? Just such a start could be the key to becoming a responsible citizen and climbing up the income ladder."[47]

To return to the question, was New Zealand unique in curbing full freedom of choice? Not really. The US, for example, rejects the sort of freedom that was advocated. The NLRA gives one union exclusive representation rights based on majority decision of workers in a bargaining unit,[48] as do many other countries.[49] In addition, NLRB-developed doctrines such as contract and election bar promote a balance between stability and freedom of choice. Under each doctrine, during certain periods of time, ranging from one year to three years, workers cannot change their representative or the unit in which they are represented.

Contrary to the NZBR, it is not the norm elsewhere to permit employers to bargain with individual employees at the termination of a collective bargaining agreement to try to persuade them to deunionise. In the United States it would violate labour law, since employers are prohibited from dealing directly with employees.[50] While the NLRA permits decertification of a union, employer involvement in the process can violate s 8(a)(2).

The proposals on freedom are striking in their dishonesty. First, other proposals and statements made it clear that there was no intention to allow the freedom promised. Second, although they claimed this freedom would benefit workers and unions, other statements show the goal was lowering wages and creating compliant bargaining partners.

3 Award coverage: If there was any one aspect of New Zealand industrial relations which most aroused the NZEF and NZBR, it was the award system. Historically, award and blanket coverage were welcomed by employers because they ensured a level field with no competitor being able to undercut another.[51] The NZEF and NZBR, however, complained bitterly when the LRA did not outlaw awards outright[52] and pressed for what they called decentralised labour relations.[53]

The key argument for eliminating uniform minimum wages and working conditions across workplaces was that it was unique: "Uniform national agreements are virtually unknown outside" Australia and New Zealand.[54] Eliminating them would improve employer–employee relations.[55] NZBR member Athol Hutton stated: "There is no incentive for Waitaki to have good relations with our employees when they delegate the task of representing them to outside officials and we ask a person whom we don't employ to undertake our negotiations. I am irresponsible to allow this to continue to happen."[56]

NZBR member Lindsay Fergusson said: "[B]y and large real progress towards arrangements that improve productivity and safeguard jobs is only possible outside the award system."[57] They made other arguments: poorer employers would be better off without awards, because they took no account of ability to pay; awards were complex and confusing, especially when multiple agreements or awards applied in one workplace;[58] only poor managers could favour awards, the sort of employers who simply did not want to "talk to their own people" or to treat them "as people with their own individual needs and aspirations, not commodities for sale at a fixed price established by some national award...."[59]

They praised the United States and Japan as successful models of enterprise bargaining[60] but overlooked the fact that both have important bargaining structures which recreate aspects of the award system. Both the United States and Japan have long had large numbers of workplaces with multi-plant and multi-employer agreements.[61] In those countries these are created through pattern and coalition bargaining, national, statewide, or regional contracts, and master contracts. These are forms of agreement common in the manufacturing, retail, hospitality, government, and transportation sectors.[62]

Factors which influence the level at which bargaining takes place include national tradition, the structure of employer and employee organisations, country size, issues, tactical considerations, and economic conditions.[63] No one bargaining structure is best for all. Employers dominant in an industry are likely to prefer enterprise bargaining because they believe they can negotiate the best deal alone and have staff experienced in bargaining. Multi-employer bargaining compensates for small employers' deficiencies in power and expertise and lowers bargaining costs.[64] It recognises that employers negotiate with an eye on their competition and ensures that competitors will make the same deal and will be hit with a strike or lockout at the same time.[65] Multi-employer bargaining can more successfully resolve industry-wide problems and promote industry training.[66]

It is difficult to explain the NZEF-NZBR's apparent ignorance of foreign practices when this information was readily available. They also seemed unaware that the system they advocated would benefit those most influential within the NZBR and NZEF—the larger, stronger employers—and disadvantage the smallest, weakest employers—the ones not represented by the NZBR.

Given their fervour, one might think that the LRA had prohibited enterprise agreements and that law reform was the only way to achieve them. However, an enterprise agreement could be achieved if an employer made an offer that was attractive to other employers and unions. Employers who were unsuccessful in achieving enterprise agreements could not blame the LRA.

Rather, they had failed to make a convincing case for their views. What they could not gain at the bargaining table, they used the force of law to give them.

4 The Labour Court: In all senses of the word, the Labour Court and labour law were a peculiar target of the NZEF-NZBR. They advocated eliminating the Labour Court and vesting its jurisdiction in the civil courts,[67] although the Labour Court's structure was similar to those in European countries and most of the world.[68]

Labour courts are not only expert bodies capable of grasping the nuances of cases, they also represent a commitment to an industrial law freed from common law contract and tort concepts. They represent a judgment that the common law has historically proven itself inadequate to deal with the work relationship.[69] Common law contract concepts are not suited to industrial reality in which one party remains subservient to the daily and ever-changing demands of the other.[70] Others have argued that private law concepts such as contract "are close to useless when we are talking about a relationship that is complex and that changes over a long time."[71]

The NZBR's statements about the employment relationship were so abstract they suggest they had not understood its complexities. Ronald Trotter suggested treating employment as a simple commercial relationship: "An employment relationship should be a relatively straightforward deal. An employee is essentially offering his or her labour services to a willing buyer, on terms and conditions which are periodically renegotiated."[72] Economist Penelope Brook claimed that the common law had been benign in its effects on workers' rights and dismissed the significance of common law criminal conspiracy which had been used to defeat union organisation as "an unfortunate flirtation."[73]

The employment relationship is complex. An appropriate law must reflect its nature, and judges must be able to understand and apply that specialised law. To create law specifically applicable to the industrial context and then leave its interpretation and application in the hands of civil judges will inevitably lead to an admixture of concepts the law was enacted to be rid of.[74]

In the end the ECA did not eliminate a specialist labour court. However, although the ECA established an Employment Tribunal and an Employment Court to exist primarily as an appellate body,[75] this result was not accepted, and the attack on the court has continued.

5 The commonality of employer and worker interests: The NZEF and NZBR argued that New Zealand industrial relations legislation needed to be cleansed of the idea that employer and employee interests conflict. In other countries, all understood that their mutual goal was productivity and that the interests of workers and unions were served by a closer identification with the employer.[76] The LRA was a failure because it was "based on the premise of an inherent on-going conflict of interest between employers and workers,"[77] which is a "shibboleth and source of confusion."[78] Employers want to run a profitable and efficient business, so "[t]he main concern of employees is that the business that employs them generates a sufficient return so that they can continue to be employed in a profitable and efficient operation." The goals of "individual employees" and employers are so consistent "it seems obvious that any external constraints that work against the common goals should be removed."[79]

It is true that in other countries, some employers and some unions have entered into cooperation agreements, just as those in New Zealand can do and did under the LRA.[80] The argument that cooperative systems are fundamentally different from and incompatible with a strong collective bargaining system is not necessarily accepted in the United States.[81]

Labour–management cooperation was central to the NZBR–NZEF campaign. They contended that cooperation, equality and fairness were the natural state for the workplace when there is no third party interference.[82]

> The idea that capitalists as employers exploit workers has been around for a long time. It has wafted around snooty circles as well as shop floors and has been absorbed through a sort of intellectual osmosis by academics, editorial writers, news reporters and others too lazy to think things through for themselves.

> . . . In a free market employers are thought to have the upper hand because they do the employing. The free market thus allows them to use their "bargaining strength" to drive down wages and so increase their profits "unfairly".
>
> . . .
>
> The theory blows up once you realise that the competition in the labour market is not between workers and employers. It is instead between employers for workers.
>
> . . .
>
> Employers thus must compete for workers. Sure, they want to get workers as cheap as they can. But they have to pay a price sufficient to get workers to work for them. The need to outbid other employers puts a floor to the wage that must be paid.[83]

The labour market was tied to the idea that workers and employers were united in making the employer as profitable as possible. Nothing else mattered. Labour–management cooperation and individual freedom would improve working conditions and the country's economy. Peter Shirtcliffe, NZBR member and Chairperson of Telecom NZ, said: "Improved customer satisfaction—giving people more of the goods and services they need in better quality, at prices they can afford—is *the* central objective of deregulation: the force driving opportunity, innovation, business growth, economic expansion, higher employment, higher wages, and better social harmony for the future."[84] This reflected the NZBR's objectives that "the interests of the business sector are closely aligned with those of the community at large."[85]

The unitary workplace was tied into the issue of freedom and autonomy in an odd way that was highly intolerant of debate and diversity of opinion. In fact, this was the problem with unions: unions advance views on employment issues that differ from or conflict with the employer's, this creates dissent in the workplace. Eliminating unions would eliminate dissent and lead to a workplace free to engage in single-minded cooperation.[86]

> [I]t is the . . . firmly held view of proponents of the [Employment Contracts] bill that the new legislation will have the . . . effect

... that divisions that have been created in the workplace by outside constraints imposed by current legislation will be removed, allowing the employer and the employees at an enterprise to have full and open communication.[87]

Under this view, unions created dissent and, oddly enough, also suppressed individuality. Peter Carroll, General Manager of the Auckland Employers' Association, claimed unions wished to have "everyone toeing the same line with no deviation" and despised those "not conforming with the union line."[88] The NZEF and NZBR failed to explain their inconsistency in advocating individual choice, insisting that employee interests were invariably the same as the employer's, and arguing that individual choice to deviate from identification with the employer is illegitimate. They claimed to respect their workers and their choices but asserted that choosing union representation was not legitimate.

Of course, it is true that unions are organs of dissent. Unions become concerned with goals that transcend one employer. Key union goals are worker solidarity across workplaces and taking wages out of competition. At times these union goals must conflict with employer goals of competition against other workplaces. It is also true that most workers, isolated in one workplace, only periodically see their common interests with employees at a competitor's. Furthermore, many unions would not equate the success of capitalism as guaranteeing the general welfare.

Intolerance of dissent and discussion was directed not only at unions. Those who supported the ECA were disciples of unitary management, an ideology which emphasised hierarchy and managerial prerogative and which saw accommodation of disparate interests as weakness.[89] Nigel Haworth attributed this anti-democratic tendency to the influence of Hayek:

> Its result in New Zealand is a clear lack of confidence in political intervention in economic activity. The universe of economic behaviour is now partially independent of the political process, and in an important sense is free from the concerns of equity and representation at the heart of the democratic process. MNC's

[multi-national corporations] are no longer to be controlled, argues the new orthodoxy; they are seen as key guarantors of well-being.[90]

NZBR Executive Director Roger Kerr confirmed that dissent was unwelcome within their ranks: within the NZBR itself, there has never been any debate "about the need for comprehensive reform or the shape it should take."[91] In April 1991, Kerr stated: "Labour relations policies are not a matter of political debate in successful countries. I would be surprised if they are a source of contention in New Zealand in a few years' time."[92]

These statements, at once overblown and untrue, while also being anti-democratic, reveal much about the ECA ideology. It was advocated by those who saw dissent, discussion, individual thought, or participation—all necessary to maintain democracy—as of no value and even as highly negative. Few asked, however, what this anti-democratic bent meant in relation to the goals the organisation advanced with such zeal.

Uncovering the Inner Vision
These proposals formed the ECA, even though, as discussed, most were demonstrably and objectively inaccurate. They were not based on reality or solid research. Their hidden vision encompassed the role to be played by unions, workers, and employers. Although the NZBR and NZEF claimed their proposals were non-partisan and that they would benefit unions, other statements displayed antagonism towards unions.

They claimed that unions were illegitimate because they owed their existence to statute.[93] This is puzzling, since most NZBR and many NZEF members were corporations and also owed their existence to legislation. Corporations were created by legislative action to do what otherwise would not be legal. A corporation is nothing but an aggregation of capital permitted to do business while not making those who benefit responsible for its actions.[94] Indeed, but for the protections law gives corporations, unions might be unnecessary.[95] Unions are aggregations of people which came into existence to permit workers to deal effectively with the aggregations of capital permitted by the corporate form.[96]

The attack on unions was relentless. Unions were aliens whose interests were inimical to workers' needs and desires: "[T]here is considerable evidence that too many union officials do not genuinely represent the interest of significant parts of their membership, and their motives for resisting moves to enable workers to exercise freedom of choice are very clear."[97] That unions were hostile to the interests of the poor and unemployed[98] was demonstrated by union support for the minimum wage.[99]

In the new system unions would be a sort of personnel agency providing services to "customers" on a competitive basis: "Thorough reform of the system, including breaking down barriers to competition, will transform unions in much the same way that the deregulation of product markets has transformed business in New Zealand and made it more productive and responsive to consumers."[100] Unions would exist in a system controlled by economic outcomes: "The bottom-line test of the performance of any employment relations system is a simple one: is it achieving high levels of employment and high levels of productivity growth?"[101] Missing were issues of justice, equality, and democracy.

What the NZEF-NZBR hoped to see was a system of workers and employers—without unions—free to engage in contracting at the lowest possible cost.[102] This raises not only the political question of what balance of power should be struck between unions and employers but also a philosophical issue, one challenging the function of institutions which exist in and as part of democracies. Democracy requires diverse interests, opinions, and views, and a process of robust discussion and election.[103] The new system had no place for these.

The NZEF-NZBR did not want discussion and workplace co-determination with equal partners. They wanted a law that would give them complete control and saw the rhetoric of labour–management cooperation as a benign-sounding way to explain their goals. The problem was that, if they achieved the law they had lobbied for, the largest New Zealand employers would have unfettered power and workers would have little protection. Labour–management cooperation is difficult to implement successfully. When used to increase production without true participation,[104] such systems often decline.[105] Similarly, grievance systems set up without union involvement have been found insufficient to replace those provided by unions, because employees fear reprisals or feel they are ineffective.[106]

This, however, was what the NZEF-NZBR advocated. The NZEF's handbook on employee involvement programs stated that "the effect of consultation should be to achieve the co-operation of employees in . . . the implementation of management decisions." Labour–management programs were not intended to provide employees with influence over workplace decisions.[107]

The NZEF-NZBR's real moral and political vision was not the enchanting portrait they advanced. The inner logic revealed a sombre portrait of a country which would be based on unilateral, oligarchic employer control and powerless unions relegated to a peripheral role. The portrait was to be filled out with worker competition and powerless workers on lower wages. The danger of radical law reform, given the history of industrial relations and the goals of the reformers, was that it would lead to a society in which deregulation ratified and cemented the current hierarchy. The public portrait was a pleasant one done in impressionistic pastels. The one beneath that surface was altogether different.

Notes

1. Roger Kerr, Letter to the Editor, *Dominion*, Dec. 5, 1989, at 10; Ronald Trotter, "New Zealand Labour Market Reform: Class Struggle or Productivity Struggle?" 8–9 in NZBR, *Labour Markets and Employment: New Zealand Business Roundtable Statements on Labour Relations* (1988); Douglas Myers, "Industrial Relations: A Better Way" in NZBR, *Labour Markets*, 6–7.
2. "Submissions of the NZEF to the Royal Commission on Social Policy: Summary," *Employer*, Feb. 1988, at 1; Lindsay Fergusson, "Labour Relations: The State of the Debate" (Institute for International Research on Managing Change in Industrial Relations, Aug. 17, 1989); *Employer*, Apr. 1989, at 5; *Employer*, Apr. 1987, at 1–6; NZBR, "Labour Markets," *Employer*, June 1987, at 5.
3. Kevin O'Connor, "Shop Floor's New Broom," *Dominion Sunday Times*, Apr. 21, 1991, at 9; Anne Knowles, "Employment Contracts Bill: What's In It for the Workers?" *Examiner*, Apr. 24, 1991, at 7; *N.Z.P.D.*, 1448 (Apr. 23, 1991).
4. See, e.g., NZBR, "Supplementary Submission to the Labour Select Committee on the Options Paper," 4 (Mar. 1991).

5. David Steele, *The Business Roundtable*, 18 (1989).
6. "A Quick-fix Solution," *Dominion*, Feb. 20, 1991, at 14.
7. Penelope Brook, *Freedom at Work: The Case for Reforming Labour Law in New Zealand* (1990).
8. Chris Trotter, "National Axes 96 Years of Boss–Worker Relationships," *National Business Review*, Jan. 15, 1991, at 17.
9. *Employer*, Apr. 1989, at 5; *Employer*, Apr. 1988, at 3; NZEF, 1988 Annual Report 3 (1988); NZBR, *Review of the Operation of the Labour Relations Act in the 1988/89 Wage Round*, 6 (1989) [hereafter Review]; Athol Hutton, "Labour Market Reform and the Labour Relations Act" in NZBR, *Labour Markets and Employment: The New Zealand Business Roundtable Statements on Labour Relations*, 6 (1988).
10. Peter Brosnan, "Introduction" in *Voluntary Unionism*, 1, 2–3 (Peter Brosnan, ed., 1983).
11. Hutton, "Labour Market Reform," 6; Roger Kerr, "Industrial Relations After Rogernomics—Why There Has to be a Better Way," 3 in NZBR, *Labour Markets*; Fergusson, 6–7.
12. Horton, "Labour Market Reform and the Labour Relations Act," 7; Loach, "Freedom in Employment," 8, 13, 14 in NZBR, *Labour Markets*.
13. Fergusson, 6–7; Loach, 13–14; NZBR, *Review*, 6.
14. Fergusson, 6–7; NZBR, *Freedom in Employment: Why New Zealand Needs a Flexible Decentralised Labour Market*, 7 (1987); NZBR, "New Zealand Labour Market Reform: A Submission in Response to the Green Paper," 47 (1986); NZBR, *Review*, 6; Douglas Myers, "Labour Market Reform: Getting It Right," 9 in NZBR, *Labour Markets*; Rowe, "Implications of Voluntary Unionism: The Employer's Perspective," 27, 29 in *Voluntary Unionism*.
15. Robert Dahl, *Democracy and Its Critics*, 48 (1989).
16. NZBR, "Submission to the Labour Select Committee: The Labour Relations Bill," 6 (1987).
17. NZBR, 1987 Submission, 6.
18. Trotter, "New Zealand Labour Market Reform," 9.
19. Ronald Trotter, "National Party Industrial Relations Policy," 4 in NZBR, *Labour Markets*.
20. Fergusson, 9.
21. NZBR, 1987 Submission, 8–9; Patricia Herbert, "Battle for Power in the Workplace," *Evening Post*, July 2, 1990, at 7.
22. Brook, 79.
23. Patricia Herbert, "Employers' Federation Almost Outdoes Itself," *Dominion*, Nov. 26, 1990, at 10.
24. Anne Knowles, "Employment Contracts Bill: What's In It for the Workers?" *Examiner*, Apr. 24, 1991, at 7.
25. John Howells, "For or Against Compulsory Unionism? Recent Ballots in New Zealand," 122 Int. Lab. Rev., 95, 100 (1983).
26. Raymond Harbridge & Patrick Walsh, "Legislation Prohibiting the Closed Shop in New Zealand: Its Introduction and Consequences,"

27 N.Z. J. Ind. Rel., 191, 199–200 (1985).
27. Harbridge & Walsh, 199–200.
28. LRA ss 82, 83.
29. Letter from M. E. Feely, Deputy Registrar of Unions (Feb. 13, 1990); Fuller, "The Functioning of the Labour Relations Act 1987—Unions" in *Evaluating the Labour Relations Act 1987*, 14 (Raymond Harbridge, ed., 1989).
30. 29 U.S.C. ss 157, 158(a)(3), 158(f), 159(a).
31. E. Cordova & M. Ozaki, "Union Security Arrangements: An International Overview," 119 Int. Lab. Rev., 19, 24, 28–29 (1980); Cullen, "Recent Trends in Collective Bargaining in the United States," 124 Int. Lab. Rev., 299, 306 (1985).
32. NZBR, Review 7; NZBR, Green Paper Submission, 48; Fergusson, 9.
33. Trotter, "New Zealand Labour Market Reform," 9.
34. Trotter, "National Party," 3.
35. "The Labour Relations Bill," *Employer*, Apr. 1987, at 3; Economic Monitoring Group, 55 (1986); NZBR, Green Paper Submission iv, 6–7, 47.
36. NZEF, *The Industrial Relations Green Paper: An Employer Perspective—Summary of the Submission by the NZ Employers Federation*, 3 (1986).
37. Kerr, "Industrial Relations After Rogernomics," 3; NZBR, 1987 Submission, 6, 13–14.
38. NZBR, Green Paper Submission, 49.
39. Myers, "Getting It Right," 17; Athol Hutton, 7.
40. NZBR, 1987 Submission, 4.
41. *Id.*, 9–10.
42. *Employer*, Apr. 1987, at 3.
43. P. K. Edwards, *Conflict at Work: A Materialist Analysis of Workplace Relations*, 145 (1986); Brosnan, 2–3.
44. ECA ss 6, 10.
45. Myers, "Industrial Relations: A Better Way," 7.
46. Douglas Myers, "New Zealand Labour Market: Breaking Moulds," 6 in NZBR, *Labour Markets*.
47. Loach, 8.
48. NLRA ss 7 and 9(b); 29 U.S.C. ss 157 and 159(b).
49. Cordova & Ozaki, 26.
50. *Medo Photo Supply Corp. v. N.L.R.B.*, 321 U.S., 678 (1944).
51. New Zealand Planning Council Economic Monitoring Group, *Labour Market Flexibility*, 47 (1986).
52. "Award Renewals," *Employer*, April 1989, at 5; "The Wage Round," *Employer*, April 1988, at 3; NZEF, 1988 Annual Report, 3 (1988); NZBR, *Review*, 7–9.
53. *Employer*, Feb. 1988, at 1; NZBR, Green Paper Submission, 5, 44.
54. Ronald Trotter, "Reforming the Labour Market—Idle Dreams or Real Prospects?", 9 in NZBR, *Labour Markets*.
55. Ronald Trotter, "Government Policy Statement on Labour Relations,"

2 in NZBR, *Labour Markets*.
56. Hutton, 4–5.
57. Fergusson, 4.
58. NZBR, 1987 Submission, 13–14; Rose, "The Pursuit of Full Employment: Macroeconomic Perspectives," 11 N.Z. J. Ind. Rel., 65, 73 (1986).
59. Myers, "New Zealand Labour Market: Breaking Moulds," 8; NZBR, *Review*, 11.
60. NZBR, *Freedom in Employment: Why New Zealand Needs a Flexible Decentralised Labour Market*, 10 (1987); Ronald Trotter, "Political and Economic Change in Britain and New Zealand," 7 in NZBR, *Labour Markets*.
61. Hendricks & Kahn, "The Determinants of Bargaining Structure in U.S. Manufacturing Industries," 35 Ind. & Lab. Rel. Rev., 181, 198 (1982); Richard Freeman & James Medoff, *What Do Unions Do?* 39 (1984); Derber, "Employers Associations in the United States," 79, 83–93 in *Employers Associations and Industrial Relations* (J. Windmuller & A. Gladstone 1984); K. Sisson, *The Management of Collective Bargaining: An International Comparison*, 171–72 (1987); Levine, "Employers Associations in Japan," 319, 346–53 in J. Windmuller & A Gladstone.
62. Freeman & Medoff 35, 39; K. Sisson 18–22, 171–72; Booth, "The Bargaining Structure of British Establishments," 27 Brit. J. Ind. Rel., 225, 231–32 (1989).
63. International Labour Organization, *Collective Bargaining in Industrialised Countries: Recent Trends and Problems*, 28 (1977).
64. Weber, "Stability and Change in the Structure of Collective Bargaining," 13, 21–22 in *Challenges to Collective Bargaining* (Lloyd Ulman, ed., 1967); Booth, 226.
65. Booth, 226; Weber, 15–17; Otto Kahn-Freud, *Labour and the Law*, 132 (1977).
66. P. Willman, *Technological Change, Collective Bargaining, and Industrial Efficiency*, 138 (1986).
67. NZBR, Green Paper Submission, iii, iv, 5–6, 11, 32, 40, 47.
68. Benjamin Aaron, "The NLRB, Labor Courts, and Industrial Tribunals: A Selective Comparison," 39 Lab. & Ind. Rel. Rev., 35, 36–37 (1985).
69. Margaret Wilson, "A Few Observations on the law Relating to Security of Employment" in *The Industrial Law Seminar*, 1, 1 (Legal Research Foundation 1979); James Atleson, *Values and Assumptions in American Labor Law*, 13, 14, 94 (1983); Roberto Unger, *The Critical Legal Studies Movement*, 71–73 (1983).
70. I.T. Smith, "Is Employment Properly Analysed in Terms of a Contract?" 6 N.Z.U. L. Rev., 341, 341, 342–42, 365 (1975).
71. Peter Linzer, "The Decline of Assent: At-Will Employment as a Case Study of the Breakdown of Private Law Theory," 20 Ga. L. Rev., 323, 392–93 (1986).

72. Trotter, "Idle Dreams," 3.
73. Brook, 6.
74. Atleson; Lord Wedderburn, "Labour Law: From Here to Autonomy?" 16 Indust. L.J., 1, 13–14, 16–17 (1987); Gordon Anderson, "The Reception of the Economic Torts into New Zealand: A Preliminary Discussion," 12 N.Z. J. Ind. Rel., 89, 91–92 (1987).
75. ECA ss 75–140.
76. NZBR, *Critique of the Labour Relations Act* 2 (n.d); NZBR, 1987 Submission, 10; Horton, 8; Hutton, 4; Myers, "Getting it Right," 16.
77. Horton, 9; NZBR, 1987 Submission, ii; *Employer*, Apr. 1987, at 1.
78. Myers, "Getting it Right," 7–8; NZBR, 1987 Submission, 4.
79. Knowles.
80. NZEF, 1988 Annual Report, 4.
81. Dept. of Lab. Bur. of Lab. Mgmt. Coop., *Labor–Management Cooperation and the Duty of Fair Representation in U.S. Labor Law and the Future of Labor–Management Cooperation, Second Interim Report* (Oct. 1987); Maryellen Kelly & Bennett Harrison, "Unions, Technology, and Labor–Management Cooperation" in *Unions and Economic Competitiveness*, 247 (Lawrence Mishel & Paula Voos, eds, 1992); William Cooke, "Improving Productivity and Quality Through Collaboration," 28 Ind. Rel., 299, 313 (1989).
82. Brook, 17.
83. Rodney Hide, "Evil Greedy Boss Class Figment of the Mind," *National Business Re*view, Mar. 13, 1991, at 16.
84. Peter Shirtcliffe, Address to the NZEF Convention 4–5 (May 13, 1992).
85. Nicola Natusch, *An Analysis of the Influence of the New Zealand Business Roundtable Since Its Inception*, 1 (1990).
86. Herbert, "Battle for Power."
87. Knowles.
88. Peter Carroll, "Towards Voluntary Unionism: Serving People, Not Institutions," *Examiner*, Dec. 6, 1990, at 23.
89. John Deeks, "Colonising the Managerial Mind: Management and Business Ideologies" in *Transition in Business and New Zealand Society* 107 (John Deeks & Peter Enderwick, eds., 1994); John Deeks, "New Tracks, Old Maps: Continuity and Change in New Zealand Labour Relations, 1984–1990," 15 N.Z. J. Ind. Rel., 99, 112 (1990).
90. Nigel Haworth, "National Sovereignty, Deregulation and the Multinational: New Zealand in the 1980's" in *Controlling Interests: Business, The State and Society in New Zealand*, 16, 29 (John Deeks et al., eds., 1992).
91. Roger Kerr, "A Small Step In the Right Direction," *National Business Review*, Apr. 17, 1991, at 7.
92. *Id.*
93. NZBR, Green Paper Submission 7; Wedderburn, "Labour Law—A Hold and a Nudge," 13 Indust. L. J., 73, 78–79 (1984).

94. Anderson, 94–95; Wedderburn, 21; see also Ireland, Grigg-Spall & Kelly, "The Conceptual Foundations of Modern Company Law," 14 J. L. & Soc., 153 (1987).
95. Martin Vranken, "Comment," 11 N.Z.J. Ind. Rel., 7 (1986).
96. Barkin, 2–3; NLRA s 1, 29 U.S.C. s 151; Marion Crain, "Feminizing Unions: Challenging the Gendered Structure of Wage Labor," 89 Mich. L. Rev., 1155, 1159–72 (1991).
97. Trotter, "National Party," 4; "Unions—Friends of Their Members?" *Employer*, Apr. 1989, at 3.
98. Myers, "New Zealand Labour Market: Breaking Moulds," 6; NZBR, 1987 Submission, 25.
99. Loach 14; Trotter, "Political and Economic Change," 13; Myers, "Industrial Relations: A Better Way," 12–13.
100. Trotter, "New Zealand Labour Market Reform," 10; Myers, "New Zealand Labour Market: Breaking Moulds," 9.
101. NZBR, *Review*, 15.
102. NZBR, 1987 Submission, 8–9.
103. John Deeks, "Ideology and Industrial Relations in New Zealand," N.Z. J. Ind. Rel., 26, 27 (1976); Atleson, 44–45.
104. D. Smith, "A Critique of Worker Participation in New Zealand," 3 N.Z. J. Ind. Rel., 71, 71, 79 (1978).
105. Elliger & Nissen, "A Case Study of a Failed QWL Program: Implications for Labor Education," 11 Lab. Stud. J., 195, 201–202 (1987).
106. Freeman & Medoff, 108–109.
107. NZEF, *Employee Involvement in the New Zealand Workplace: An Introduction and Guide to Worker Participation*, 35 (1977); *Employer*, Oct. 1989, at 2.

5

The 1990 Election Campaign— Unions Prepare for Change

Just Prior to the October 1990 Election
Long before the October 1990 elections it was clear the Labour Party could not win election to a third term. Labour had used its two terms from 1984 to 1990 enacting a business agenda.[1] Labour's natural constituency felt betrayed as they watched their party privatise state services and remove protective regulations. Others who had benefited from these changes supported Labour until the 1987 sharemarket crash was followed by ever-rising unemployment. Labour could not win without the support of its traditional constituency, but it could not regain the loyalty of working class New Zealanders and the Left because the party was still advancing its business agenda.[2]

Labour could also no longer turn to those who had supported it and its program of liberalisation and deregulation. It had declared a "tea break" from further reform.[3] When Labour said it was rethinking its economic liberalisation program, the business community decided it was time to return to its natural ideological home, the National Party.[4]

Labour tried to improve its standing in the polls by replacing Prime Minister Geoffrey Palmer with Mike Moore on September 4, 1990, one month before the election and less than one year after Palmer had replaced former Prime Minister David Lange. So many changes so late only made Labour look desperate and in disarray.[5]

In contrast, the National Party serenely campaigned under its manifesto (party platform), "Creating a Decent Society." After the ECA was introduced, many claimed that they would not have voted for National had they known that it intended to introduce such radical legislation.[6] However, labour market reform was a major issue in National's campaign,[7] and National spelled out the specifics:

We will:
1. Reintroduce voluntary unionism.
2. Encourage more flexible bargaining arrangements between employers and employees.
3. Allow employees to choose their own bargaining agents.
4. Give industrial agreements the status of binding contracts.
5. Give workers greater flexibility to decide who will represent them in dispute procedures.
6. Introduce a minimum code of wages and conditions.[8]

National explained that "flexible bargaining arrangements" meant introducing a system in which workers could negotiate "individual contracts, through workplace or enterprise agreements, to industry and national awards."[9] It said it planned to "allow employers and employees to jointly choose their own bargaining arrangements; be they workplace, enterprise or industry arrangements" and "[a]llow employees to choose their own bargaining agents, be it a union or otherwise, to represent them in industrial negotiations."[10]

In July 1990, columnist Patricia Herbert predicted that within 100 days of taking office, National would amend the LRA to achieve these goals. She said: "The focus will be threefold. They will allow workers to go outside their unions and appoint their own independent bargaining agents and they will give each worker absolute discretion over (A) whether or not to join a union and (B) which union to join."[11] Three months before the election, the Public Service Association (PSA), the union which represented many public sector employees, accurately spelled out National's policies and their consequences. It said that unions would have no special role, that workers would be encouraged to move to individual contracts, and that worker free choice meant unions had no guaranteed membership.[12]

It is true that National occasionally soft-pedalled its positions and was not always united during the election. However, if National's manifesto left anyone unclear as to its plans, its language ought to have prompted voters to inquire further and not to have assumed the best. Despite this, some unions insisted that change would be minimal, just outlawing union security or compulsory unionism. Other unions saw that radical change was on the way.[13] Rosslyn Noonan, leader of the New Zealand Educational Institute Te Riu Roa, disputes after-the-fact claims that National was elected only because no one knew they would make such a radical change in industrial relations. "[T]hey were very clear. Don't let anybody tell you that the National Party did not spell out what it intended to do in the industrial relations area, because it was very unclear in a number of areas, but in the industrial relations area, it was absolutely clear."[14] To be fair to those who were caught by surprise, National had, in the past, used radical rhetoric in its election campaigns, but then moderated once in office.[15]

Whatever the reason, on the eve of massive and devastating change many trade unionists were not prepared for life under a hostile legislative regime.[16] So extreme have the changes been that, within two years under the ECA, even some in the union movement admitted there was no turning back.[17] Just how true this was became clear when Labour presented its proposed Employment Relations Act prior to the 1993 elections. It built on the ECA rather than rejecting its principles. It provided free choice of bargaining representative (although with limits on change during contract bargaining to ensure stability), no compulsory interest arbitration, and the loss of blanket coverage.[18]

Union Preparations for Change
On the eve of the ECA, some New Zealand unions were highly entrenched within the old system, even dependent on it for existence. Others were undergoing fundamental change as new leadership emerged. They were attracted to strategic ways of thinking and were implementing what they hoped would be more effective tactics, including making greater use of their delegate

(shop steward) structures and increasing the education level, involvement, and activism of their staff and members.[19]

Of the small sample of unions examined here, certain qualities seem to stand out as accounting for their distinct actions in the pre-ECA period. Those with creative, intelligent, and democratic leadership seemed best able to make themselves aware that times were changing and to force themselves to prepare. They approached the threat as a problem to be solved. They searched actively and broadly for solutions. They thought about the nature of their current memberships and tried to share information and power within the organisation. The job of preparation included mental preparation, skills training, and organisational streamlining. There were also important differences among these unions.

1 The Service Workers Federation of Aotearoa: The Service Workers Federation of Aotearoa (SWF) was an umbrella organisation of unions which represented a broad range of mostly unskilled and part-time workers, including restaurant workers, custodians, nursing home workers, security staff, and musicians.[20] The SWF's membership is roughly equivalent to that of the Service Employees International Union and Hotel Employees and Restaurant Employees Union in the United States. In late 1990, the SWF represented approximately 70,000 workers, of whom 70% were women, as well as many Maori, Pacific Islanders, and South-East Asians.[21] In May 1991, its constituents amalgamated, and it became the Service Workers Union. After two and a half years under the ECA, its membership was 25,900.[22]

This decline in members may be shocking, but, given the jobs its members performed and the industries in which they worked, it should come as no surprise. SWF members were among the most poorly paid in New Zealand,[23] with full-time wages in the range of $14,800 to $18,500 a year.[24] The presence of large numbers of women and minorities among its membership would suggest to many that they would have hard work to keep these groups organised.[25] However, more recent work suggests this may not be true.[26] Some suggest that the "difficult to organise" label may have resulted from different styles of organising among

66   WORKING FREE

women-centred unions,[27] or may reflect stereotypical thinking on the part of some unions.[28]

The SWF's National Secretary, Rick Barker, was one of the union leaders who tried to prepare for change. He thought that one of National's first actions would be new labour law.[29] Barker thus urged massive change within the union on a number of fronts. The union looked abroad to predict what could be expected and for successful strategies, in particular to the more contentious American environment. The union then promoted education programs for union officials, including importing American trade unionists to teach American organising techniques. These exercises were to equip SWF organisers to operate competently in a new collective bargaining environment.[30]

> I would like to say that the object was for us to have sufficient numbers of our people having an appreciation first hand of what the likely environment of this was to be. This was so they would be able to say, "Well, this is what people have survived, and they can do these things," and to have enough personal reserves and confidence to tackle the future. That was what I saw the objective to be. We were not certain what we were facing at that point.[31]

The exercise provided information on others' mistakes and an opportunity to devise ways to avoid them.

> The most useful thing I learned was the statistic of decertification. Seventy percent of all decertification ballots was because of the perception of lack of service. As I understand, that is the figures of both the UFCW [United Food and Commercial Workers] and the Hospital/Hotel employees and the generally accepted figures are right around the 70% mark. I find it very clear if that's the experience in America why people leave unions, it would be no different here. We don't have any statistical base here about why people leave, so you have to build a system that ensures a good level of service to the membership.[32]

The SWF decided to use the organising model of unionism to set up committees within each worksite to maintain organisation on the job,[33] in contrast with the traditional servicing model. In the servicing model, the union acts as a body with expertise which provides problem-solving services to its members for a fee, essentially the role the NZEF-NZBR advocated for unions. In the organising model members solve their own problems and promote higher organisation, empowerment, and success.[34] The SWF wanted the central union to providing the workplace committees with information, expertise, and assistance, that would support the committees' activities rather than control them. It tailored communications with each of its groups through newsletters targeted to their special needs.

The SWF also tried to negotiate new agreements in place of the pattern set by the awards.

> When it [the award covering tearooms, restaurants, and fast-food outlets] was written in 1900, no one had ever heard of the fast food industry, in particular the chains, the type of place, the language and the structures in the award. So people in McDonald's would pick it up and would not see any reference to swing shifts; they would see no reference to all the phrases that were commonly used.
>
> And for people who were flipping hamburgers they were cooks. They were cooks engaged to reconstitute precooked or pre-prepared foods. This was just a nonsense to them. It seemed that the document was irrelevant in terms of the sick leave. It was written in terms of full-time staff who worked regular shifts. And there was sort of an add-on to it to deal with the casual nature the industry had become. The whole document was written upon the basis of full-time code with occasional part-time code as an appendage to it, when in reality, the industry had become almost completely casual and to read one entitlement for sick leave for a casual, part-time worker was pretty hard to interpret. But all of those things were turned around so it became very clear. It was written from the perspective of an employee, the type of person who was engaged by McDonald's.[35]

In early 1990, the SWF began breaking down its Restaurants Award into four agreements to cover different sorts of establishments.

This effort was a harbinger of things to come. Only a year or two earlier, employers would have welcomed this. By 1990, however, most employers were no longer interested. They knew significant change that would benefit them was on the way. The one exception was McDonald's. In June 1990, it agreed to a plain-language contract drafted specifically for it. The SWF–McDonald's negotiations included direct member involvement in formulating positions through in-store meetings and a national meeting attended by approximately thirty-six McDonald's employees from around the country.[36]

The SWF's preparations included the more prosaic work of restructuring itself to survive on a reduced dues income. According to Barker, the industries it represents have only 3% of the workforce organised worldwide. He therefore predicted that SWF membership would drop toward this figure once the LRA's protection was gone. As a result, the union began to remove redundant functions, centralised operations, and tried to have its staff specialise so it could provide higher-quality, more effective service to members and potential members. It organised itself by the specific areas it represented so it could be more focused and could ensure that specific tasks were not overlooked. It also hoped this would encourage members to identify more strongly with their divisions than they could with the more general union. In addition, it borrowed business tools in information collecting and analysis to improve its management functions. Finally, on the eve of the enactment of the ECA, it completed its amalgamation and became the Service Workers Union of Aotearoa.[37]

2 *The Engineering & Related Trades Union:* The Engineering & Related Trades Union (Engineers), a union made up largely of automotive and metal trades workers, began changing its operations as early as 1987. Two things prompted this. First, the downturn in New Zealand's manufacturing industries after the sharemarket crash depleted the ranks of the Engineers and forced them to think about survival. At the same time, the LRA opened up the range of issues that could be bargained about.[38]

As did the SWF, the Engineers looked abroad for models it saw as negative, such as the United Kingdom and the United

States, and positive, mainly Europe and Northern Asia and particularly the Swedish and Finnish metal workers unions. The Engineers saw those countries as pursuing a strategy of developing high-tech, high-skilled, high-wage industries with productive manufacturing bases and high rates of unionisation. As a union, they wanted to become service and membership driven in order to cope with a deregulated environment. The Engineers wanted to break out of what was defined as "the union point of view" to expand their role to include economic issues. To this end, the Engineers advocated an integrated approach to economic policy and labour relations. They embraced the 1987 legal changes and even some of those in the ECA because they removed what the union saw as the system's past inflexibility.[39]

The Engineers decided that member satisfaction depended on member contact with their organiser. Each organiser was required to visit every worksite at least twice a year and, preferably, several times a year, instead of appearing only for negotiations or when problems arose. A pool of organisers worked with jobsite delegates, and the number of delegates increased and their role was made more visible. In this way, the union had a continuous noticeable presence on the job. Union organisers were to give support to the steward only as needed and to legitimise the steward's authority. Organisers were instructed to involve their stewards during site visits and to have stewards play a larger role in grievance handling.[40]

The Engineers also began to recruit paid staff from sources other than the workplace. The union hired graduates of professional programs, people from the Labour Department, who were sympathetic towards the union movement, and other non-traditional union employees. "[T]hey even got down to wearing blue suits and nice ties to make themselves more presentable and more acceptable to the employers that they were meeting with."[41] Different sorts of stewards were also recruited:

> The union has a public image of being a white male trades union, even though the majority of our members are not highly skilled workers.

Historically shop stewards had been white male tradesmen, usually someone from the tool shop. In a plant of 300 people where the union covered both the maintenance areas and all the production workers, the representation system was difficult. Quite often production workers would be of different social groups—for example, Polynesian women. They deferred to the seniority of the trades group. At times this was unproductive because information didn't flow through or was in the wrong format for most of the members. It also meant a biased view would come back from the delegate structure about what they wanted.

In order to improve representation, the union aimed to improve the delegate ratio. If a workplace had 12 members, it should have a delegate. In a plant of 300, for example, we would have 4 or 5 delegates rather than relying on just one person to do the job. By boosting representation the delegate structure became much more reflective of and responsive to the membership.[42]

Accompanying these personnel reforms were changes in the written materials sent to the membership. The Engineers wanted written contracts to "put unionism on the job" by offering workers different ways to become involved in their union. Jobsite delegates were given detailed information about important issues accompanied by resources they could hand out to the workers, such as a flyer, a pamphlet, or a sticker. These written communications were intended to be material that was useful and actually read and which would lead workers to see themselves linked to the union and as getting more out of their union. The Engineers also used written materials to build a membership that was better informed on issues affecting them in and out of the workplace.[43]

For example, when the government began restructuring medical services under the Accident Compensation Corporation (ACC), the union paper, *Metal*, contained articles and a small tear-out pamphlet on the changes.[44] The delegates' kit had background information on the changes accompanied by attractive stickers saying "ACC Cuts Can't Heal," as well as a petition if the delegate was interested in seeking signatures, and other related materials that could be put to use.

The Engineers were strongly influenced by Australian workplace reform[45] long before the ECA was introduced. They began to focus negotiations on non-traditional issues, such as productivity, worker incentives, redesigning skills, and training. This led the Engineers to want a collective bargaining document focused on the industry, as opposed to an occupational award.[46] In 1987, the Auckland branch negotiated what was known as the "Nissan Way" agreement with Nissan Manufacturing. This was influenced by agreements at other Nissan plants in the United Kingdom and the United States.[47]

> The decision was to change from some of the more staid elements in trade unionism. To move on from just bargaining about wage increases to looking at the whole picture about what productivity meant. The decline in manufacturing forced some of this. To survive as a union, we needed to have members in jobs. If we were going to represent manufacturing workers, then we had to ensure that the manufacturing sector survived at a time when it was evident that it was going under in this country. So we started looking at strategies for manufacturing and began promoting a much wider agenda.[48]

This should seem strange only to those who believe that there is "a causal connection between workers forming a union and productivity declining, as if workers were more interested in 'loafing' than in helping to maintain the source of their livelihood."[49] On the other hand, it brought the Engineers close to the NZEF and NZBR position that employee interests were in productivity, with the exception that the Engineers made a place for unions. Murray French of the Wellington Employers Association observed: "And that union very much was promoting a sympathy with employers on the basis that if employers were successful, their members would benefit."[50] This focus on helping employers be more efficient made the Engineers a target of criticism by other unions.

By late 1989, the Engineers began to prepare for the expected change in government and the impact it would have on the union:

We looked far and wide, combing through speeches of Bill Birch [then the Opposition National Party's shadow Minister of Labour]. While the National Party made big statements that they were going to reform labour legislation they were very tight-lipped about exactly what they were going to do. Some thought they would just bring in voluntary unionism. But we could see that they were going to go far further and wanted to know how far. At that time there was a strong emphasis on individual choice and individual freedoms along with the usual cries for labour market flexibility.[51]

The report prepared for the Engineers' July 2–6, 1990 meeting at Hastings reflects these pre-election preparations. It advocates creating "an ability to handle the radical change a National Government could impose upon us."[52] The Engineers predicted that union recognition would have to be earned, rather than being a matter of registration; that National would remove controls on the labour market and give individuals the right to choose "how they wish wages and employment conditions to be negotiated and disputes resolved."[53] It then analysed how each of the specific predicted changes—voluntary unionism, flexible bargaining arrangements, free choice of bargaining representatives, and the like—would function.[54] The report even included a model collective bargaining contract, something not needed before.[55]

3 The New Zealand Educational Institute Te Riu Roa: In 1989, the New Zealand Educational Institute Te Riu Roa (NZEI-TRR), a union of primary school teachers and workers, was forced into self-examination as the result of pressures to restructure New Zealand's public schools.[56] These pressures would only increase once National came to power. Ruth Richardson, National's Minister of Finance and a major force in the drafting of the ECA, advocated imposing fees beginning at kindergarten. She explained that the government was opposed to putting more money into a "statutory monopoly" like a kindergarten.[57]

Two years before National took office, pressures to act more like the private sector forced the NZEI-TRR leadership to change its structure:[58]

> We were very clear that this is what was going to happen, and we had a good look at how the organisation was operating and how it represented the interests of different groups of members, whether every group member genuinely could feel they had a voice in the union and a say on the matters that affected their lives and a very rigorous review of what was being provided and how it could be improved.
>
> ... [A]s part of the process, we completely reviewed what we called a recruitment and retention campaign. ... It was ... a systematic review of all aspects of the way the organisation operated and where members came in contact with the organisation and what the quality of their contact was and what could be done to improve that. And so we focused as much on retaining existing members, because I think in a way, because we were a compulsory union, there was a fear that we would lose some members once it ceased to be compulsory. And so we focused, not just on recruiting new members, but what was required to retain all of our existing members.[59]

The union wanted to change Maori attitudes from seeing the union as uninterested in them and uninvolved in their concerns to wanting to take an active role. NZEI-TRR created a new structure "from the grass roots up," called Miro Maori (Maori Thread).[60] Union publications affirmed the value of Maori culture and tradition by featuring issues of concern to Maori and including articles written in Maori. Union meetings respected Maori tradition, including welcomes from the tangata whenua at meetings. Maori participation increased and strengthened the organisation's ability to respond to members' interests and needs. This meant setting up a structure so that Maori could set policy on Maori issues and that those structures were given adequate resources and funding. In addition, to prevent Maori and Maori issues from being isolated, information was shared with members about the changes.[61]

Women and women's issues were also given prominence. "And similarly now, we have women's networks as well, we have a woman's officer. The position was established in late '88. That is another identification of the extent to which targeting a membership group that needs support to become more involved and active and to be able to see that the union was actually affecting the interests and needs."[62]

As a result, NZEI-TRR entered 1990 having already restructured in the face of stress to become a union as efficient and representative as possible.

4 The Clerical Workers Union—NZ: Many, if not most New Zealand unions, entered the ECA era ill-prepared.[63] One of the least prepared was the Clerical Workers Union—NZ (CWU). The CWU was New Zealand's second largest union, with 40,000 members in 1985. Nine months after the ECA's enactment it was defunct,[64] except for COMPASS, which represented private-sector clerical workers in the northern part of New Zealand and in Southland and which eventually amalgamated with the SWU.[65] This meant the loss of a large group active in support of women's rights.[66]

The CWU was aware it had to meet the challenge National posed. However, it was a union by nature dependent upon the award structure. It tried to expand union services, marketing and recruiting unorganised clerical and administrative workers.[67] Its one advantage was that about half its members were covered by an award that did not expire until February 1992, so it had time to adjust.[68]

However, other factors were more important. Rather than strengthening the CWU, its recent amalgamation led to an internal power struggle and difficulty integrating the constituent unions into a new structure.[69] Even had there been no internal struggle, the CWU represented difficult-to-organise workers.[70] Its typical member was one of only two clerical workers at a worksite. Worksites were separated and scattered throughout the country. Thus, the union faced an enormous—perhaps impossible—task just to visit all its members at their worksites.[71]

Survival for the CWU meant relying on compulsory union membership and supportive legislation. This is not to say that clerical workers did not want to support their union or that they became members only under compulsion. According to Clerical Workers organiser Maxine Gay:

I found members hid behind the legislation. People who did want to be union members found it difficult. They were largely women, largely nervous and anxious, so for them having legislation meant that, well, of course, I don't want to be a law-breaker, Mr. Employer, so I am going to be a member. And this was really in small towns where nobody could police it anyway. So although the law was there, it was pretty well self-regulating. People retained their membership.[72]

In fact, the CWU reported losing only 160 members from a total of 15,000, one month after the ECA.[73]

The final difficulty facing the CWU came from the union movement itself. It was Council of Trade Unions (CTU) policy to support only industry-based unions. CWU members worked across all industries and thus could never meet this goal.[74] The union was aware if it met with difficulty, it could not expect support from the CTU.

In late August 1991, the union announced that it was considering liquidating and turning its membership over to the industry union in the workplace which employed the particular clerical worker. The CTU promoted this as a way to rationalise union structures. In November 1991, the CWU announced it would dissolve itself in February 1992, even though it was still losing no more members than other unions.[75]

The Northern Clerical Workers Union resisted liquidation. It had just restructured itself in June 1991 as a white collar workers' union and renamed itself COMPASS for Commercial, Professional, Administrative, Secretarial Staff Union of New Zealand. This change signified its goal of attracting members of middle management who had not been protected by industrial relations legislation before the ECA.[76]

The CWU's dissolution took place in an atmosphere of disarray amidst accusations of betrayal. Some union staff complained that they had agreed to cut their redundancy payments to save the union. Union vice-president Sandra Bishop complained that the dissolution of the union had been "steamrollered" by the union secretaries and the CTU. Other union officers echoed this complaint or protested that the union had failed to consider other options. Even worse, the union's sudden discontinuation left many members with no coverage or home to go to in the union movement. Among these were 300 union organisers who had been represented by the Clerical Workers.[77]

> All it succeeded in doing was deunionising huge numbers of clerical workers. If there had to be a dissolution and if they were to go to other member unions, they ought to have gone at the time that those other unions were negotiating their contract and then the clerical workers included into them. But what happened was here's shut-off day now so clerical workers were simply in limbo, and I think what was really significant is even after it had closed and all the announcements had been made, people still continued to pay their fees. People still remained members.[78]

Some organisers simply continued to perform their former duties, as freelancers.

> By that stage I had started negotiating employment contracts for a number of firms, and I felt an obligation to finish those contracts. I had asked in December when we were made redundant on that day, I simply asked that question—what about my work in progress, what about the personal grievance cases that I'm handling at the moment, and what about the employment contracts that are in the process of being negotiated?...
>
> And then at that stage also my former colleague, Dolly Larkins, and I had established the Administrative and General Workers Union. Dolly was made redundant in October, so she became [the AGWU's] first unpaid paid worker, and we made a pact at that time that we would split whatever income we could get. And so from October I shared my salary with her, and she worked attempting to set up the new union out of the ashes of the Clerical Workers Union.[79]

By May 1992, four organisers worked for the newly formed Administrative and General Workers Union, primarily in the Palmerston North area: Dolly Larkins, George Larkins, Maxine Gay, and Robert Reid, all with no pay. Together they were representing about 120 members. Eventually, they affiliated with the

Manufacturing and Construction Workers Union as a white collar workers' division. Leon Morel of the Canterbury Clerical Workers Union also announced that he would set himself up as a bargaining agent for clerical workers and would form a new union.[80]

5 Manufacturing and Construction Workers Union: The Manufacturing and Construction Workers Union (MCWU) is essentially an umbrella organisation for a number of small unions which amalgamated as a result of their shared interests and to meet the LRA's requirement that a union have a minimum of 1000 members. It operates as more of a confederation than a full amalgamation.[81] The MCWU's membership has remained steady at about 3,000 since 1991.[82] The greatest number of its members have been in the metal industry, an industry mainly represented by the Engineers. The two unions have had long-standing jurisdictional disputes as the result of overlapping coverage in their registrations. This long-running battle has been exacerbated by the ECA.[83]

This is not the only area of disagreement between the two. The MCWU opposes the workplace reform policies the Engineers advocate and, instead, has taken a strongly confrontational stance towards management. It views itself as part of a "world-wide tradition of workers . . . prepared to take militant action when, as responsible unionists, we find that this is the only way in a right cause."[84]

The MCWU's philosophy on the role of unions "is basically that a union should do what its members want, and that should be determined by the members in meetings. As a result of that, the members ought to have meaningful control over the union. They must control its resources."[85] The MCWU policy of decision-making in meetings based on majority rule resembles the International Longshore Workers Union on the west coast of the United States.[86] The union promotes democratic action by paying its officers no more than the members,[87] a policy that has helped union finances, no small matter in surviving in a hostile situation.

The MCWU has tried to make itself visibly relevant to its members by involving them in and giving them power over core financial decisions.

78 Working Free

> So, unlike unions that are increasingly centralising funding, and then respond to people's needs in accordance with a centrally determined policy, our funding is decentralised. We have about eight accounting centres, which means there are eight sets of meetings looking at expenditures, eight different areas that the people concerned can approach for resources to carry out this or that. Within each occupational group or industry group, they have autonomous control within the policy of the union as a whole over their own affairs. You can't elect a superior group that will dictate policy to any section.[88]

It also involved defining the union's areas of concern broadly to meet those of the members.

> And the union should be looking out for the interests of the members in the broadest terms. If that means that you put some of the union's funds into giving kids Hepatitis B injections, well, that's what you do. If it means that members' income is affected by State house rent increases, well, you try to organise a rent strike. If it affects the members in any way and people are interested in it, then the duty of the officers is to carry that out.[89]

An example of this was the MCWU loan fund. In 1988, when the union discovered that members were being exploited by loan sharks charging 1000% interest, it created a fund that would loan up to $500 with an administration charge of $22, to be repaid at a rate of $29 per week. In 1991, the union loaned $147,000 to about 500 workers.

> Now, to people who do not have that facility, when you go around the plant shelling out money to people when they need it, so they don't have to go and borrow it from people at high interest rates or don't even have to leave the job to get it, all they have to do is ask the delegate—other people look at that and they say: "Why can't our union do that for us?"[90]

Policies like these had an impact on making membership attractive after the ECA came into effect:

A third of the people that left the Engineers Union and joined us would have done so because they wanted a union. Another third would have done so because the others did. One-third would have left simply to get a loan. So, doing what the members want, even if it's off-beat and not really a traditional union activity is something that will persuade people that "Yeah, okay, we'll join that organisation, because it's meeting a need that we have. We can't meet it anywhere else." People on lower pay, the ability to get a $500 loan to smooth out your income to meet the unexpected bills is a really incredible thing to have, and the cost of it is so low—$22 for $500.[91]

The MCWU was not the only union to expand services to meet members' needs. Other unions, including the Engineers, were providing services such as group discounts on medical and life insurance, setting up union medical centres where less expensive medical services could be provided, and providing legal representation in areas other than just labour relations.[92] In doing so, they were meeting the NZEF and NZBR prescription that unions should provide services members wanted as a way to increase their market share.

6 *New Zealand Council of Trade Unions:* In 1991, 65% of New Zealand unions representing 87% of union members were affiliated to the New Zealand Council of Trade Unions (CTU).[93] The CTU pursued a strategy which largely paralleled that of the Engineers. It saw itself as taking a creative approach to union issues that would enlarge its role in New Zealand society beyond traditional union issues to pursuing integrated strategies attacking issues such as full employment, trade and labour policy, productivity, industrial democracy, and other social issues; participating as an equal member in tripartite bodies with government and capital; focusing on creating growth and wealth, as opposed to focusing solely on the equitable distribution of resources; pursuing these goals within and without the workplace; and creating educational and research services.[94] As part of this effort, the CTU promoted a rational structure for New Zealand unions. In 1989, it proposed amalgamating the union movement

into fourteen unions from 112 at that time. These larger unions would have greater resources and a wider bargaining focus.[95]

The CTU was hampered in its plans from 1984 to 1990 by the Labour Government. "The supply-side victory in the Labour caucus made the union perspective on economic policy irrelevant, even obstructive. It also disestablished the unions as the key client group of the Labour Party in power. Not only were union economic priorities not relevant but the channels of influence expected to open with a Labour victory were blocked."[96]

The CTU's alliance with the Labour Party left it unable to criticise when labour's own party privatised government agencies and deregulated industries. When the public looked to the CTU for leadership, it heard nothing. Not criticising policies that hurt working people broke faith with them and left their needs unheard within their party. As the October 1990 election drew closer, there were no easy choices. It was one thing to criticise the Labour Party for policies which had caused workers genuine suffering but another thing to let criticism help National win. If voters elected National by voting to punish Labour, they would be choosing the party most likely to implement the very policies they did not like. On the other hand, Labour did not deserve to be re-elected or at least deserved to be punished or criticised.

The more unpopular Labour became, the less the CTU could criticise it, for fear this would only lend support to the National Party. The CTU also could not wholeheartedly endorse Labour. Its only option appeared to be silence, but silence destroyed its credibility. The run-up to the election left unions and unionists demoralised and divided. Some continued to be actively involved in the Labour Party. Some supported Labour reluctantly, feeling that no alternative party could win election. Others, especially those close to the New Zealand Communist Party, such as the MCWU, accused the CTU of collaborating with Labour in its "Big Business" policies.[97] The Building Trades Union opted to support Labour and educate its members about what electing a National government meant, but its members rebelled. "These meetings gave the union hierarchy a roasting for suggesting that members should cast their vote for Labour. The view that was expressed was that the Labour Government had let them down and anything would be better than another term or at least it couldn't be worse."[98]

With but a few months left till the election, the Labour Party tried to heal the rift with the unions. In July 1990, CTU officials and Helen Clark, Minister of Labour, began negotiations for a Compact Council, which would consult on policy-making.[99] On September 17, 1990, the CTU reached a Growth Agreement with the Labour government, which set a 2% ceiling on wage increases, unless justified by higher productivity. With inflation at 5% and Members of Parliament having just received a raise of 31%,[100] the 2% limit was not well received. The CTU had hoped that this would show that unions should have a role with government and industry on policy setting and that this would prove the value of unions and legislation that protected workers, making it more difficult for a National government to repeal them.[101]

They might as well not have made the effort, because the agreement fell apart almost as soon as it was put together. National called the deal a stunt. The NewLabour Party charged the CTU with selling out workers. The NZEF called the agreement positive[102] but "wanted no part of such a formalised, predetermined structure."[103] It called the Tripartite Wage conference "ritualistic" since employers made their decisions based on the market and not on government or union wishful thinking.[104] Several major unions, such as the Engineers Union and Harbour Workers, tried to demonstrate the viability of the agreement by quickly limiting their wage demands to 2%.[105] Two percent quickly became the benchmark for settlements, even though before the agreement was announced, wages had been closer to inflation at 4.5 to 5.5%.[106]

By the early 1990s it was clear "that the mood of the country was for a change and that any National government coming in was going to make quite sweeping changes to the industrial legislation."[107] A May 1990 opinion poll had Labour holding only eight seats.[108] In the opinion of former CTU counsel, Robyn Haultain:

[E]verybody at CTU knew at least three months out from the election that Labour was going to lose and probably more like six. [CTU President] Ken Douglas was very reluctant to admit

> that. He didn't want to believe that, I don't think. He was hopeful that Labour would get back in. There was quite a lot of internal discussion about whether we should start meeting with Bill Birch, from the National Party, and with people who we knew were going to be at the forefront of the charge as far as voluntary unionism and so on was concerned.
>
> . . . [A]ll of the people who worked in the technical services division had a very strong opinion that we ought to be meeting with Birch and as many of other National Party people as we could. The writing was on the wall. The Nats were going to win and at the very least we were going to have voluntary unionism. Some of us thought that we were going to have a hell of a lot more which would turn out to be a hell of a lot less from the point of view of workers. . . . [109]

This meeting never occurred.

> [Meeting with Bill Birch] was personally abhorrent to [Ken Douglas] and he didn't want to go and meet with him. He didn't want to do it. And he kept on thinking that workers would see the writing on the wall and realise that even though Labour had done the dirty on them in pretty horrendous ways that they would still be better off with a terrible Labour government then they were going to be with a National government which would be far more brutal for them in terms of their working lives. So he just hung on to the hope that they would vote Labour and Labour would get back in so that he would never have to talk to Bill Birch.[110]

With National's victory having come to pass, the public seemed to take a deep breath while it waited for events to unfold. National, meanwhile, already was making preparations for massive changes in labour law.

Notes
1. Chris Trotter, "New Industrial Relations Era Frogmarching History to the Door," *Examiner*, Feb. 28, 1991, at 7.
2. Owen Harvey, "Towards a Union Strategy for the 1990's" (June 1988).

3. For one inside account of events affecting Lange's decision, see Bruce Jesson, *Fragments of Labour: The Story Behind the Labour Government* (1989).
4. Jane Kelsey, *The New Zealand Experiment: A World Model for Structural Adjustment?* (1995); Jane Kelsey, *Rolling Back the State: Privatisation of Power in Aotearoa/New Zealand* (1994).
5. Kelsey, *Rolling*, 21, 147; Herbert Roth, "Chronicle," 15 N.Z. J. Ind. Rel., 291 (1990).
6. New Zealand Clerical Workers Union, Submission to the Labour Select Committee on the Employment Contracts Bill 9 (Feb. 1991); *N.Z.P.D.*, 913 (Mar. 19–20, 1991).
7. Jonathan Boston, "The 1990 General Election: Economic Strategies" in *The 1990 General Election: Perspectives on Political Change in New Zealand*, 79, 85, 87 (E. McLeay, ed., 1991); National Party, *New Choices in Industrial Relations*, 1 (May 8, 1990); 511 *N.Z.P.D.*, 493 (Dec. 19, 1990).
8. National, *New Choices*, 1–2.
9. *Id.*, 2.
10. *Id.*, 1.
11. Patricia Herbert, "Battle for Power in the Workplace," *Evening Post*, July 2, 1990, at 7.
12. "Nats Plan For a Future Without Unions," *PSA Journal*, Sept. 13 – Oct. 10, 1990, at 3, 8–9 ; "National Promises More Unions—Fewer Rights," *PSA Journal*, July 12 – Aug. 8, 1990, at 4.
13. Interview with Hel Loader, Research Advocate, New Zealand Engineering & Related Trades Union, in Wellington (May 13, 1992).
14. Interview with Rosslyn Noonan, National Secretary, New Zealand Educational Institute, at Wellington (May 26, 1992).
15. Letter from Brian Easton, economist, to Ellen Dannin, 1 (Mar. 21, 1994).
16. Interview with Rick Barker, National Secretary, Service Workers Federation of Aotearoa, in Wellington (May 14, 1992).
17. Angela Foulkes, "The Culture of Tripartism: Can European Models Be Adapted for New Zealand Use?" 18 N.Z. J. Ind. Rel., 185, 185 (1993).
18. Helen Clark, "Employment Relations—The New Direction Under Labour," 18 N.Z. J. Ind. Rel., 153, 154, 159–60 (1993).
19. Nigel Haworth, "Unions in Crisis: Deregulation and Reform of the New Zealand Union Movement" in *Organized Labor in the Asia–Pacific Region: A Comparative Study of Trade Unionism in Nine Countries*, 282, 282 (Stephen Frenkel, ed., 1993).
20. Service Workers Federation of Aotearoa, "The Employment Contracts Bill: Submissions of the Service Workers Federation of Aotearoa," 1 (n.d.).
21. SWF, "Submission," 1.
22. Raymond Harbridge & Kevin Hince, *A Sourcebook of New Zealand*

Trade Unions and Employee Organisations 67 (1994).
23. Marlene Kim, "Overview: Losing Ground, Increasing Hate—Workers and Minorities Today" in *Building on Diversity: The New Unionism*, vii, viii–ix (Lab. Res. Rev., ed., 1993).
24. SWF, Submission, 1.
25. Dorothy Cobble, "Introduction: Remaking Unions for the New Majority" in *Women and Unions: Forging a Partnership*, 3, 6 (Dorothy Cobble, ed., 1993); Marion Crain, "Feminizing Unions: Challenging the Gendered Structure of Wage Labor," 89 Mich. L. Rev., 1155, 1159–72 (1991).
26. Linda Hill, "More Than a Cuppa and a Scone," *Labour Notes*, Sept. 1992, at 11.
27. Marion Crain, "Feminism, Labor, and Power," 65 S. Cal. L. Rev., 1819, 1870–85 (1992); Crain, "Feminizing Unions," 1173–74.
28. Patrick Renshaw, *American Labor and Consensus, 1935–1990*, 152–168 (1991).
29. Barker.
30. Id.
31. Id.
32. Id.
33. *Let's Get Moving! Organizing for the '90's* (Lab. Res. Rev., ed., 1991); Marion Crain, "Images of Power in Labor Law: A Feminist Deconstruction," 33 B.C. L. Rev., 481 (1992).
34. *An Organizing Model of Unionism*, 1, 2 (Lab. Res. Rev. ed., 1991).
35. Barker.
36. Id.
37. Id.; Haworth, 301; Ruth Needleman, "Space and Opportunities: Developing New Leaders to Meet Labor's Future," in *Building on Diversity: The New Unionism*, 5, 13 (Lab. Res. Rev., ed., 1993).
38. N.Z. Amalgamated Engineering and Related Trades Industrial Union of Workers, *Strategies for Change: Representing Workers in a New Environment*, 3 (1987).
39. John Deeks et al., *Labour and Employment Relations in New Zealand*, 300, 352–54 (2d ed. 1994); Engineering Union, *Strategies*, App. 2–3.
40. Engineering Union, *Strategies*, 20, 26–27.
41. Interview with Murray French, Manager Labour Relations Services, Wellington Employers Association, in Wellington (May 14, 1992).
42. Loader.
43. Id.
44. "Public Health—A Terminal Disease?" *Metal*, Feb./Mar. 1992, at 2; "ACC Submission," *Metal*, Feb./Mar. 1992, at 3; "Health Hazards of Metals," *Metal*, Feb./Mar. 1992, at 4–5; *Metal*, Apr./May 1992, at 6.
45. N.Z. Engineering Union, Inc., *Workplace Australia: The New Zealand Link* (June 1991); *Workreform: The Newsletter for Workplace New*

Zealand No.2, at 1 (undated); Patricia Herbert, "Ripples of Change for the Workplace," *Dominion*, Nov. 3, 1992, at 6.
46. Steve O'Neill, *Labour Market Deregulation: The New Zealand Experience*, 11 (Parl. Res. Serv. Background Paper No.5 1993).
47. Deeks et al., 352–54.
48. Loader.
49. Edmund Byrne, *Work, Inc.: A Philosophical Inquiry*, 139 (1990).
50. French.
51. Loader.
52. Engineering Union, *Strategies*, 5.
53. *Id.*, 5–7.
54. *Id.*, 7–10.
55. *Id.*, App. 6.
56. Noonan; Hugh Lauder et al., "The Labour Market, Education Reform, and Economic Growth," 15 N.Z. J. Ind. Rel., 203 (1990).
57. Colin James, "Now For the Main Course: A Recipe for Self-reliance," *National Business Review*, Jan. 16, 1992, at 11.
58. Noonan.
59. *Id.*
60. *Id.*
61. Bill Hamilton, "Unions Getting to Grips with Issues of Maori Sovereignty," *Labour Notes*, Dec. 1995, at 5.
62. Noonan; see also Crain, "Feminizing Unions," 1180.
63. Interview with Donna Payne, Organiser, New Zealand Nurses Association, in Wellington (May 8, 1992).
64. Russ Francis, "New Zealander Warns of Free Trade Havoc," *Vancouver Sun*, Jan. 16, 1992, at E3.
65. Harbridge & Hince, 67–68.
66. Peter Franks, "The Employment Contracts Act and the Demise of the New Zealand Clerical Workers Union," 28 *N.Z. Journal of History*, 194 (1994).
67. Franks, 206.
68. Rebecca Macfie, "Clerical Union Weighs Liquidation Proposal," *National Business Review*, Aug. 21, 1991, at 4.
69. Interview with Maxine Gay, Organiser, Public Service Association, in Palmerston North (May 17, 1992).
70. Crain, "Feminizing Unions," 1182 n.168.
71. Franks, 194.
72. Gay.
73. Macfie, "Clerical Union."
74. Franks, 203.
75. Macfie, "Clerical Union"; Herbert Roth, "Chronicle," 17 N.Z. J. Ind. Rel., 119 (1992); "Clerical Union," *M&C Workers News*, Dec. 1991, at 2.
76. Roth, "Chronicle," 16 N.Z. J. Ind. Rel., 209 (1991); Macfie, "Clerical Union."
77. Amanda Cropp, "Union Dissolution Angers," *Dominion Sunday*

Times, Dec. 1, 1991, at 14.
78. Gay.
79. *Id.*
80. Cropp.
81. Letter from Graeme Clarke (Nov. 13, 1996); LRA s 6(2).
82. Harbridge & Hince, 49.
83. Interview with Graeme Clarke, General Secretary Manufacturing and Construction Workers Union, at Wellington (May 5, 1992).
84. Manufacturing & Construction Workers Union Charter (1992).
85. Clarke interview; MCWU Charter.
86. Howard Kimeldorf, *Reds or Rackets? The Making of Radical and Conservative Unions on the Waterfront,* 10–11 (1988).
87. MCWU Charter.
88. Clarke interview.
89. *Id.*
90. *Id.*
91. *Id.*
92. French.
93. Kevin Harbridge & Kevin Hince, "Unions and Union Membership in New Zealand 1985–1992," 18 N.Z. J. Ind. Rel., 352, 358 (1993).
94. Owen Harvey, "The Unions and the Government: The Rise and Fall of the Compact" in *Controlling Interests: Business, the State and Society in New Zealand,* 59, 64 (John Deeks & Nick Perry, eds., 1992). Haworth, 293; Foulkes, 188–89.
95. Haworth, 299–300.
96. *Id.,* 288.
97. Harvey, "The Unions and the Government," 68, 72.
98. Murray Reid, "New Union Centre: New Direction," *Labour Notes,* Dec. 1992, at 11.
99. Sarah Heal, "The Struggle Over the Employment Contracts Act, 1987–1991" in *Labour, Employment and Work in New Zealand 1994,* 274, 275 (Philip S. Morrison, ed., 1994); see also Trade Union Education Authority, *The Compact and Current Union Issues* (n.d.).
100. Roth, "Chronicle," 16 N.Z. J. Ind. Rel., 294 (1991); Rebecca Macfie, "CTU Wants to Retain Growth Accord," *National Business Review,* Jan. 23, 1991, at 5.
101. TUEA, "Compact," Ind. Dem., 4.
102. Roth, "Chronicle," 15 N.Z. J. Ind. Rel., 291–92 (1990).
103. Steve Marshall, "Time for Employers to Have Their Say," *Employer,* Apr. 1990, at 3.
104. "Wage Talks Ritual," *Employer,* Sept. 1990, at 2.
105. Herbert Roth, "Industrial Summary Sept.–Oct. 1990," Indus. L. Bull., 88 (Nov. 1990).
106. Brian Easton, "Alternative Systems of Industrial Relations: The Impact of the Employment Contracts Bill," 17 (Feb. 5, 1991).

107. Gay.
108. Raymond Harbridge, "The Impact of Economic Liberalisation on Labour Relations in New Zealand 1984–1990," *British Review of New Zealand Studies*, 4, 69, 69 (1991).
109. Interview with Robyn Haultain, lawyer, in Wellington (May 19, 1992).
110. Haultain.

6

Drafting and Introducing the Employment Contracts Bill

ON OCTOBER 27, 1990, LABOUR NOT ONLY LOST THE ELECTION, it retained only twenty-nine of ninety-seven seats in Parliament.[1] The economy was in such desperate trouble that it would be four more years before it began to turn around. There was general bad news about the high balance of payments deficit and foreign debt, but what was of immediate interest to most people were mortgage and loan interest rates stuck between 12% and 14.5%, and 239,700 jobless out of a working-age population of 2,219,500 with no sign of improvement.[2] This level of unemployment represented a tripling since 1985 when Rogernomics began to take effect.[3] This figure would soon soar. Two months after the election, unemployment figures which included discouraged job seekers increased to 15–20%, from levels closer to 10% through 1990.[4] After adjusting for inflation and increased taxes, workers experienced a 1.5% decline in purchasing power.[5]

Unemployment played a complex role with regard to the ECA. It drove the election results, making the enactment of the ECA possible, and it made the ECA's impact harsher than would otherwise have been the case. The ECA was to be introduced only two months after the elections in the midst of a devastated economy.

The campaign which the NZBR and NZEF waged for the ECA moved to a new forum once National took power. The official terms of the debate were in the briefing papers presented by the Treasury, a department now headed by Minister of Finance Ruth Richardson, and by the Department of Labour, now headed by William (Bill)

Birch. There was also an internal cabinet debate added to the external public debate on facts, theories, and principles.

Treasury's 1990 Briefing Paper
Treasury urged labour law reform because the current labour laws allowed wages to rise too high, thus causing high unemployment. It contended that the only way to bring down unemployment was to lower benefits because, at their current generous level, they gave workers the ability to demand high wages and to hold out against reasonable lower ones. Lower benefits would induce people to work.[6] Treasury supported "a balanced approach that makes benefits less attractive than work, reduces laws and regulations that lead to the low-skilled being priced out of the market, and adopts approaches to benefit administration that help people back into the workforce."[7] The government's 87-page policy statement on social assistance contained at least 72 references claiming that beneficiaries were intent on cheating the system, that fraud and abuse were rampant, that those receiving benefits were different from the ordinary, honest New Zealanders who were paying taxes to provide the benefits, and that benefits were the cause of unemployment.[8]

Treasury argued: "To break the vicious cycle of rising unemployment and increased benefit dependency, it is important to get those able to work back into jobs. To achieve high employment will involve real wage restraint and in some cases real wage declines."[9] This meant there had to be fundamental change in the industrial relations system.[10] Issues concerning the industrial relations system would seem to have been more the concern of the Labour Department, but the new government saw the labour market and labour law as having a pivotal role in reshaping the economy.

Treasury identified three "fundamental flaws" in existing labour law, flaws which also resembled those identified by the NZEF and NZBR:

1. it placed collective bargaining in the hands of unions and employer associations even though individual companies

and workers "have better information and incentives to reach agreement."
2. unions were not accountable to employers or workers.
3. the law made it virtually impossible to alter bargaining arrangements.[11]

Fundamental reform would "allow individual workers the freedom to contract with their employer" individually or collectively and with or without a bargaining representative.[12] Treasury acknowledged that some were concerned "that [its recommended] less-prescriptive regulation might allow employers to exploit workers by driving down wages, and that incomes could fall for groups who already do worse than average."[13] This was short-sighted, because, in the end, workers would gain more from economic growth than through collective bargaining gains.[14]

Given the number of analysts available to Treasury and the bold assertions that the ECA would yield positive results, getting access to its economic analysis of the gains to be achieved under the legislation or of its impact on the economy was not easy.[15] In response to a question in Parliament as to what advice the National government had received on the "anticipated effects of the Employment Contracts Bill on real wage levels," Minister Birch responded that the *Department of Labour* had advised him that it was "not expected that the reforms will lead to further significant moderation or reductions in real wages across the board."[16] Either Treasury had said nothing on the subject, or National did not wish to reveal it.

In some cases the facts Treasury relied on in formulating its proposals were subject to dispute. It argued that New Zealand's minimum wage was unusually generous at 48% of average earnings. However, European minimum wages when measured as a percentage of either average blue collar wages or average wages varied from Ireland's low of 50.2%–62.4% to France's high of 71.8%. Treasury paid little attention to the social and personal impact its recommendations would have if introduced at a time of high unemployment. If people could not find jobs and now had inadequate benefits to sustain them through a time of very high unemployment, the impact was likely to be severe.[17]

Treasury believed that if wages could be lowered more people would be hired. It thought that an employer would hire two workers if it could get them for the price of one rather than simply lowering the pay of the worker and adding the difference to its profits. However, it does not necessarily follow that being able to pay a worker less for the same output means that the wages not spent will be used to increase the number of jobs rather than to increase profits.[18] John Deeks of Auckland University asserted that this leap of faith was taken because of an unwavering belief in

> the ability of the deregulated market to deliver both economic performance and an equitable society. Questions of market regulation or deregulation were not argued in relation to outcomes, that is, in relation to the demonstrable efficiency or inefficiency of the market as a creator of wealth and a regulator of goods and services. Rather they were argued in relation to beliefs, to ideology. The market was given moral authority; it was *a priori* "good" rather than good as a consequence of what it could and did deliver.[19]

Others, in addition to Deeks, pointed out methodological or other flaws in the Treasury recommendations. The New Zealand Planning Council concluded that it would require a drop of at least 28% in unskilled wages to make a dent in unemployment.[20] Another study concluded that the nominal unskilled wage rate would have to fall by 10% for each reduction of the unemployed by 10,000, a wage adjustment which would be "between the infeasible and inhumane."[21] There were a number of studies available which could have given Treasury pause in this great experiment, but did not do so.[22] National chose policies based on theories without empirical studies or social research and without using other means of investigation available to them.[23]

Brian Easton pointed out that Treasury's analysis ignored the lessons of history and the complex dynamics of the existing system:

> There is a quaint naivety here: the Treasury seems to be arguing that by destroying the entire system and rebuilding from nothing,

the problems of the complexity of interrelationships can be avoided, while the design and construction of the new system can be done with a purity and precision that past generations failed to do. This generation supposes it is superior to previous ones, without providing any evidence, other than its arrogance.[24]

There was also evidence that Treasury's claim that decentralised bargaining would facilitate training was seriously flawed when one considered how training programs had come to exist in the first place. Cooperation through the award system had originally set up training programs as a way of overcoming employer fears that their investment in training might be lost should the employee decide to depart with the new skills.[25] The award system also overcame individual incentives to choose short-term investments over longer-term investments, such as training.[26]

To the extent Treasury and others advocated change without adequate analysis, they had the country embark on a voyage into unknown territory with little evidence that it was a wise or safe course.

The Department of Labour's Briefing Paper
The Department of Labour's briefing paper to the new government presents the other side of the internal argument that was taking place within the government. However, although there were fundamental differences of opinion, the department's analysis demonstrated that Treasury was transforming the way New Zealanders perceived and discussed policy, values, and society. Most important, the department accepted that changing benefits would prompt people to seek work. Labour, however, recommended tighter means-testing to ensure that only those entitled to received the benefit did so, reducing benefit fraud and abuse, and applying a meaningful work test rather than reducing benefits.[27]

The Labour Department also contradicted fundamental Treasury assumptions. It argued that people are more restricted than capital and cannot move as easily as money can, that "restrictions on geographical mobility mean labour markets operate very differently from financial markets, which now operate globally."[28] A system of industrial relations must provide for individuals with bargaining power as well as the 60% of the workforce too weak to consummate an agreement.[29] In addition, the new system had to create bargaining structures "appropriate for both a buoyant and depressed labour market" which were "better able to reflect differing circumstances in differing industries and/or enterprises."[30] The Labour briefing paper also warned: "There is a danger in assuming that efficient adjustment is the same as an ability for firms to unilaterally change terms of employment of staff, rather than a process which involves firms and employees in an exchange of information, negotiation and sometimes modification of changes sought."[31]

The NZBR and NZEF
For the first time in a decade, the NZEF and NZBR had the problem, not of lobbying for reform, but of preparing to live with the reality of their industrial relations system. In November 1990, the NZEF issued *The Benefits of Bargaining Reform* "to change employer attitudes so that they will take full advantage of the menu of opportunities National is offering them."[32] The employment utopia in "The Vision" has a successful company complete its five-year strategic plan (which is updated annually). "[E]ach employee is committed to a set of operational and personal objectives, through participation in the planning process." The workers are self-managing, individually fulfilled, problem-solving team workers who work through "[s]taff associations, [which] where they exist are strong and loyal" and facilitate the sensitive and rapid defusing of controversy to obtain mutually satisfactory results. Management provides information freely and regularly and shares profit with the workers, "after capital retention and dividend decisions have been made."[33] In the new world of contract and negotiation, conflicts never arise.

"The Reality—A Picture of Many Enterprises" depicts a rule-bound, inflexible, hierarchical organisation controlled by "[p]ower, secret information, unpublished agendas, prejudices". Its employees "display all the expressions of low self esteem, lethargy and hostility." Life is grim: "Innovation is suspect. Quality is the preserve of the quality control manager. Service means servitude. Going the extra step can be tantamount to betrayal of one's colleagues, an Uncle Tom of the industrial system."[34]

"Reality"'s unions limit communications to wage demands, grievances, or "an alleged infringement of long held rights; usually trivial and rarely an expression of concern about improving the performance of the company, or the long term futures of the employees' jobs and livelihood." "Reality"'s collective bargaining is irrelevant to the employer. "There is no concept of 'win/win'." Unions try to thwart the enterprise and their members in order to retain control. Otherwise, bargaining freedom would be "the first step in which workers and employers decide their own destiny. That success would highlight the superfluous nature of union involvement."[35]

Abolishing "Reality" would lead to a world in which "[u]nions and their captive audiences would be forced into the world of reality, and employers would be foolish not to communicate that reality. Ultimately employer and employee would resolve their differences and bargaining would take on a very different aspect." Communication would improve "because wage bargaining is a natural forum on which to build communication."[36]

Thus, ideology permitted the NZEF and NZBR to believe that the free market could lead only to good. If, however, the workplace always had some degree of conflict or unions were not the cause of that conflict, then their proposals failed to address important problems.

Drafting the ECA—Giving Ideology Form
The National Government began drafting the ECA even before the election so that it could be introduced as quickly as possible once it took office. In part this was to fulfil the central element of its election campaign promises. National also saw early enactment of new labour law as the key to victory in the 1993 elections. Rick Barker of the SWU explained:

> I had predicted that it would be one of the first acts National would bring in, because when they brought in an anti-union

law before [in 1983], they privately admitted that they had been too slow in doing it. . . . But had they done it much earlier, they would then have been able to hobble the unions more. And to have blunted the effect that the unions would be able to have on the election in 1984.

They were pretty angry that the union movement was able to mobilise as much support as it was able to in 1984 [in support of the Labour Party], and they thought that they had lost a chance. So I always anticipated from that they would do it first up, so it would have its maximum effect and maximum time to run. The full three years. So when the next election came they would have the union movement in the most vulnerable and depressed state it could be.[37]

In August 1990, two months before the elections, Paul Bell, a former Wellington Employers Association lawyer, and Department of Labour personnel began the groundwork in preparation for drafting new industrial relations legislation.[38] Bell tried to resolve important issues while others were occupied with winning the election. In a November 16, 1990, memorandum to W. F. Birch, Bell noted that certain matters "had been fully considered and accepted by industrial relations practitioners in my preliminary meetings prior to the formulation of the paper to you in August."[39] Consultation throughout the entire process was, however, quite limited. No one identified with the union movement was mentioned.[40]

Drafting the ECA by refusing to consult widely and to learn what opponents' concerns were was not limited to this situation. In some ways, the form of government at the time, which placed all power in the hands of a small caucus within the dominant party, promoted taking unilateral action, simply because it was easy and possible.[41] Concentrated power and control, with few constraints on it, rewarded those willing to act undemocratically. "[H]ealthy participatory democracy was a threat to the success of the reform programme, and indeed to the national interest itself."[42] Discussion, compromise, and deliberation were seen as impediments to efficiency, rather than as a slow but valuable way to work toward the wisest approach to a problem. For example, in 1991, Simon Upton, Minister of Health, explained that elected boards of health had been eliminated because voting for representatives, meetings of consultative committees, "and the potential for political paralysis doesn't add up to choice in my vocabulary."[43]

Before the October 1990 election the NZEF had criticised legislation introduced without wide consultation.[44] However, the NZEF demonstrated no similar concerns that it was the only non-governmental body consulted prior to the release of the ECA.[45]

The ECA was introduced on December 19, 1990, just before the Christmas and summer holidays, and scheduled to become law on May 1, 1991. Time for comment on the complex and important legislation was brief, so the NZEF's early involvement gave it valuable additional time to prepare a response. When the ECA was returned to Parliament four months later from the Select Committee process, the details had been settled only the day before. National was in such a hurry that it began debate before Members of Parliament had copies of the bill to read and to refer to. Labour Minister Birch said that "the lack of copies would not affect the debate in Parliament because the second reading debate was about the principles of the bill, which had not changed."[46]

One columnist opined that imagination was now an important quality for MPs:

> This week, especially, MPs found themselves having to pretend they knew all about legislation they had never clapped eyes on.
> The Employment Contracts Bill, in its post-select committee form, did apparently exist. But confirmed sightings of the document were limited to some ministers.
> They said copies of the bill had not been printed in time, so everyone would just have to take their word for it that there was a bill, and that certain things were in it.
> These certain things the House would now debate, sight unseen.[47]

The unavailability of copies led to an interesting confrontation during the debate.

Ian Revell (Birkenhead): The member for Eastern Hutt has just demonstrated conclusively to the House that he does not understand the Bill. I suspect that he has not even read the Bill. That has been clear from his comments.

Rt. Hon. Mike Moore: I raise a point of order, Mr. Speaker. I seek your guidance. Can the member accuse another member of not having read the Bill? The reality is that the Opposition does not have a copy of the printed Bill in front of it. We would like to debate the matter all night, but the point has been made. Here is the most important Labour legislation in 100 years and there is no printed copy of the Bill available.[48]

The process that would lead to this situation began in earnest on November 2, when Minister of Labour Bill Birch met with Secretary of Labour C. J. McKenzie and General Manager of the Industrial Relations Service Ralph Stockdill. Birch wanted the new legislation ready in one month.[49] Unfortunately, the drafters encountered serious problems almost immediately. On November 12, Ralph Stockdill and D. J. Martin, Assistant Commissioner of the State Services Commission, warned Bill Birch that the "tight timetable" for producing the legislation did not allow "time to explore the issues identified [in connection with the change in the law] in any detail."[50] For example, the bill was being drafted based on how the law would operate when unemployment was high, but the same law that gave employers power in a time of high unemployment would see employers weakened in a buoyant economy. If the legislation was to provide for more than the short term, it was important to think through how it would function in all situations, especially since industrial relations inevitably affects more than just the single employee and employer.[51]

In addition, there were fundamental technical problems that had not been addressed in the drafting instructions. The process for worker representation and bargaining agent recognition was confusing. Parties seemed able to enter into new agreements during the term of an existing one. Prohibiting recognition strikes and lockouts would create problems. The memorandum warned that the principle of individual choice, followed to its logical end, would result in a high "level of uncertainty that will compromise the whole basis and stability of any settlements." It would be necessary to name each individual worker who would be party to an agreement, an expensive and time-consuming undertaking.[52]

The memo also forecast problems growing out of employers' right to decide whether to recognise the worker's designated bargaining agent. Workers' freedom to choose their representatives would be nullified by employers' absolute power to decide whether to recognise the workers' choices. The government decided that the way to resolve all such conflicts was to leave them to unfettered freedom of choice and the market, a decision that was likely to lead to unproductive strikes, lockouts, or other workplace unrest. In addition, the government had directed the drafters to give individual agreements primacy over collective agreements as a central principle.[53]

Furthermore, the proposed structure invited the re-emergence of second- or even third-tier bargaining, so that a worker or group of workers would have more than one contract that set the terms of employment.[54] Although many employers liked the flexibility of second-tier agreements, they disliked the ratcheting-up they caused. The NZEF had long battled against them and had only recently won when the LRA prohibited more than one set of negotiations.[55] Now, only a few years later, the NZEF was promoting freedom of choice, a system that guaranteed constant change and second-tier contracting. The only way to explain the change in positions is to recall that the NZEF and NZBR contended that employment problems were rooted in unions. Once contracts were negotiated individually, there would be no dissension or difference as to conditions. In other words, the problem of second-tier agreements would disappear. However, the issue created a problem for the drafters.

On November 16, Birch proposed creating a working group to review "Labour Relations Institutions and the rest of the Act not directly addressed in the pre-Christmas legislation." Included in these deferred issues would be whether to retain a Labour Court. The NZEF and NZBR's deep suspicions of the Labour Court and its decisions were shared by important groups within the National Party. National said the Labour Court's "social engineering" stood in the way of a judicial system consistent with free market ideology.[56] Birch even questioned whether there should be a role for any State organ in resolving disputes.[57]

On November 20, the Cabinet agreed to introduce the ECA before the Christmas and summer holidays. There would then be a second bill in 1991 to "integrate any institutional arrangements that flow out of the initial draft legislation, with the two Bills being brought together in consolidated form during the Select Committee stages."[58] Except for a minimum code of wages and conditions, the new legislation would be founded on "the right of individual employers and workers to freely select their own representational arrangements and their own bargaining arrangements (either of a collective or individual nature)."[59]

Treasury vigorously opposed this plan because it did not "achieve as comprehensive a reform as is possible. In particular, it [did] not bring labour market contracting firmly within the law of contract and general law."[60] Treasury and Ruth Richardson demanded a complete free-market approach, which they interpreted as meaning only the common law would apply to labour relations. This position is one premised on the idea of "a minimalist state, believing that government intervention must inevitably be inferior to market ordering supported by the common law."[61]

The commercial law they advocated, however, was not that in effect in New Zealand at the time. Had the government adopted the law covering general commercial contracting, it would have legislated to protect a weaker bargainer from overreaching (victimisation) by a stronger party. The High Court had recently provided protections on a par with those under the LRA for wrongful termination of non-unionised workers. In addition, laws such as the Hire Purchase Act or the Sale of Goods Act protected commercial contracting parties if one was more vulnerable.[62] The sort of contract law envisioned was not to include these sorts of protections.

The differences between the two camps in the National caucus were extreme. The new regime as envisioned by the Minister of Labour provided:

(i) Individuals choose whether they wish to be represented individually or collectively. Employer must recognise that decision.
(ii) Individuals are entitled to individual contracts, subject to employer agreement. Similarly, employers may only conclude collective contracts with a group of workers or their representative bargaining agent.
(iii) Voluntary unionism (no closed shops or non-union shops).
(iv) Collective contracts may only be concluded on a voluntary basis.
(v) Right to strike or lockout where no collective contract exists (e.g. after expiry). No right to strike or lockout where there is a collective contract.
(vi) During the term of a collective contract, sanctity of agreement and provision for new matters.
(vii) Collective contracts expire after their term.
(viii) Collective contracts to contain rights and grievance resolution procedures.
(ix) Collective contracts legally enforceable.
(x) Institutional arrangements to complement above.[63]

Treasury's outline of the new legislation was a clear contrast:

(i) Labour relations to be dealt with under the general law of contract, which, inter alia, allows collective contracts.
(ii) Individuals may seek to bargain individually or collectively.
(iii) No special rules concerning union membership (closed shops and non-union shops may be negotiated).
(iv) Striking or locking out constitutes a breach of the contract of employment, allowing the other party to treat the contract as terminated. The full range of legal remedies are available (including damages).
(v) Contracts may be renegotiated during their term, provided both parties agree.
(vi) Contracts expire after their term.
(vii) Contracts do not include any rights or grievance resolution procedures, unless agreed.
(viii) Contracts legally enforceable.

(ix) No specialist institutions required.
(x) Workers acting jointly in a way that causes a concerted breach of their contract(s) may be held severally liable to the extent of an equal proportion of the damages caused.
(xi) Default and transitional provisions as per the draft legislation attached.
(xii) Effective date 1 April 1991.[64]

Treasury's draft "Labour Bill 1990" was attached. It was three pages long.[65]

At its meeting on November 21, the Cabinet decided to follow the Minister of Labour's recommendations, rather than those of Treasury.[66] In the month remaining before the ECA's scheduled introduction, the drafters worked feverishly. On November 29, Stockdill wrote Birch to ask how to deal with renegotiating expired collective contracts.[67] This was a serious problem. If a party used its freedom of contract to refuse to negotiate—and it seemed likely that many employers would—there would be stalemates all over the country and existing conditions would remain in place indefinitely. Another outcome could be that at stand-off when the contract expired, the employment relationship simply ended. Yet another would give one party the power to impose its will on the other so that new terms—terms acceptable to at least one of the parties—would control. This, of course, could only happen if one party lost its freedom to contract.

Stockdill reasoned that "as long as a worker continues to work there is always a contract of service, whether it be individual or collective, in force. There can never be a period of work when there is no contract governing the conditions of employment."[68] He recommended cutting the baby in half by providing that, if a collective contract expired with no agreement on a new contract, the worker would continue to work but on an individual contract "based on" the terms of the prior collective contract. Any terms involving collective rights would be dropped.[69] This recommendation, adopted in the ECA, would prove inadequate as a way of resolving bargaining impasses, so that very quickly the courts interpreted the law to permit employers to impose their terms under a doctrine which would be called a partial lockout.

Although Stockdill was able to flag many of the problems that would arise under the ECA, in retrospect some of his speculations seem naive. For example, he believed individual workers would choose lawyers or industrial relations consultants to represent them in bargaining. He does not explain where the bargaining representatives would come from to negotiate millions of individual contracts or how the average worker would pay for personal representation. Stockdill also glossed over some fundamental problems:

> Individual workers may choose to negotiate individual contracts, but this choice will be subject to the agreement of the employer. Similarly although a group of workers may have chosen a particular bargaining agent, recognised by the employer as required by the legislation, the employer will have the right to refuse to negotiate with any particular person or organisation or grouping of person or organisations. In that case the workers might feel obliged to change their choice of bargaining agent in order to gain agreement to negotiate and conclude a contract.[70]

Where in this system would there be employee freedom of choice, and how would this operate in a country in which employers had long had freedom to set workplace conditions? Who could spend the time to capture the numerous complex rules and interactions that workers operate by during the minutes and through the days and years they are at work? As new situations arose, would the parties stop to renegotiate each change? If the rules were not agreed to, then someone was making unilateral decisions and the contract was breached. Failing to define all terms of such an important relationship—one that almost alone defines status and the lives of workers, their families, employers, and their communities—meant that the goals of the ECA were not achieved.

This was not an abstract problem. One New Zealand employer gave its workers a twenty-word two-sentence contract to sign containing only the hourly rate. When this proved unsatisfactory, the employer presented the workers with a six-page contract with blanks left for the wages and other conditions to be inserted and with a provision that the contract's terms would be suspended and others provided upon request by particular clients.[71]

Pure contract can apply only to employment in which few problems arise and must be limited only to the moment the relationship is formed. Once the employment relationship moves into its day-to-day operation, contract would prove inadequate and would create problems. The ECA thus would usher in a highly complex system in which contract law and theory were stretched to their limits in an attempt to make them appropriate to a long-term work relationship. If anything betrays the naivety of those who advocated the ECA, it is that they failed to understand that important attributes of a successful workplace are dependent upon the complex interplay of factors which are difficult to state explicitly in contractual form.[72] This limited view was reflected in the change of terminology from "industrial relations system" to "labour market." The lack of attention to resolving impasses and the problems of a continuing relationship were symptoms of the problem of building an industrial relations system on a narrow view of the workplace as private and economic with no impact on society beyond the economic.

The contract model was also a poor choice for promoting workplace peace. A contractual regime is based on an adversarial, arm's-length relationship, deceitful negotiations, and the advancement of narrow self-interest.[73] Anyone who has studied the law of contracts is exposed to thousands of court cases and ways that contracting parties have come into conflict through the centuries. The common law did not develop out of peace and cooperation but out of disagreement. ECA proponents recognised that the workplace requires cooperation—and cooperation which is more than mere formal adherence to work requirements—but they failed to see how difficult it is to elicit cooperation within a pure contractual regime.

The regime was even more confused because, while some ECA proponents valued freedom of contract with an almost religious zeal, others saw it as a means of achieving other ends, such as lowering wages, increasing measures of productivity, or making employers more competitive. These splits and philosophical abstractions led to a confused law that stated it was based on freedom of contract but which compromised that freedom at key points. The instrumentalist view could be seen in the failure to examine the law of corporations. Corporations, more than workers, are vehicles for buying and selling. If anything or anyone should be freed by exposure to the full rigours of the marketplace surely it should be corporations and their shareholders.[74] Yet no one recommended freeing corporations to face the full consequences of their actions freed from their refuge behind limited liability laws.

One month after starting the process, on December 3, 1990, the draft bill was ready for review by the Cabinet.[75] Stockdill warned: "All of the Bill is likely to be contentious."[76] Not only was this true of its content but also of the undemocratic process leading to its enactment. No effort was made to solicit or provide for the concerns of most who would be affected by the law. The drafters confessed they had failed to consult with those likely to be interested in the legislation, including the Council of Trade Unions, "workers, unions and employers in general" and admitted: "There has been limited consultation on the Bill."[77] Although the only non-governmental body consulted was the NZEF,[78] when asked who had been involved, Birch claimed that, though the policies paralleled those of the NZEF, they were "arrived at by an independent course involving wide consultation."[79]

When, in 1994, the International Labour Organisation criticised this failure to consult, then Minister of Labour Doug Kidd argued that National's electoral majority based on its campaign meant there had been consultation. Kidd charged that the ILO's criticism "directly challeng[ed] the democratic and parliamentary process of member states" and that "the ILO risks being portrayed as a partisan advocate in domestic policies."[80]

On December 6, 1990, the Cabinet Legislative Committee referred the draft bill for approval and submission to the Caucus.[81] Most of the last-minute changes appear to have incorporated changes desired by those who favoured a total free-market approach. (1) Clause 2A provided: "Nothing in this Act limits the right of any person to negotiate for an employment

The Employment Contracts Bill 105

contract in a manner other than that provided by this Act." This allowed parties to "contract out" of the ECA. (2) Clause 2B conferred joint jurisdiction in the general courts to hear employment contracts cases. This was meant to "normalise" employment law, since non-specialist judges would not appreciate the unique aspects of the employment relationship and would apply the law they were most familiar with, the common law of contract. (3) Clause 10 provided that procedural aspects of the bargaining relationship, such as the choice of collective or individual employment contracts, the number of applicable contracts, and the relationship between applicable collective and individual contracts, would be subject to negotiation. (4) Clause 20 restricted appeals from personal grievances to questions of law only. Before this time, the Labour Court could consider appeals de novo, which meant that the Labour Court could essentially retry the case.[82]

Clauses 2A and 10 together potentially nullified the ECA. Negotiating employment terms could be postponed indefinitely as one side exhausted the other in discussing procedural preliminaries. A party could prevent or delay agreement by holding out for setting up a personal labour regime. A party could use its power over negotiations, a power enhanced or limited by prevailing economic conditions, to force the parties outside even the meagre protections of the ECA. Bargaining under this system was thus likely to take one of two forms: non-existent, in the sense that the stronger party would set all the terms, or chaotic and thus functionally non-existent.

On December 7, Stockdill cautioned Birch that the new legislation would cause far-reaching changes and great controversy.[83] On the eve of the bill's introduction, the memorandum raised perplexing problems left unsettled by the vague provisions concerning representation and bargaining procedures. First, Stockdill asked, might the system not create instability since the legislation allowed workers who were not satisfied with an agreement to withdraw their agent's authority after the fact. Negotiations would have to begin again, with all the preliminary matters to be resolved anew.[84] Any limitation on this right would, however, violate freedom of choice.

Second, employers might have to deal with more bargaining agents.[85] Representation was not limited to job classifications, as under awards, so there could be many representatives for one job classification, all seeking different terms. Under the ECA the potential number of agents was not even limited to one for each worker employed.[86] Schism was likely as different representatives fought for workers. Each representative would have to demonstrate it was the most vigorous, increasing divisiveness and worker demands.

Third, the ECA did not address problems inherent in certain industries. Construction contractors, for example, would have trouble making bids with no pre-job contract to project labour costs. There could be no contract until the workers for the project were hired and the contract or contracts negotiated. Subcontractors could have conflicting provisions which would have to be resolved on an ongoing basis after the project had started, adding expense and disruption.[87]

Fourth, the ECA would disrupt any industry reliant on apprentice training tied into the award system. The ECA promoted atomistic bargaining which could not support long-term, ongoing cooperation. Focusing only on a single workplace's existing needs meant that New Zealand was likely to lose a vital source of worker education.[88] Unions had been the only institutions capable of fostering certain forms of industry-specific training.

Individual employers have little incentive to provide training, since they lose the costs if the employee can then seek a better job. Government may not be able to ascertain training needs accurately[89] and, when a philosophy of individualism is dominant, government may not feel that training is its role. Individuals may not be able to pay for training. Thus, even necessary training may go undone in a society with a low level of unionism, low pay, and highly competitive employers.[90]

On December 19, 1990, one week before Christmas, the National Government introduced the Employment Contracts Bill as part of a package aimed at radical change in the welfare state. This Economic and Social Initiative, which made major cuts in social welfare benefits, had the potential for intensifying the ECA's impact. Indeed, it was intended to do just that. Social

Welfare Minister Jenny Shipley said that benefits were too high compared to wages and needed to be lowered in order to "encourage" workers "to compete for work opportunities."[91] The NZBR supported this view and blamed unemployment on overpaid workers and a "social welfare system . . . [which] restricts job creation by giving people almost as much through benefits as they could expect to earn."[92] The unemployment benefit for single workers paid from 47.3% to 59.9% of the lowest award rate, with the comparable figures for those with one or two children being from 70.7% to 76.2% and for married workers being 85.6% to 94.3%.[93] Many employers paid above-award rates. If these benefits were too high, any reduction would barely sustain life.

The new benefits law provided that any unemployed worker who rejected "suitable employment" faced a six-month "stand-down period",[94] where the prior stand-down period had been six weeks.[95] Anyone who resigned without good reason, who was fired for misconduct, or who turned down a job offer of at least minimum wage could be denied welfare benefits for six months.[96] The minimum wage was to become $245 a week or $6.125 an hour for those older than twenty years,[97] so benefits had to be lowered to provide an incentive to work. The new legislation lowered welfare benefits for those younger than 25 years to $108.17 from the prior figure of $114.86 a week.[98]

In addition to the increased stand-down period the social legislation lowered wages payable to large segments of the workforce. The youth rate or sub-minimum wage was raised to age 20. For those under age 20 there was no minimum wage.[99] Raising the age of eligibility for adult rates had a discriminatory impact on the non-Pakeha (non-European) as a consequence of the different median ages of the groups. The median age for Pakehas at this time was 33 years but was 21 for Maori and Pacific Islanders. Thus more of the latter were consigned to lower wages.[100]

Auckland University Director of Labour Studies Maryan Street observed: "The logical consequences of this are extreme for low paid workers. Where jobs, the skills for which can be learned quickly on site, are available or are currently held, the potential to depress the rates of pay for those positions, given the structure of individual and collective contracts, is clear and frightening."[101] Indeed, high unemployment, competition and the long stand-down period became an effective tool to lower wages for more than just low-skilled workers once the ECA was enacted. Rick Barker commented on the impact they had on even skilled trades in early 1992:

> Carpenters used to be on an average rate of about $12 an hour with travelling time and with guarantees of pay when the building was stopped because of bad weather. All of that is gone. Carpenters are now being employed in the Lower Hutt on a rate of $8 an hour. So they've lost $4 an hour. No travelling time and no downtime. There is no overtime. Job and finish. Flat rate.
>
> Well, it's very difficult on those carpenters. . . . But they have families to feed and the unemployment benefit is below eight bucks an hour. And if they turn the job down, they face twenty-six weeks' stand-down. So they are being press-ganged into accepting terrible rates.[102]

The impact of these changes were even more painful than intended. It was intended that "the substantial reductions in unemployment benefits—some of the cuts were over 20 percent—plus harsher entitlement conditions" would "reinforce the changes in industrial law, by keeping unskilled wage rates lower." This was done in the hope that it would generate jobs. "Unfortunately the fiscal impact of the package—involving substantial reductions in social welfare spending—collapsed a fragile economy into its sharpest post-war contraction, so the harsher welfare measures and the changes in the industrial relations law, compounded the social pressures of an economic downturn."[103]

The new social welfare payments led people to refer to Minister of Social Welfare Jenny Shipley as "Jennicide."[104] The nickname was not fully merited, since she had prevailed over the Minister of Finance who wanted far greater cuts. "[T]he Minister of Finance originally put forward a proposal in which sickness and unemployment beneficiaries with one child would have their benefits cut by $88.50 a week if married (the eventual cuts were

$9.22 and $25.20 respectively) or by $40.71 if single (the eventual cuts were $27.21 in both cases)."[105]

Although the new benefit figures were severe, it appears that their severity may have been more the product of poor mathematics than intention. This is not to say that National did not mean to institute severe cuts; mistakes or not, National intended the most onerous cuts possible, since at each point the lowest figures of a range were chosen.[106] The figures assumed food would be bought from supermarkets and in bulk, even though many New Zealanders, particularly those without cars, could not do this. They were also based on the prices for in-season fruits and vegetables for the Dunedin area, close to the major fruit-growing regions, which were also not the most populated parts of the country. The figures were then further reduced 25% for an austere level of diet. This food share of a budget was then multiplied by 4, assuming that food was 1/4 of a budget. However, current government data had food as 1/6 of a family's budget. Multiplying by 4 instead of by 6 reduced the total by 1/3.[107]

The new social welfare system would have had little effect in robust economic times. These, however, were not robust times. In May 1991, official unemployment was 10.1% or 163,800 unemployed.[108] By June 1991, the figure had soared to 253,000.[109] Unofficial unemployment was likely to be higher. Employers could take a hard line, confident they had a large pool of unemployed on low benefits or in a 26-week stand-down who would be desperate for any work at any price. Workers would be at a tremendous disadvantage in negotiations, since, once they lost or gave up a job, they were unlikely to find another. It was easy to foresee workers bidding against one another for ill-paid jobs. Collectivity would be impossible to achieve.

Understanding these conditions is important to assessing the enactment of the ECA. As Alan Geare commented:

> The EC Act presumes an individual employee can negotiate on an equal footing with an employer. One must assume the drafters and supporters of the Act are strongly unitarist and believe all, or certainly the vast majority of employers will *always* operate

in the best interests of everyone. If not, they demonstrate a callous disregard for the weaker members of society.[110]

Notes
1. Raymond Harbridge, "The Impact of Economic Liberalisation on Labour Relations in New Zealand 1984–1990," *British Review of New Zealand Studies*, 4, 69, 69 (1991).
2. Keith Rankin, "The New Zealand Workforce: 1950–2000," 18 N.Z. J. Ind. Rel., 214, 235 (1993); Colin James, "Midweek: Captain Richardson and Her Starship Enterprise," *National Business Review*, Jan. 16, 1991, at 9; Herbert Roth, "Chronicle," 15 N.Z. J. Ind. Rel., 289 (1990).
3. Ian Shirley, "Unemployment—Its Realities and Human Costs" in *Towards a Just Economy*, 21, 36 (Pelly ed., 1991).
4. Roth, "Chronicle," 16 N.Z. J. Ind. Rel., 98 (1991).
5. Roth, "Chronicle," 15 N.Z. J. Ind. Rel., 199 (1990).
6. Treasury, "Briefing to the Incoming Government, 1990," 11–12 (Oct. 27, 1990).
7. *Id.*, at 145.
8. Natalie Jackson, "Youth Unemployment and the 'Invisible Hand'—A Case for a Social Measure of Unemployment" in *Labour, Employment and Work in New Zealand 1994*, 177, 186 n.4 (Philip S. Morrison, ed., 1994).
9. Treasury, "Briefing," 11.
10. *Id.*, 7–8.
11. *Id.*, 150.
12. *Id.*, 152.
13. *Id.*, 154.
14. *Id.*, 154.
15. Gordon Campbell, "Bill's Act of Faith," *Listener & TV Times*, May 27, 1991, at 15.
16. N.Z.P.D., Question No.176, 644 (Mar. 20–Apr. 3, 1991).
17. Brian Easton, "A Commentary on the Treasury View of the Labour Market," 4, 16 (Feb. 11, 1991).
18. Easton, "Commentary," 4–5.
19. John Deeks, "Introduction: Business, Government and Interest Group Politics" in *Controlling Interests: Business, The State and Society in New Zealand*, 1, 10–11 (John Deeks et al., eds., 1992).
20. Campbell, 15.
21. Easton, "Commentary," 5.
22. Bob Stephens, "Budgeting with the Benefits Cuts" in *The Decent Society? Essays in Response to National's Economic and Social Policies*, 100, 105, 106 (Jonathan Boston et al., eds., 1992); David Thomson, *Selfish Generations? The Ageing of New Zealand's Welfare State*, 123–24 (1991); Paul Dalziel, "Policies for a Just Society" in *The*

Decent Society? Essays in Response to National's Economic and Social Policies, 208, 216 (Jonathan Boston et al., eds., 1992).
23. Paul Dalziel & Jonathan Boston, "Preface," in *The Decent Society? Essays in Response to National's Economic and Social Policies*, vii, x (Jonathan Boston et al., eds., 1992); Brian Easton, "Alternative Systems of Industrial Relations: The Impact of the Employment Contracts Bill," 5, 6 (Feb. 5, 1991).
24. Easton, "Commentary," 13.
25. *Id.*, 14.
26. Thomson, 96, 98, 196–97; Peter Brosnan, "Labour Market Flexibility and the Quality of Work: A Case Study of the Retail Industry," 16 N.Z. J. Ind. Rel., 13, 29–30 (1991).
27. Dep't of Labour, Ministerial Brief, October 1990, 4, 43 (1990); Jane Kelsey, *The New Zealand Experiment: A World Model for Structural Adjustment?*, 271–283 (1995).
28. Labour, Brief, 126.
29. *Id.*, 132.
30. *Id.*, 129.
31. *Id.*, 35.
32. Patricia Herbert, "Employers' Federation Almost Outdoes Itself," *Dominion*, Nov. 26, 1990, at 10.
33. NZEF, *The Benefits of Bargaining Reform*, 3 (1990).
34. *Id.*, 4.
35. *Id.*, 4.
36. *Id.*, 9.
37. Interview with Rick Barker, National Secretary, Service Workers Federation of Aotearoa, in Wellington (May 14, 1992).
38. Memorandum from Paul Bell to W. F. Birch, Minister of Labour, 1 (Nov. 16, 1990); letter from W. F. Birch, Minister of Labour to John Robertson, Chief Ombudsman, 1, 2 (n.d.); interview with Murray French, Director, Wellington Regional Employers Association, in Wellington (May 14, 1992); *N.Z.P.D.*, 1433 (Apr. 23, 1991); *N.Z.P.D.*, Question No.65, 2114 (Dec. 6–27, 1990); Pat Walsh & Rose Ryan, "The Making of the Employment Contracts Act" in *Employment Contracts: New Zealand Experiences*, 13, 17 (Raymond Harbridge ed., 1993).
39. Bell, Nov. 16, 1990 Memo, 1; Birch, Letter, 1, 2.
40. Memorandum from R. A. Stockdill, General Manager, Industrial Relations Service, to William Birch, Minister of Labour Annex, 2 (Dec. 3, 1990).
41. Margaret Wilson, "Employment Equity Act 1990: A Case Study in Women's Political Influence, 1984–1990" in *Controlling Interests: Business, The State and Society in New Zealand*, 113, 113 (John Deeks et al. eds., 1992); Brian Easton, "From Rogernomics to Ruthanasia: New Right Economics in New Zealand" in *Beyond the Market: Alternative to Economic Rationalism*, 149, 154–55 (Stuart Rees et al., eds., 1993); Ian McAndrew, "From Regulation to

Deregulation in New Zealand Labour Relations: New Models of Bargaining Under the Employment Contracts Act 1991," 1 (Jan. 5, 1993) (45th Annual meeting of the Industrial Relations Research Association).
42. Jane Kelsey, *Rolling Back the State: Privatisation of Power in Aotearoa/ New Zealand*, 28 (1993).
43. *Id.*, 34.
44. "Substandard Lawmaking," *Employer*, Sept. 1990, at 4.
45. Memorandum from R. A. Stockdill, General Manager, Industrial Relations Service, to William Birch, Minister of Labour Annex, 2 (Dec. 3, 1990); NZEF, 1991 Annual Report, 4 (1991).
46. Simon Kilroy, "Contracts Bill Being Rushed Into Law," *Dominion*, Apr. 24, 1991, at 1; CCH Dispatch, New Zealand Employment Law Library Personnel Management, "Employment Contracts Bill Taking Final Shape," 1 (Apr. 24, 1991); N.Z.P.D., 1436 (Apr. 23, 1991).
47. W. Pember Reeves, "Imagination an Essential Asset," *Dominion*, Apr. 26, 1991, at 2.
48. N.Z.P.D., 1462 (Apr. 23, 1991).
49. Memorandum from C. J. McKenzie, Secretary of Labour, to Bill Birch, Minister of Labour (Nov. 2, 1990).
50. Memorandum from R. A. Stockdill, General Manager of the Industrial Relations Service of the Department of Labour, and D. J. Martin, Assistant Commissioner of the State Services Commission, to Minister of Labour and Minister of State Services, 1 (Nov. 12, 1990).
51. *Id.*, 3, 10.
52. *Id.*, 4.
53. Stockdill & Martin, Nov. 12, 1990 Memorandum, 4–5, 9–10.
54. *Id.*, 5.
55. LRA ss 152–55.
56. Bell, Nov. 16, 1990 Memorandum.
57. Memorandum from Bill Birch, Minister of Labour to the Chairman, Cabinet Strategy Committee, 3 (Nov. 1990).
58. Memorandum of Cabinet Strategy Committee, Development of the Government's Industrial Reform Package, 1–2 (Nov. 20, 1990).
59. Birch, Strategy Memorandum, 2.
60. *Id.*, 4.
61. Peter Strauss, "Review Essay: Sunstein, Statutes, and the Common Law—Reconciling Markets, the Communal Impulse, and the Mammoth State," 89 Mich. L. Rev., 907, 908 (1991); Nick Wailes, "The Case Against Specialist Jurisdiction for Labour Law: The Philosophical Assumptions of a Common Law for Labour Relations," 19 N.Z. J. Ind. Rel., 1 (1994); Penelope Brook, *Freedom at Work: The Case for Reforming Labour Law in New Zealand* 175–76 (1990); NZEF, "Forward to the Past: the Labour Opposition's Industrial Relations Policy," 18 N.Z. J. Ind. Rel., 205, 207 (1993).

62. Rose Ryan & Yvonne Oldfield, *Your Employment Contract: A Handbook for Workers*, 11 (1991).
63. Birch, Strategy Memorandum, App. I.
64. *Id.*, App.II.
65. *Id.*, App.II; French.
66. Memorandum of Cabinet Strategy Committee Meeting, 1 (Nov. 21, 1990).
67. Memorandum from R. A. Stockdill, General Manager, Industrial Relations Service, Department of Labour, to Bill Birch, Minister of Labour, 1 (Nov. 29, 1990).
68. *Id.*, 3.
69. *Id.*, 3.
70. *Id.*, 2.
71. Jason Barber, "Staff Given 20-Word Contract," *Dominion*, July 30, 1992, at 11.
72. Thomas Mahoney & Mary Watson, "Evolving Modes of Work Force Governance: An Evaluation" in *Employee Representation: Alternatives and Future Directions*, 135, 140 (Bruce Kaufman & Morris Kleiner, eds., 1993).
73. Mahoney & Watson, 142.
74. Stephen Presser, "Thwarting the Killing of the Corporation: Limited Liability, Democracy, and Economics," 87 N.W. U. L. Rev., 148 (1992).
75. Letter from R. A. Stockdill, General Manager, Industrial Relations Service, Department of Labour, to Bill Birch, Minister of Labour (Dec. 3, 1990).
76. Memorandum from Bill Birch, Minister of Labour, to Cabinet Legislation Committee Annex B-1 (Dec. 1990).
77. *Id.*, Annex B-3.
78. *Id.*, Annex B-2.
79. "Bill Birch Spells it Out," *PSA Journal*, Dec. 1990, at 6.
80. Doug Kidd, Speech to the Plenary Session of the ILO, 2 (June 8, 1994).
81. Memorandum of Cabinet Legislative Committee, Leg (90) M 28/6 Pt.2, 1 (Dec. 6, 1990).
82. *Id.*, Pt.2, 2–3.
83. Memorandum from R. A. Stockdill, General Manager, Industrial Relations Service, Department of Labour, to W. F. Birch, Minister of Labour, 1 (Dec. 7, 1990).
84. *Id.*, 2.
85. *Id.*
86. *Id.*
87. *Id.*, 4; cf. NLRA s 8(f), 29 U.S.C. s 158(f).
88. Stockdill, Dec. 7, 1990 Memorandum, 5.
89. Joel Rogers, "Reforming U.S. Labor Relations" in *Restoring the Promise of American Labor Law*, 15, 25 (Sheldon Friedman et al., eds., 1994).

90. "Need for Ongoing Bargaining, Employee Training Stressed During Atlanta Hearing by Dunlop Panel," 8 *Daily Lab. Rep.*, Jan. 12, 1994, at D9; Hamid Azari-Rad, Anne Yeagle & Peter Philips, "The Effects of the Repeal of Utah's Prevailing Wage Law on the Labor Market in Construction" in *Restoring the Promise of American Labor Law*, 207, 209, 212–220 (Sheldon Friedman et al., eds., 1994).
91. Patricia Herbert, "Stripping Away Workers' Protection," *Dominion*, Feb. 20, 1991, at 14.
92. Hugh Barlow, "Report Blames High Wages for Unemployment," *Dominion*, Feb. 18, 1991, at 7.
93. See Brian Easton, "Labour Market Issues," 8–9 (Sept. 12, 1990).
94. Finance Bill s 15(3).
95. Kelsey, *Rolling*, 83.
96. Herbert, "Stripping Away Workers' Protection"; John Hughes, "Termination of Employment and the Benefit Stand-down," Empl. L. Bull., 3 (Jan. 1994).
97. NZEF, *Employment Kit: Employment Related Legislation* (1991); Ryan & Oldfield, 22; Peter Brosnan & David Rea, "An Adequate Minimum Code: A Basis for Freedom, Justice and Efficiency in the Labour Market," 16 N.Z.J. Ind. Rel., 143, 149 (1991).
98. Herbert, "Stripping Away Workers' Protection."
99. Finance Bill s 34, Schedule (1990). Jonathan Boston, "Redesigning New Zealand's Welfare State" in *The Decent Society? Essays in Response to National's Economic and Social Policies*,1, 11 (Jonathan Boston et al., eds. 1992); Colin James, "Stay Tuned In—There's a Lot More Drama," *National Business Review*, Dec. 21, 1990 at 10.
100. Jackson, 184.
101. Maryan Street, "The New Act's Effect on Low Paid Members," 12 (n.d.).
102. Barker.
103. Letter from Brian Easton (Mar. 27, 1994).
104. Easton, "From Rogernomics to Ruthanasia," 150.
105. Stephens, "Budgeting with the Benefit Cuts," 107.
106. *Id.*, 111–13.
107. *Id.*, 111–13.
108. Rebecca Macfie, "Unemployment Rate Tops 10%," *National Business Review*, July 9, 1991, at 1.
109. Roth, "Chronicle," 16 N.Z. J. Ind. Rel., 317 (1991).
110. Alan Geare, "The Proposed Employment Relations Act," 18 N.Z. J. Ind. Rel., 194, 196 (1993).

7

In the Shadow of the ECA

The NZEF
The weeks just before the Employment Contracts Bill was introduced were weeks of anticipation for employers and unions alike. Although unions appeared most likely to suffer from the enactment of the new legislation, employers and employer advocacy groups would also have to adjust to the new environment.

Some speculated that the NZEF's success might do it out of a job.[1] Under the LRA, the NZEF and its affiliates had played key roles in the centralised bargaining system. Decentralised bargaining might have no use for a central employers' organisation, since individual employers were expected to do their own bargaining. The NZEF would be an outsider, just as unions would be. Indeed, those employers who preferred enterprise bargaining also favoured doing bargaining in-house.[2] As employers became more familiar with enterprise bargaining, more would probably opt not to use outside representation.

Steve Marshall, the NZEF Director-General, began to reinvent the NZEF. He insisted that it could fill new roles such as monitoring and reporting on international trends, lobbying, and providing research and advice.[3] As part of its restructuring, the NZEF produced a mission statement which provided: "We will support quality representation and support services to our members in the furtherance of employers attaining their enterprise objectives."[4] It began to promote management techniques, basically versions of labour–management cooperation, as ways to elicit employee support and offered itself as a consultant equipped to assist employers in learning and applying the new skills.[5]

The NZEF also found a niche created for itself as a result of the ECA's taking government out of the business of compiling bargaining data. Employers would still want to look over each other's shoulders. The NZEF moved into the gap by starting a database of employment contract provisions on wages and other payments, work conditions, and other relevant details. Access to the database was contingent on employers' making their own contracts available.[6]

Providing this service, however, created internal conflict within the NZEF. On the one hand, the NZEF was promoting freedom of contract by eliminating information about contract terms that might be used to recreate the award system of level wages and conditions. NZEF executives urged that it was crucial not to make information about other companies available. If employers bargained knowing what their competitors paid, this would distort or distract enterprise bargainers from reaching an agreement relevant only to their workplace and its unique needs.[7] In addition, the only way to keep workers from being concerned about conditions elsewhere was to prevent them from getting information.[8]

On the other hand, even though it was behaving inconsistently, key NZEF officials felt it was impossible to stick to theoretical purity on this issue. The NZEF would have competitors in the new environment, and some of its competitors recognised that employers needed and wanted information about their competitors. Teesdale-Meuli advertised that it would provide services that included allowing employers to compare their bargaining proposals with "contracts in your industry or other employers in your district."[9] In addition, potential adversaries were setting up databases. The Public Service Association announced that its Dan Long library planned to hold as many collective employment contracts (CECs) as it could obtain, "enabling union, researchers and delegates to compare wages and conditions."[10]

If the new world of industrial relations was a trackless wilderness, the NZEF was willing to put ideological scruples aside as long as it was hired as guide. It advertised its database as an important resource for its members. The kit prepared by the Wellington Regional Employers Association says:

> With the demise of awards it will be more difficult for individual employers to gain access to information on the wages and conditions of employers in their locality or industry. However many employers will need information on these matters. We therefore see an increased demand for wage and condition surveys and your Association will become more actively involved in this area.[11]

By having supported ending the government's role as a repository of information important to the public, the NZEF effectively privatised this function and then tried to sell it.

Thus, the NZEF took a complex route in the days just prior to the introduction of the ECA. It prepared to meet the future both by creating resources that would be important to its constituents and by trying to bring its membership along with it to a place many were reluctant to go.

Unions

After the 1990 elections, unions were more concerned for their very existence and had little time to reinvent themselves. Unions had been shut out of the process which shaped the legislation. National "didn't want to sit around having cups of tea with Ken Douglas talking about how terrible it was going to be for workers."[12] With their normal channels of communication blocked, unions tried to learn what was in store for them:

> There was lots of scurrying around trying to find out, trying to see things on paper. We knew that Paul Bell was preparing things, and Wellington leaks like a sieve and usually you can get your hands on things quite easily. That was quite a subject of discussion at the technical services division meeting about "this thing is as tight as a drum. How come there is no paper around? There must be something falling off the back of the truck." But there didn't seem to be.
>
> It was a weird atmosphere. We kept on being given dates. The Nats won the election and Ruth Richardson was going to have—what was it?—40 days of action or 60 days of action or something like that. It gave a time frame when they were going

to blast off with the foundations of their vision for the next three years of the country.[13]

It was not until the text of the Employment Contracts Bill was released on December 19, 1990, that they knew just how enormous the changes would be. The ECB's very language was strange. It did not talk about unions and workers but about representatives, employees, freedom of association, incorporated societies, and efficiency. Unions were not mentioned. Some argued this was more than substituting one word for another of similar meaning.[14]

Negotiations were to take place between the employer and the employee or between their chosen representatives. Unions could only play a role in collective bargaining if they could prove a specific employee had designated the union to act as an agent for the specific task. A union with authority to negotiate might not have authority to take a strike, and, even if designated as a bargaining agent, the employer had freedom to refuse to negotiate. The ECA provided, finally, that it would be effective on May 1, 1991[15] — May Day—a choice of date which some found highly offensive.

Unions faced more than philosophical or semantic problems with the new legislation. Many had awards that had expired or would expire soon. Most union awards at that time were for one-year periods, so even those which expired after May 1 would soon have to be renegotiated. As CTU President Ken Douglas put it: "[Employers] didn't need to wait for the actual passage of the Act—the legal intention and the revamped welfare system shattered power relationships and employer behaviour changed from then."[16]

Thus virtually all unions had to make difficult tactical decisions immediately. They could renegotiate their awards while still under the Labour Relations Act, but that would inevitably mean making major concessions to induce an employer to enter into an agreement. They could stand firm and wait to renegotiate and see how they fared under an untested and hostile law. The price of security was known: accepting concessions. The price of standing firm was less clear, but might be higher than even a concessionary agreement.

In addition to bargaining strategy, unions had to decide how to react to the bill. The labour movement desperately needed to overcome its state of factionalism, needed solidarity of purpose and to build alliances within and outside the house of labour if they were to have any chance. The danger was so clear that unions should have had no difficulty in overcoming their past differences, seeing their common purpose, and uniting. Even trade unionists who had foretold its contents with fair accuracy read their copies of the ECA with dismay. Rick Barker observed:

> I thought we had overstated the case. It went beyond what I thought. I always saw myself as being one of the more extreme in what my views were. And it had gone beyond what I expected. . . . I had passing admiration for the skills of those who had thought of it, drafted it. I thought it was an extremely clever piece of legislation. . . .
>
> Well, quite often the legislators who are anti-union put in place legislation or laws which could completely hinder unions in what they do by directing them to do this or not to do the other. And the net effect of that is you can see the legislators are anti-union. This law didn't do any of them. It was anti-union because it de-recognised unions and transferred them all to societies.
>
> Bill Birch was able to say—not that I think he's the main one either—what they were able to say to unions was not that you can't do this or can't do that. You can do whatever you like. They simply prescribed for a completely open situation and by creating a system of almost total anarchy, there's going to be the complete antithesis of organisation. . . .
>
> They didn't disappoint me with that, with the extremeness of the legislation. In fact, I was surprised. It went beyond what I thought was possible.[17]

Negotiating in the Shadow of the Employment Contracts Act
Before its enactment, some employers believed the ECA would give them unfettered freedom to control their workplaces. Unions certainly feared this was true, particularly those with large numbers of unskilled and easily replaced members. Everyone could read

the unemployment statistics, each point representing so many people who could replace a current worker or at least bring wages down. Some industries were facing severe competition after trade barriers were lowered and were desperate to survive. The situation was not a happy one for unions.

By mid-March 1991, two months before the ECA was scheduled to become law, collective bargaining entered a phase of "panic buying." "Major concessions have been agreed to by unions negotiating documents under the shadow of the bill, concessions that would have been considered sacrilege by the union movement even twelve months ago."[18] Employers, such as Chemby Vinyl in Onehunga, which had declared a half-year profit of nearly $350 million felt confident enough to demand a 25% pay cut.[19] Agreement after agreement was settled on terms that can only be explained by their having taken place in the shadow of the ECA.[20]

The situation, however, was not simply one of employers exercising muscle over supine unions. While some employers leapt at the chance to make a good deal, others were fearful. They embraced the opportunity to renew their awards to buy time to adjust to an alien system.[21] The Plumbers and Gasfitters organisation explained it had renegotiated its award because of its "terrible uncertainty" over the bill and its belief it could not survive under the new regime.[22] Ultimately, this was a motivation for settling the hotel industry award on March 13, 1991,[23] a settlement that astonished many since ECA proponents had "repeatedly cited [it] as a likely benefactiary of the Employment Contracts Bill."[24] Of course, the hotel employers achieved substantial savings through their early agreement.[25] Even though fear prompted both employers and unions to settle, they were not on an equal footing. Even where employers wanted to settle, settlements were on the employers' terms, usually concessionary.[26]

Even before the ECA became law, unions and employers behaved as if the ECA would be enacted as drafted.[27] It was a no-lose situation for employers, almost regardless of what became of the bill. A management consultant summarised the advantages to employers as including:

IN THE SHADOW OF THE ECA 121

The opportunity to delay their exposure to the coming period of instability.

The chance to get a good deal now from unions keen to retain coverage of workers for as long as possible.

Agreements under existing law will bind new employees who join the company.

The opportunity through composite agreements to have all or most employees under one agreement with one expiry date rather than face separate negotiations with a fragmented workforce under the new system.

Employees fearful of the new system are prepared to make concessions to postpone its impact.

Unions may opt for longer-term agreements to guarantee their coverage for a longer period. This offers employers a longer period of stability but may mean delaying future change.

The opportunity to include provisions which constrain what employers see as potentially troublesome possibilities under the Bill such as second tier bargaining via individual employment contracts.[28]

Events during the five months from the introduction of the bill to its enactment could be used to forecast the future.

1. *The Distribution Workers Unions:*[29] The Distribution Workers Unions (DWU) represent mainly workers in retail businesses. It faced the same sorts of organisational difficulties as did the Clerical Workers Union. Both had members spread over tens of thousands of small worksites. In 1990 the Northern Distribution Union had members distributed as follows: 7211 sites had 1–5 members; 181 sites had 6–15 members; 112 sites had 16–50 members; 37 sites had 51–100 members, and 18 sites had over 100 members.[30]

The organisational task facing the DWU was enormous and not one they had been successful in meeting. Under the benign LRA the DWU had organised only 27% of the workers in their jurisdiction. This lack of organisation included both small and large enterprises.[31] Part of their problem was due to employers' strong anti-union feelings. "[T]he Second Sweating Commission

(1990) uncovered a strong, almost obsessive anti-unionism among retail employers. This was strongest among the owners of small shops who resented any intrusion of 'outsiders' into the affairs of their business. But it was also evident in the attitude of management in some large chains too."[32]

Weak organisation meant that the DWU could not keep pace with workplace conditions in other industries. It depended on compulsory interest arbitration to set wages, rather than organisational strength.[33] In 1985, compulsory interest arbitration ended and so did wage increases in the retail industry. Workers saw their pay packets decrease and found they were making concessions, such as increased hours, a higher proportion of youth workers to more highly paid adults, and a lower number of minimum hours for casual workers.[34] Thus, when the ECA was introduced, the DWU faced negotiations with retail employers accustomed to concessions and, now in a position of even greater power, with the union poorly organised.

Even worse, employers were driven both by feelings of power and desperation. The retail non-food industry had been depressed since at least 1984, when deregulation had allowed overseas firms, such as K Mart, to enter the New Zealand market. Price competition pushed retailers. The retail industry extended hours of operation to entice consumers, especially those who could not shop during regular business hours.[35] As hours increased, overtime became a greater factor in labour costs.

The DWU had no choice about postponing negotiations. On November 6, 1990, just before the ECA was introduced, the union settled the national Grocery and Supermarket Award, covering 25,000 workers, for a 2% increase. This was considerably better than the employers' original offer of a 2% wage increase in exchange for penal rates for night and weekend work.

However, there were a number of other awards still unsettled, including the Retail Non-food Award, covering all shops that were not supermarkets or food-related shops. It expired December 21 with no replacement and remained unsettled through late 1990. In November 1990, employers offered a 2% increase as a trade-off for eliminating Saturday penal rates. The union picketed stores and announced a consumer boycott for

Christmas, while employers received support from the NZEF and the Hotel Association. In February 1991, the union proposed that new negotiations begin in April. By then, however, the employers said they saw no need for an award because things were going very smoothly without it. When the union, in desperation, offered to settle by agreeing to the same concessions which the employers had originally sought, employers had no interest in settling.[36]

2. *The Engineering Union:* The Engineers settled their major award, the Metal Trades Award on October 11, 1990, two months before the ECA was introduced. Settlement may have been possible only because the new agreement was so attractive to employers. It allowed individual workplaces to vary shifts and hours if approved by a vote of the workers rather than with approval from the central union.[37]

Negotiations for the Motor Trades Award—covering mechanics and service station attendants—demonstrated the pressure the ECA could place on a strong, well-prepared union even before it was law. This award covered the very sorts of service workers the DWU, SWU, and CWU represented, often low-skilled workers employed in small numbers in many widely scattered workplaces. The employer representatives said they were under pressure from employer groups to achieve conditions equal to those that they thought would be available under the ECA. Wellington Regional Employers Association manager Murray French, however, says that demands to remove penal rates and lower pay were motivated solely by individual employers' desires to avoid more job losses and to deliver better weekend service.[38] The Engineers saw employers as using the Act to claw back concessions in return for settling an award just before the ECA became law.

In the end, the union accepted its inability to settle unless it split the mechanics and service station attendants into two groups. This meant that the more skilled and thus powerful group could not lend support to the less powerful one. On April 25, just days after the revised ECA was reintroduced into Parliament, the Engineers agreed to cut 1500 service station attendants from the new award.[39] Once this was done, the new Motor Industry Award was settled easily and covered automotive repair and parts workers but left the pump attendants with no agreement and with little bargaining power.[40]

The decision to break the award was a pragmatic one that arguably sacrificed principles of solidarity. The Engineers took the position that it was better to get coverage and a wage increase for as many workers as possible than to have allowed the talks to break down or take a pay cut for all those covered.[41] If this agreement was the best a union could achieve for skilled workers with bargaining power, it demonstrated just how weakened the Engineers were in the pre-ECA environment. The agreement compromised the union principle of a level playing field by allowing individual companies to vary shift provisions and also eliminated double-time pay.

To the extent there was capitulation, however, it was not complete. The award provided a 2% raise and extra tool money, grandfathered existing penal rates, and figured double time into the new base rates so employees would receive comparable pay for a week's work. Engineers also saw the agreement as tailored to industry needs by providing for training. Most important, the union maintained multi-employer bargaining, a difficult achievement indeed, given the drive for enterprise bargaining.[42]

The service station agreement, however, was heavily attacked by independent operators.[43]

> They saw the Act was coming in and then they could do what they liked. The award was therefore irrelevant to them. They intended to use the threat of the Act, the depressed economy, and poor organisation in the sector to get concessions. The whole service sector is a nightmare to organise. It's very casual, highly mobile with shifts worked all around the clock.
>
> The unions used the employers' desire for and promotion of a high service industry to force a better settlement. At the time, a number of companies had TV ads running which highlighted service. We pointed out that if 'You pay these people peanuts, you'll end up with monkeys'. They agreed, and some progress was made.[44]

3. *Service Workers Union:* Early March 1991 found the Hotel Workers Unions, affiliates of the SWU, all but ready to concede to the employers' demands, which would end penal rates, institute youth rates, and give employers more freedom to use casual workers, in exchange for a 2% raise. The union despaired of reaching a better settlement, because it had no support from its membership to work for improvements. Members had failed to attend stopwork meetings and were willing to accept whatever the employers offered. The union's weakness was no secret from the employers who said their own offer was "a package deal, not a negotiating position."[45] The March 13 agreement had no weekend penal rates and youth rates but did increase wages and provided pay for learning new skills.[46]

This still left the SWU's main award, its Tearooms and Restaurants Award covering 20,000 workers, unrenewed. Employers offered a 2% raise in exchange for removing all penal rates, premiums, and other "restrictions on employment" and demanded a ten-hour day, four-day week and eliminating the union's right of access to employers' premises.[47] In mid-April, after employers refused to retreat from their demands, the SWU decided to abandon efforts to renew the award and began bargaining within each site. The union felt it had "nothing to lose by moving to enterprise bargaining, given the 'extreme' claims of the employers on an already low-paid document." The union's tactic seemed bold for the time, but, in retrospect, it was probably no worse than buying time with a poor settlement. Rick Barker, SWU National Secretary, felt employers might take a less severe stance in bargaining with their own employees than when insulated by bargaining through their representative body. Inevitably, however, this also meant many of the small worksites would be lost to the union.[48]

Even though it seemed prudent to have the security of any agreement, one year later, Rick Barker had concluded that settling just to buy time had not been a wise strategy, because it gave employers the greatest opportunity to use the law to their advantage. In addition, it gave employers time to learn how to use the ECA before the next negotiations. Furthermore, if agreement meant concessions, it meant that the next negotiations would take place with a prepared employer starting from concessionary terms.⁴⁹

4. *Seafarers Union:* The Seafarers Union was a small union with a membership of 1500 who worked in an essential industry. The Seafarers had not allied itself with the CTU for fear it "would in fact dampen or kill the fighting spirit of the trade union." It became a member of the Trade Union Federation in 1993, by which time its membership had declined to 1061.⁵⁰ It saw itself as philosophically aligned with the Manufacturing and Construction Workers Union:

> It is a union based in its rank and file and, moreover, all of its decisions taken are rank and file decisions. It's been a source of our strength in fact. In some ways, it's stood us in very good standing, maybe a little bit apart from the mainstream unions in New Zealand in respect to that decision making process. Sometimes, the members have turned the leadership around and what have you. They bump up underneath us all the time in terms of progressing. Often, we find that a decision taken or a recommendation made gets turned around and somehow we don't do it.⁵¹

In 1991, management proposed employing workers directly and eliminating the hiring hall system or register of seafarers, referred to as "the corner."⁵² Access to the corner and work depended on membership in the Seafarers Union. The government assigned workers to ships, with the employer and employee having the right to veto an assignment. In fact, individuals generally returned to the same ship after each period at sea ended, so there was actually a great deal of stability in employment.⁵³

The NZEF contended:

> The corner system gives the Seafarers' Union a classical pre-entry closed shop, and all the bargaining strength that goes with this. . . . The relationship between employee and shipowner is not seen as a strong one: the employee's loyalty is with the union which gave access to the "register", and therefore to jobs.

Employees frequently refer to the union as the employer and union officials frequently describe themselves as employers.[54]

The NZBR said the corner was "inconsistent with the principles of the Employment Contracts Bill" and thus likely to lead "to monopolistic behaviour . . . not conducive to staff development, company loyalty and productive employment relationships."[55]

The Seafarers took on the employers' demands by making a credible threat of a prolonged strike to begin April 10. Although this industry had seen turmoil and some painful work stoppages, in the prior seven years, 97% of all 24,500 sailings scheduled on an 11 per day, seven days basis had been met. What changed this and led to the strike were government plans to open coastal shipping to foreign ships.[56]

The Labour government had begun rearranging port business, and a year earlier, on August 3 and 4, 1990, the Seafarers had demonstrated in Wellington and New Plymouth against the state-owned enterprise Petrocorp's using a Panamanian ship to export oil to Australia.[57] In March 1991, the Seafarers picketed the tanker *World Spring* in New Plymouth to protest Petrocorp's registering the ship under the Panamanian flag and using a Korean crew.[58]

The Seafarers' power was easily explained by New Zealand's situation as a three-island nation dependent on its ports.[59] Even this power might not have been adequate, given the forces marshalled against the union. It faced not only employers but also the government as a committed opponent which also had been taking actions which made the union more vulnerable. The government's announcement made employers worry that they would soon be competing against employers with lower-priced workers.[60] Taking on and paying a permanent workforce at the rates the union demanded was undesirable. Furthermore, the ports had just gone through a period of upheaval so that the Seafarers were fighting deregulation both in labour law and in their industry.

The Seafarers suffered from popular feeling against it for prior strikes. The news media had exacerbated these feelings in the past by focusing on the union's actions and the inconvenience they caused, while not explaining what motivated the union.[61] National's election manifesto had a photo of a ship in its section on industrial reforms. "Asked if this was significant, [then] Opposition Leader Jim Bolger chuckled and said they had been careful to ensure the illustrations were 'appropriate'."[62]

The Seafarers benefited from being in an essential industry. They also benefited and were weakened from having recently met deregulatory pressures and by improving competitiveness. The changes had saved $58 million but at the cost of jobs. These enormous savings and dramatic changes provided the immediate context in which these negotiations took place. They had forced the Seafarers to face and deal with change but they also whetted employers' appetites for more reforms.[63] Employers wanted to reduce the Seafarers' power.

Settlement did not come easily or quickly, which is not surprising, given the situation and recent history.[64] April 9, the Seafarers reaffirmed their threat to strike the next day. Federated Farmers, the umbrella organisation of farmers of New Zealand, maintained that additional cuts could be achieved, given Seafarers' pay rates, their two days off for each day on schedule, and fourteen weeks' annual leave.[65]

The strike began April 10 with 1100 Seafarers out.[66] Dave Morgan, Seafarers President, said that unless they chose to fight then, employers would walk all over them under the ECA.[67] By April 15, the effects of the stoppage were severe. The New Zealand Air Force was mobilised to fly stranded passengers and their cars across Cook Strait. Fifty thousand metric tons of freight was abandoned.[68] April 15, five of the ten employers—Union Shipping, Tasman Express Line, Milburn Cement, Pacific Management, and Pacifica Shipping—agreed to a twelve-month award that continued the "corner" and gave a 2% wage increase.[69]

New Zealand Rail, the state-owned enterprise which operated the interisland ferry between the North and South Islands, was one of the hold-out employers. The government was restructuring it with an eye to privatisation.[70] On April 19, New Zealand Rail accepted the same terms earlier agreed to but with nine jobs cut and a commitment to agree to savings of $5 million by June 1991.[71] Federated Farmers called the settlement a cowardly cave-in by incompetent management.[72] Once NZ Rail settled, only Golden Bay held out.[73] The government immediately discounted the agreement's value and said that now work would be opened up to competition by non-New Zealand crews paid minimum wage.[74]

Even the Seafarers' clear victory was a mixed blessing coming at this time. Anti-union forces seized on the strike and settlement as evidence that strikes should be banned or restricted.[75] Prime Minister Jim Bolger called the union "bloody-minded" and "warned that the system which brought their excessive pay and conditions would end under the bill."[76] The *National Business Review* observed:

> Meanwhile, the government has reacted to the disruption with all the intelligence used in handling industrial disruption during the 1970's. From the sidelines it has added heat by abusing the union side of the argument, shipping up anti-union feeling to the best of its ability, and moving in the armed forces.[77]

In Parliament, the government tried to have it both ways, both condemning and praising the ferry settlement. Bill Birch called the settlement a victory. Labour MP Richard Prebble responded: "In light of the fact that all New Zealand Rail Ltd has actually got is a commitment for everybody to go along to have 'talkies', will the Minister take any notice of the suggestion of the president of Federated Farmers that the board ought to be fired?" Birch denied this would be appropriate since the settlement was the means of achieving "an immediate saving of $1 million" and "a unique arrangement whereby the conditions in the award will be subject to renegotiation at an early date." When Mike Moore, Leader of the Opposition, responded: "Is the Minister saying that all those great achievements were achieved under the old industrial relations Act?" Birch was quick to attribute only the strike to the LRA.[78]

5. *Public sector bargaining:* At the same time as it was crafting legislation that controlled industrial relations, the National government was bargaining as employer with the Public Service Association (PSA) which represented government workers. As a

result, these negotiations could be taken as a model and signal for both employers and unions. The PSA was a union in which membership was voluntary, with "the union relying on delegates and organisation to keep membership levels high."[79]

The PSA's high membership levels in December 1990, just before the ECA was introduced into Parliament, made it optimistic about negotiations. PSA President Sue Piper predicted a 2% settlement without concessions. At the same time, the union was planning to seek as contract terms matters which had before been provided by law, including union recognition, education leave for delegates, union access to worksites, and document enforcement. It noted:

> At present these rights are guaranteed by legislation but the Government has made it clear it intends to change the law. These provisions will need to be determined between individual employers and workers in each collective agreement. All future PSA claims will include these as "insurance" for members.[80]

At the same time, the PSA began to get unsettling signals from the government. Bill Birch—both Labour Minister (then in the midst of drafting the ECA) and State Services Minister (employer of the PSA's members)—stated that employers and employees should not have equal rights to determine bargaining structures, because employer views were more important. When asked if this meant that the employer could compel a worker to belong to a bargaining unit which the worker had not chosen, Birch responded:

> If the individual employees all said, "Look, these are the bargaining structures we're going to impose on you, the employer, in your particular firm," that would make life impossible.... In a particular workplace an employer has to say, "Am I going to get involved in individual contracts, or am I going to have one bargaining structure for the whole of the workplace?"[81]

When the PSA heard National speaking generally about labour policy, it heard hints of the bargaining it would face as it began to deal with the 130 documents it then had up for negotiation.

By February 1991, optimistic PSA forecasts had changed tone. The *PSA Journal* headline read: "Gov't Takes Out Contract on Your Pay" and continued saying, "PSA members may be among the first workers in the country to feel the full effects of a new bill introduced to Parliament only a few days before Christmas.[82]

In mid-April 1991, the PSA offered either to roll over its current terms or a 1.5% wage increase with a 32% reduction in other terms for fifty documents not set to expire for several months.[83] Although this offer telegraphed the PSA's fears about bargaining, on May 8, only a week before the effective date of the ECA, the government agreed to roll over the fifty documents with no wage increase.[84]

The PSA's motives were easy to understand. It saw that other unions were either settling for concessionary contracts or not settling at all.[85] In its first issue after the ECA had become law, the *PSA Journal* counted itself lucky. Of 600,000 New Zealanders who were union members, 50,000 had lost collective coverage because their agreements had not been renewed. The PSA knew that it had only a moment to pause before it would have to take on Electricorp's threats to put its workers on individual contracts and Radio New Zealand's threats to impose unilateral pay cuts.[86]

It is harder to understand why National settled on these terms or at all. This could have been National's opportunity to be a model for how structural and other changes were achieved. This was precisely the situation the ECA was created for,[87] but the government passed up the opportunity. One explanation is that the government had begun to fear that employers might be tempted to take very strong action under the ECA, so it wanted to soft-pedal the radical nature of the ECA by not taking advantage of the situation, thus quelling fears.

Many more contracts were up for negotiation during this period. Some of these negotiations became part of the protests against the ECA. That was the second prong of union action during these five months—finding a way to protest against and defeat the ECA.

Notes

1. Patricia Herbert, "Employers' Federation Almost Outdoes Itself," *Dominion*, Nov. 26, 1990, at 10.
2. Ian McAndrew & Paul Hursthouse, "Southern Employers on Enterprise Bargaining," 15 N.Z. J. Ind. Rel., 117, 124 (1990.
3. Herbert, "Employers' Federation."
4. "New Structure Shows Federation's Wider Role," *Employer*, 4 (Apr. 1992).
5. NZEF, *Human Resources: An Introduction to Best Practice*, 11 (1992).
6. "Employment Contracts Database," *Employer*, 11 (Feb. 1992).
7. Anne Knowles, "Four Months Down the Track: Is the Employment Contracts Act Working?" *Examiner*, Sept. 5, 1991, at 19. A part of Knowles' theory was to isolate workers from the concerns of fellow workers through this lack of information. *Id.*
8. *Id.*
9. Paul Loof, "Bargaining Style in Sudden Switch," *National Business Review*, Aug. 14, 1991, at 18; McAndrew & Hursthouse, "Bargaining," 126.
10. "Secret Pay Deals Snub Freedom Act," *PSA Journal*, July 1991, at 1.
11. NZEF Memorandum in Wellington Regional Employers Association, *Employment Contracts Act 1991: Resource Kit for Employers* (1991).
12. Interview with Robyn Haultain, lawyer, in Wellington (May 19, 1992).
13. *Id.*
14. Maryan Street, "The New Act's Effect on Low Paid Members," 11 (n.d.); Jane Kelsey, *The New Zealand Experiment: A World Model for Structural Adjustment?*, 335–36 (1995).
15. ECB s 1(2).
16. Ken Douglas, "The Impact of the Employment Contracts Act," *Economic Alert*, 1, 2 (Aug. 1994).
17. Interview with Rick Barker, National Secretary, Service Workers Federation of Aotearoa, in Wellington (May 14, 1992).
18. Rebecca Macfie, "Unions Fold Under Pressure," *National Business Review*, Mar. 20, 1991, at 2; Richard Long, "Cook Strait Strife Boosts Birch's Contracts Bill," *Dominion*, Apr. 22, 1991, at 2.
19. Herbert Roth, "Industrial Summary December 1990 – January 1991," Indus. L. Bull., 12 (Feb. 1991); Roth, "Chronicle," 16 N.Z. J. Ind. Rel., 101 (1991).
20. Macfie, "Unions Fold."
21. Rebecca Macfie, "Workers Get 3%–3.25%," *National Business Review*, Feb. 14, 1991, at 1.
22. Brad Tattersfield, "Flaw Singled Out in Contracts Bill," *National Business Review*, Mar. 7, 1991, at 1.
23. Roth, "Chronicle," 16 N.Z. J. Ind. Rel., 202 (1991).
24. Rebecca Macfie, "Hotel Industry Opts for Familiar," *National*

Business Review, Feb. 21, 1991, at 1.
25. Long, "Cook Strait Strife."
26. Macfie, "Hotel Industry."
27. Stick Welcome, "Now for Carrots," *National Business Review*, Apr. 12, 1991, at 6; John Drinnan, "Employers' Head Hits Out at 'Misleading' Criticism," *Dominion*, Apr. 9, 1991, at 2.
28. Paul Loof, "Pre-empting the New Labour Bill," *National Business Review*, Mar. 27, 1991, at 16.
29. Although discussed here as one union, prior to the ECA, there were three distribution unions: the Northern Distribution Workers Union and the New Zealand Distribution and General Workers Union. These amalgamated and then covered all workers except those in Nelson and Marlborough, who were covered by a separate Nelson Marlborough Distribution Workers Union. See Janet Hector, Jon Hemming & Mary Hubble, "Industrial Relations Bargaining in the Retail Non-food Sector: 1991–1992," 18 N.Z. J. Ind. Rel., 326, 330 (1993).
30. Peter Brosnan, "Labour Market Flexibility and the Quality of Work: A Case Study of the Retail Industry," 16 N.Z. J. Ind. Rel., 13, 21 (1991).
31. Hector, Hemming & Hubble, 330–31.
32. Brosnan, 21.
33. There are two types of arbitration: interest arbitration and rights arbitration. Interest arbitration essentially sets the terms of a contract, agreement, or award. In fact, it was this sort of arbitration that accounts for the word "Arbitration" in the IC&A Act. When there is a dispute as to the application or interpretation of an agreement, this is referred to as rights arbitration. Either sort of arbitration can be either voluntary or compulsory, depending on the system.
34. *Id.*, 24–25.
35. Hector, Hemming & Hubble, 328–29.
36. Roth, "Chronicle," 16 N.Z. J. Ind. Rel., 97, 99, 103 (1991); interview with Paul Kimble, Organizer, Distribution Workers Federation, in Wellington (May 12, 1992).
37. Roth, "Chronicle," 15 N.Z. J. Ind. Rel., 295 (1990).
38. Rebecca Macfie, "Attack Continues on Penal Rates," *National Business Review*, Mar 22, 1991, at 3.
39. "Service Station Attendants Cut Out of Industry Award," *Dominion*, Apr. 26, 1991, at 3.
40. Roth, "Chronicle," 16 N.Z. J. Ind. Rel., 204 (1991).
41. "Service Station Attendants."
42. Roth, "Chronicle," 16 N.Z. J. Ind. Rel., 204 (1991); "Service Station Attendants."
43. Rosalie Webster, "Operating Under the Act: One Union's Experience" in *Employment Contracts: New Zealand Experiences*, 237, 242 (Raymond Harbridge, ed., 1993).

134 WORKING FREE

44. Interview with Hel Loader, Research Advocate, New Zealand Engineering Union, in Wellington (May 13, 1992).
45. Rebecca Macfie, "Hotel Unions Ready to Concede," National Business Review Mar. 4, 1991, at 1.
46. "Penalty Rates Dropped," Dominion, Mar. 14, 1991, at 1; Roth, "Chronicle," 16 N.Z. J. Ind. Rel., 202 (1991).
47. Roth, "Chronicle," 16 N.Z. J. Ind. Rel., 204 (1991).
48. Rebecca Macfie, "Union Ready for Enterprise Bargaining," National Business Review, Apr. 15, 1991, at 2.
49. Barker.
50. Raymond Harbridge & Kevin Hince, A Sourcebook of New Zealand Trade Unions and Employee Organisations, 66 (1994).
51. Interview with David Morgan, President of the Seafarers Union, in Wellington (May 14, 1992).
52. Rebecca Macfie, "Foreign 'Threat' Forces Port Talks," National Business Review, Apr. 4, 1991, at 1; Jason Barber, "CTU Ponders Unions' Call for General Strike," Dominion, Apr. 5, 1991, at 2.
53. Jason Barber, "Stoking the Boiler for a Fight With the Seamen," Dominion, Oct. 30, 1991, at 9.
54. NZEF, Employment Contracts Bill 1991: Submission B-29 (Jan. 30, 1991).
55. NZBR, Submission to the Labour Select Committee on the Employment Contracts Bill 30 (1991).
56. Macfie, "Foreign 'Threat'"; N.Z.P.D., 1469–70 (Apr. 23, 1991); David Barber, "The Worst Job in the World," National Business Review, May 1, 1991, at 9, 9.
57. Roth, "Chronicle," 15 N.Z. J. Ind. Rel., 291 (1990).
58. Roth, "Chronicle," 16 N.Z. J. Ind. Rel., 202 (1991).
59. Hugh Barlow, "Trade 'Disaster' Feared if Seafarers Go On Strike," Dominion, Apr. 8, 1991, at 8.
60. Macfie, "Foreign 'Threat'," 2.
61. Patricia Herbert, "Industry Fixes Sights on the Seamen's Corner," Evening Post, Oct. 24, 1989, at 7. A good example was the ferry strike in late 1989, which was caused not only by employers' refusal to abide by the terms of the parties' award but by their doing so in a way designed to inflame union anger.
62. Patricia Herbert, "Wharfies Ready for Fight," Auckland Star, Sept. 25, 1990, at A9.
63. Herbert, "Wharfies"; Herbert, "Seamen's Corner"; Roth, "Chronicle," 16 N.Z. J. Ind. Rel., 97 (1991).
64. Rebecca Macfie, "Shipping Sector Still Faces Strike Threat," National Business Review, Apr. 9, 1991, at 2.
65. Barber, "Worst Job," 9.
66. Rebecca Macfie, "Firms Hold Out Against Seamen," National Business Review, Apr. 16, 1991, at 2; Roth, "Chronicle," 16 N.Z. J. Ind. Rel., 205 (1991).
67. Roth, "Chronicle," 16 N.Z. J. Ind. Rel., 205 (1991).

68. Martyn Gosling, "Air Force Prepares for Cook Strait Airlift," *Dominion*, Apr. 16, 1991, at 1; Rebecca Macfie, "Strait Airlift Is Not Strike-breaking Move, Says Govt," *National Business Review*, Apr. 17, 1991, at 2.
69. Macfie, "Firms Hold Out"; Roth, "Chronicle," 16 N.Z. J. Ind. Rel., 205 (1991).
70. Rebecca Macfie, "Rail Ready for the Long Haul," *National Business Review*, Apr. 19, 1991, at 1.
71. Long, "Cook Strait Strife"; Roth, "Chronicle," 16 N.Z. J. Ind. Rel., 205 (1991); Rebecca Macfie, "Ferry Deal Sets Up Reform, Says NZ Rail," *National Business Review*, Apr. 23, 1991, at 3; Barber, "Worst Job," 10.
72. Roth, "Chronicle," 16 N.Z. J. Ind. Rel., 205 (1991).
73. Macfie, "Ferry Deal"; Barber, "Stoking the Boiler"; Morgan; *New Zealand Seafarers' Union v. Golden Bay Cement Co.* [1991] 1 ERNZ 932.
74. Rebecca Macfie, "Coastal Shipping to Open Up: Storey," *National Business Review*, Apr. 24, 1991, at 3.
75. "General Opposition to Contracts Act: Poll," *National Business Review*, May 15, 1991, at 4.
76. Long, "Cook Strait Strife."
77. Gareth Morgan, "Consumers Pay the Ferryman," *National Business Review*, Apr. 23, 1991, at 6.
78. N.Z.P.D., Question No.1, 1406 (Apr. 23, 1991).
79. "National Promises More Unions—Fewer Rights," *PSA Journal*, 4 (July 12 – Aug. 8, 1990).
80. "No Clawbacks as Award Round Begins," *PSA Journal*, 5 (Dec. 1990).
81. "Bill Birch Spells it Out," *PSA Journal*, 6 (Dec. 1990).
82. "Pay Deal Beats New Contract Law," *PSA Journal*, 1 (May 1991); "Gov't Takes Out Contract on Your Pay," *PSA Journal*, 1 (Feb. 1991).
83. Rebecca Macfie, "PSA Close to New Awards Deal," *National Business Review*, May 8, 1991, at 3; Rebecca Macfie, "Redundancy Issue Not Solved by PSA Options," *National Business Review*, Apr. 17, 1991, at 2; Roth, "Chronicle," 16 N.Z. J. Ind. Rel., 205 (1991).
84. Macfie, "PSA."
85. "Pay Deal Beats New Contract Law," *PSA Journal*, 1 (May 1991).
86. "50,000 Lose Award Protection," *PSA Journal*, 1 (June 1991).
87. Macfie, "Unions Fold"; Mike Munro, "Tempers Flare in Employment Contracts Bill Hearings," *Dominion*, Apr. 2, 1991, at 2; Loof, "Bargaining Style"; Brian Easton, "Alternative Systems of Industrial Relations: The Impact of the Employment Contracts Bill," 8 (Feb. 5, 1991).

8
The General Strike That Never Was

WHILE UNIONS FOUGHT TO SECURE THEIR SHORT-TERM FUTURE BY REACHING new agreements, for their long-term survival they needed to mobilise opposition to the ECA. Trade unionists were expecting the new legislation and listening for leaks about what to expect, but details were unusually difficult to come by. Meanwhile, the country, unions included, prepared for Christmas and the summer holidays. Most union offices would be closing after about December 20th.[1] Not only were holidays occupying people's attention, the Gulf War and military build-up in the Middle East was a growing concern.

The CTU had scheduled a December 20 meeting in anticipation that the ECB would be released by then, so unions were able to meet the day after it was available. As a result, they had an early opportunity to examine the bill and begin to formulate strategy.[2] Even so, unions were slow in deciding how to respond. Part of the slowness may have been shock at seeing the bill and realising it meant the end of society as they had known it. One commentator said trade unionists were "shell-shocked" by its extremism.[3] Up to its release, many had convinced themselves that things would still be "business as usual."

A second reason unions may have been slow in responding was that the ECA is a very long, complex statute and was radically different from any prior New Zealand labour legislation. Its implications can be difficult to appreciate even after many readings. Robyn Haultain, then a lawyer working for the CTU, described the situation within the unions when they first met to deal with the new legislation:

So a meeting was called of as many union labour people and advocates and officers—basically anyone who thought they had anything to say about the legislation. . . . Most of the people who came to the meeting had not read the Bill. Many of them who would have read the Bill would not have—they are not legally trained people, and the implications of some of the stuff that was in the Bill I think missed people. It was a real pressure cooker kind of a meeting.[4]

The CTU began preparing short analyses of the bill written in plain English and disseminating pamphlets directed at constituencies from the individual worker or person on the street to the members of Parliament and employers. "Your Union: The Protection You Need" explained to the average worker that the most basic terms of employment could be lost if the worker could not negotiate an agreement that included them. It claimed that the ECA's freedom would permit tyranny by small groups. For example, "[i]n a workplace of mostly women, a group of men might sign an agreement that wipes out maternity leave. . . . Or some workers can change their negotiators in the middle of bargaining, delaying or stopping a contract for the remainder—and putting extra costs on the employer and other workers." It raised the impact the large number of unemployed could have on wages: "Another possibility is the employer could simply hire unemployed people off the street for half the wages and conditions. This can't happen now because all existing conditions apply to new workers."

The CTU's series of analyses ranged from a plain English summary, health and safety issues, the interaction of the ECB, the Finance Bill and the current economic situation, the status of ILO conventions, and the role of the NZBR. On February 4, it issued all its affiliates a kit entitled "Turning Up the Heat."

These propaganda efforts were essential, because unions had a serious problem just in educating their members. Many people assumed the new law meant nothing more than outlawing compulsory unionism. Others knew only that the ECA was about freedom. Unions had to convince people that more was involved than unions' losing dues and that it was worthwhile opposing the ECA's sort of freedom.

... [O]ne of the good things about the Employment Contracts Act was that it really impelled union officials and organisers out of their offices and into workplaces. There were lots and lots of stop-work meetings and workplace meetings, and also public town hall meetings, organised by unions about the Employment Contracts Act.

The interesting thing was that at this special affiliates' meeting, when the decision was made about whether there should be a 24-hour strike against the Employment Contracts Act, that a lot of the officials got up and said that their personal view was that there probably wasn't a hell of lot of point in taking 24-hour strike action at that stage, but they were required, because of the message that they received from their membership, to come to that special affiliates' meeting and say "Vote yes" in favour of 24-hour strike action. So they obviously did quite a good job when they went out and had those workplace meetings explaining the consequences of the Act for workers and workers, it was reported, wanted to take action.[5]

The big question, however, was not when, but, increasingly, if the CTU would call a general strike. In the end, the CTU decided against a general strike. Its vacillation in the weeks before it reached this decision meant that there was no cohesive visible leadership opposing the ECA. Other groups tried to move into the leadership void left by the CTU. The Otautahi Coalition Against Benefit Cuts gradually moved its focus from public protests against Labour government policies to opposing the December 19 legislative package. Unions became one of the community groups that participated in the Coalition's work rather than being at the forefront of opposition.[6]

In Palmerston North, 60 people from various groups met on December 18 to form the Peoples Alliance, a coalition of community and union groups.[7] Its members included significant numbers of women, church groups, community aid agencies, individual unionists and unions, including the Service Workers, Hotel Workers, Clerical Workers, Footwear Workers, Clothing Trade Employees, and Manufacturing and Construction Workers Unions.

[W]e did things like thin Santas and carol singing. It was right at Christmas, December 19th, and so one of the first activities was rewriting all of the Christmas carols to make them quite political and getting the thinnest person that we could find and dressing him up in a Santa Claus suit and marching around the square. And for many people that was their first public street protest.[8]

The CTU's refusal to call a general strike was both a symptom of a split in the trade union movement and a cause of further schism. Years later some unionists still bitterly denounce the CTU. Graeme Clarke of the MCWU, for example, supported active opposition and believes that what public protest there was helped rein in employer excesses after the ECA was enacted.[9] Dave Morgan of the Seafarers goes further:

> We ended up with [the ECA], I think rather because of the fact that people just were not prepared to fight around it. There was no leadership for them to do that. . . .
>
> I think had they called a national strike at that time, the CTU, they would have achieved as an absolute minimum a sixty percent participation, which would have to be counted as a success rate but probably would have been higher. We will never ever know. But . . . I don't think . . . that the employers would have leaped into [the excesses that have since gone on] with the alacrity that they have, in regards to whacking people and to implementing the Act to its nth degree.[10]

Others supported and still support the CTU's *realpolitik* and condemn its critics. Rosslyn Noonan of the NZEI-TRR, for example, says:

> In fact, the calls for a national strike came on the whole from union officials who could not actually deliver their members. They wanted our members and their state sector unions to take action because we could deliver our members. They would claim that CTU was a sell out, but the reality was that a lot of that was old sectarian divisions amongst the union officials. I've got very little time for that.[11]

The position one took on a general strike marks a deep dividing line to this day in New Zealand union politics.

Given that the CTU did oppose the ECA and that in the past it had been willing to take to the streets, why did it refuse to do so when the union movement's life was at stake? So many people faced personal losses that it should have seemed possible to build a strong public opposition. If ever there had been a time when it could have enlisted general support, this would seem to be the best. Many previously inactive people were frightened and angered by the severe benefit cuts coming amidst high unemployment. Such people might have been enlisted to oppose the loss of legislative support for collective bargaining. For example, the ad hoc Action on Benefit Cuts (Wairarapa) put out a flyer that addressed the benefit cuts and, on the other side of the flyer, discussed the ECA. The ECA meant: "Back to the 19th Century! 'The poor are too well off!' 'The reason you aren't rich is You're Lazy!'" It asked: "Who's going to stop you getting the sack? How are you going to protect your wages? How are you going to pay your rent or mortgage? How are you going to feed your kids—or yourself? Will there be family support? Do we want to go back to the 19th Century? STAY WITH YOUR UNION JOIN THE FIGHTBACK."

Early on, some unionists urged the CTU to make common cause with the groups springing up to oppose the ECA and the benefit cuts.

> So an idea was proposed that the CTU should facilitate meetings with all sorts of people like all the church charity groups, because within the Anglican church, they have a commission of social responsibility, whose job and the staff's job is to comment, to give the church's views on various aspects of government policy and what it will mean to the people that they represent. There's people like the Anglican church and groups like women's refuge and rape crisis and all of those organisations that have reported in the past that the poorer people be, the more demand there is for their services. Basically, anybody who did any kind of charity or public helping kind of work, it was thought that a coalition should be formed with those people so that the union

movement's voice was stronger in making its complaint against the Employment Contracts Act and also so that there would be a pan-movement of people representing workers and other dispossessed, powerless people.[12]

However, this plan was not endorsed.[13] "It meant that the CTU did not do anything to promote that coalition. It happened anyway because people like Pat Kelly went ahead and organised it."[14] Disparate groups began to take an interest in and to sympathise with the union position on the ECA.

> They were very interested. It was really heartening. I enjoyed it a huge amount working with those people. And there was no hint of "Unions are just a bunch of communist rabble rousers trying to bring the country to its knees and we don't want to be associated with them." That attitude didn't surface at all.[15]

In late February 1991, the CTU announced a week of protests combined with a $150,000 media campaign to oppose the ECA.[16] It requested affiliates to present proposals for the protest, including stoppages, rallies, and minor disruptions.[17] To those who felt there had to be a general strike, this was too weak and modest a response. Some thought that the CTU was afraid it could not make a credible showing and that if it failed to do so, it would be severely weakened.[18]

> There was a general feeling it was a fait accompli and marching down the streets wasn't going to make any difference, although there were demonstrations organised by some union groups. The Service Workers Federation seemed to be quite a leader in that area. The NZNA [New Zealand Nurses Association] finally got with other health unions. Again the Service Workers is also involved in the health sector. We started to organise the membership to oppose the Bill, and we had demonstrations throughout the major cities in the country. They were incredibly well attended by our membership.[19]

When the CTU refused to spearhead a general strike, unions began to pursue separate strategies. The NZNA, which represented nurses in public sector hospitals, used its publications to broadcast what it saw as the legislation's threats and also joined its ECA protests to a strike concerning its contract negotiations.[20] The political nature of the strike was clear. When Judge Colgan enjoined the strike, he said:

> This is not a case about the content or effect of proposed legislative reform of the labour laws of New Zealand. To the extent that the Employment Contracts Bill currently before the House of Representatives features in this case, it is as a catalyst of strike action scheduled to take place in hospitals next week.[21]

He added that his decision "is not, and should not be interpreted as, this Court's views of the moral correctness of the position of any party or other group in the community concerning the proposed legislation."[22]

The NZNA strike was called off as a result of a compromise reached in the face of an injunction. This weakened the demonstration against the ECA but did give employers notice of how deeply nurses were concerned. In place of a strike, the NZNA held educational seminars and organised other forms of protest against the ECA.[23]

Some have blamed the Engineers Union as much as the CTU for the CTU's failure to take a more active stand against the ECA, such as a general strike. The Engineers say that, before taking action, they had found the public opinion was complacent on the ECA for two reasons: people believed that union opposition was purely a matter of self-interest and that the only impact the ECA would have was to mandate voluntary unionism. The Engineers were also concerned that the public had not been aroused by the recent and unsuccessful union opposition to legalising Sunday store openings. In the public mind, unions had so overstated the consequences of Sunday trading that they had lost credibility.[24]

The Engineers concluded that nothing could be done unless they first disseminated information to members about the ECA. Calls to action would only be dismissed as "trying to whip up hysteria." Once the membership was informed, it could then decide how to react. The informational campaign included providing resources, increasing organiser rotations, and holding workshops to explain the ECA and to dispel the idea that it only involved voluntary unionism.[25] One method was a poster captioned, "Bill Birch Bares All", with a caricature of a nude Labour Minister Bill Birch surrounded by questions and answers about the Employment Contracts Bill.

> We tried to get people's attention. It was a serious issue, and we needed to get people to focus on it. The 'Bill Birch Bares All' poster was a humorous way of getting people to look at the bare facts. It had questions like 'Will I still have a union?' 'What will happen to my wage rates?' It grabbed people's attention, and they read it. They became informed.
>
> We initially printed the poster in our newsletter, *Metal*. It proved popular, and we reprinted it for wider use. It was plastered up through central Wellington before the main protest march, all around the Employers Association and Government Buildings. It wasn't graffitied either.
>
> If we had gone out and said 'This Act is bad. Your union says protest!' they would've ignored us, and thought that the union was looking after its self-interest. We did not force members on to the street to wave banners. We gave them information about the bill. They were free to do what they wanted: Believe us, not believe us, take part in industrial action, not take part. Many of them wanted to protest and did, union officials and organisers stood next to them on the streets.[26]

The Engineers succeeded in arousing member awareness and concern. Once members were aroused and wanted to take action, there were marches for Engineers members to participate in. These marches were not, however, organised by the Engineers nor by the CTU. They were organised by groups such as the Public Service Association, the Communist Party, and the Unemployed Workers League.

There is some plausibility to the Engineers' strategy of providing information and letting members decide what to do. However, how effective and appropriate is such a strategy and such a role for a union? It is fair to say that unions play special roles as a government of members, as a representative for members' views and interests, as a vehicle for expressing and channelling individual members into a collective force, and as a means of providing experience with participatory democracy.

The Engineers' actions contradicted its general policy of providing multi-layered information tied to specific coordinated action the Engineers had developed. Stewards were not left with information and then required to decide what to do with it. Here, however, when members had been galvanised into action, their union was not there to lead them. Furthermore, even if protest could only have been symbolic or quixotic, failing to protest meant, at worst, lost opportunities to defeat or wound the legislation and, at best, a lost opportunity to be perceived by their members and by the public as playing a vital role in the important issues of the day.

The MCWU is and was one of the most vocal opponents of the Engineers. Oddly enough some of its actions were at least overtly similar. The MCWU assessed member awareness and support and then acted on that knowledge. In areas where its organisation was weak, it circulated pamphlets. Elsewhere, it held stop-work meetings where union members discussed the issues and tried to work out a position on the ECA. At the national level, it urged colleagues in the trade union movement to support a general strike. At its annual conference held on April 16 and 17, 1991, it resolved to support "effective organised national stoppages and national strikes in opposition to the Employment Contracts legislation" and to provide financial support to support opposition to the bill.[27] When the CTU failed to endorse a general strike, the MCWU decided it could not effectively call a strike.[28] Thus neither the MCWU nor the Engineers called a strike of its members, although their motives differed.

However, the MCWU's decision differed significantly from the Engineers. The Engineers was large enough to have called a credible strike whether or not the CTU did. The MCWU, on the other hand, had a very small membership spread throughout the country. The decision by the CTU not to call a general strike prevented some from being able to take actions they would have liked to.

Although there was no general strike, there were many protests against the ECA, including some strikes. The anti-ECA campaign, from April 1 to May 15, had unforeseen effects, even though it failed in its main goal. By organising members and increasing public awareness, it increased sympathy for unions as institutions and left unions with more highly organised members as they went into the post-ECA period. It may also have made some employers more reluctant to press their advantage than they might otherwise have been.

> So from the point of view in a depressed economy, those people that stayed in for six months longer than they otherwise would have represent six months of income with which to try and organise and make sure that you hang on to the base areas, if you like, of the union. So, people became aware of what was going to happen, and now that things have happened along the lines that were predicted, then people can say: "Well, yeah. It was correct."
>
> You know and that this is where the source of their problem is. If nothing had been done, people would have looked at what happened ... and they might have had a variety of explanations for it, but it's unified a core of opinion that the problems we are now experiencing derive from this Employment Contracts Act.
>
> Now, in terms of shaping people's opinions, it was quite successful, because the Minister of Labour was forced to respond with a householder's leaflet which is now widely quoted and shown to be a lie. He lied to the constituency about the intentions of his legislation and did so, in writing, to every household in the country.[29]

Indeed, as the protests gathered force, the bill was delayed in emerging from the select committee so it could be rewritten.

As the enactment of the ECA drew nearer, protests took place throughout the country. In early March, a number of unions, including teachers and health workers, announced a "day of action" for April 4, even though the public sector unions had voted unanimously against a general strike. In fact, some of the strongest action in opposition to the ECA came from unions which represented teachers and early childcare workers. Their actions took a range of forms, including stop-work meetings and announcing their readiness to strike to oppose the ECA.[30]

The day of action evolved into a Week of Action beginning April 3. It included strikes, stopwork meetings, rallies, and marches involving 300,000 to 500,000 New Zealanders out of a population of 3.2 million. Actions included a 24-hour strike by 50,000 education workers on April 4 and 50,000 health workers who engaged in a two-hour stopwork meeting. There was concerted action by members of the Nurses Association, Public Service Association, Service Workers Federation, Local Government Officers Association, and the Association of Salaried Medical Specialists. In the private sector, there were strikes by storeworkers, drivers, and engine drivers of the Northern Distribution Workers Federation; the Seafarers Union; the Harbour Workers Union; workers at the New Zealand Steel plant; and a march by the members of the Railway Trades Association.[31]

Rallies, strikes, and marches took place in all the major centres and in many minor centers, such as Whangarei and Invercargill. Inland Revenue staff in Nelson struck. Wildcat strikes drew out meatworkers at AFFCO in Moerewa and Whangarei and at Weddel New Zealand, also in Whangarei; Hutt Valley railway workers; Kinleith pulp and paper workers; and journalists at the Wellington *Evening Post*, the *Dominion*, and the New Zealand Press Association. It was the first time education sector unions, formerly friendly rivals, joined together.[32] The ECA cost the country over 50,000 lost working days in the first week of April 1991 alone.[33]

To have as many as one-sixth of the population actively opposing a government action demonstrated an extraordinarily high level of public concern, especially in the absence of a central organisation supporting the actions. Some strikes were spontaneous demonstrations. For example, a two-hour stopwork meeting by the Northern Distribution Union led to a one-day wildcat strike after a worker made a motion from the floor. The public became concerned that worker anger, without a stronger outlet provided by the CTU, might lead to more generalised wildcats.[34]

It would seem that this level of opposition would have mandated at least reconsideration of the law. However, the government was controlled by persons dedicated to an ideology and bent on ensuring the ECA was enacted. The National government criticised the opposition as illegitimate and particularly condemned teachers. Speaking as State Services Minister, Bill Birch blasted teachers for setting an "appalling example" by going on strike and for inconveniencing thousands of families.

> The unions have had ample opportunity to make submissions to the select committee. That should be the responsible way of addressing any concerns.
>
> Teachers, more than anyone else, should be setting standards. They should be ashamed that as the guardians of our children they are setting an appalling example to them.[35]

In late April, the CTU again felt increasing pressure to call a general strike. The matter was to be taken up at the April 18 delegates meeting; however, CTU leadership telegraphed its opposition in advance. CTU president Ken Douglas declared publicly that there had to be some other solution than leading a protest parade.[36] The CTU leadership offered a compromise resolution for a national day of activity on April 30. Rick Barker moved to amend the resolution to have a one-day general strike, because all of his union's affiliates had made unanimous calls for a twenty-four hour strike.[37]

Barker's amendment was defeated 250,122 to 190,910, with the PSA, Engineers, Post Primary Teachers Association, Nurses Association, Post Office Union, NZEI-TRR, and Financial Sector Union voting against.[38] Instead, each individual union was to decide what action to take on a national day of activity on April 30, the day before the ECA was scheduled to become law.[39] It was assumed that this CTU-sanctioned action would be too late to have any impact on Parliament's deliberations, since the vote would be taken before then. At least it would send a timely message about the readiness of workers to oppose any draconian measures taken against them.

The votes reflected and created confusion among unions and

workers. In an interview a year later, an organiser for the Clerical Workers Union captured the complex feelings of the time:

> [A] lot of people in our union didn't have any particular trouble with the CTU's strategies. One rank-and-file member went to the CTU town meeting in the Town hall where Ken Douglas spoke. From what he said, it seemed that Ken would have liked to see a general strike but didn't think he could be the one to call it, simply because he wasn't the one with the members. It had to be the unions that called a general strike.
>
> A lot of officials interpreted what the CTU was saying as opposition to a general strike, so I'm a bit confused about the whole thing. But I quite firmly accept what Ken Douglas has said for years now at each award round: "Unless unions get themselves organised, there's very little the CTU can do overall."
>
> The whole thing of providing leadership is a very interesting issue. I think it's better if the focus is on the unions themselves. I don't think there's much point in suddenly trying to provide leadership if no groundwork has been done and if there's actually nothing there to lead. And I think that was our problem. You can't just point the finger at the CTU and say it was all their fault. There hadn't been enough done over the years, quite long, for there to be anything to be led. Who's to blame for that? . . .
>
> But yes, I was frustrated with the CTU leadership. We hammered them for a general strike, but they were saying to us, "Can you get your members out?" We knew we in the Clerical Workers Union didn't have much of a chance unless a general strike was called. . . .[40]

This division cost the union movement solidarity at a time it could ill afford division. For one thing, the vote at the CTU meeting did not reflect unions members' sentiments in many cases. For example, 87% of the Nurses Association members voted for the strike.[41] The PSA split shortly after the ECA came into effect, in part as a result of anger over its vote against a general strike.[42] Two years later, a competing union federation, the New Zealand Trade Union Federation (TUF), was created primarily out of groups who had supported a general strike.[43] By late 1993, only 57% of New Zealand unions belonged to the CTU, and there was speculation there might be more defections.[44] In the meantime, the CTU saw union membership drop from 514,000 in May 1991 to 376,000 by December 1994.[45]

Given the negative consequences, why was stronger action not taken? One intriguing possibility is that this may have grown out of the CTU's recent role as a partner in government and as an important regulator of social and economic policy.

> [T]he CTU's position at the spearhead of the protest must seem a painfully retrograde step for an organisation that has spent over three years attempting to establish a constructive social and economic policy agenda for the union movement, shaking off the traditional union pre-occupation with wages and conditions to the exclusion of all else and establishing a quasi-official role in the process of government.[46]

The CTU tried to hang on to this role after the ECA was enacted by talking "past the act directly to employers, on the basis that only unions can deliver the stable, co-operative relationship basic to both profitability and job security."[47]

The decision not to support a general strike may have been based on the accurate assessment that the ECA could not be defeated. Douglas observed, quite accurately, "[T]he government ha[s] the machinery to ram the bill through parliament."[48] The battle was uphill all the way, and time was too short. A January 1991 CTU poll found that the public had little awareness or understanding of the ECA. To the extent that the public had views, it supported the government's claim that the legislation would boost productivity.[49] Those numbers did not suggest that a general strike had any chance of success.

Hindsight tells us that public opinion underwent a massive change very quickly and largely as a result of union education campaigns. In the end, only 7% of the public believed the ECA would bring productivity gains.[50] Unfortunately for the CTU, by the time this change in public opinion was visible, it was too late to change strategy and lead the forces it had mobilised.

Notes

1. Interview with Robyn Haultain, lawyer, in Wellington (May 19, 1992).
2. "Leading from the Rear," *Listener & TV Times*, June 3, 1991, at 30; Haultain.
3. *Id.*, 30.
4. Haultain.
5. *Id.*
6. "Building Against Benefit Cuts," *Race Gender Class*, 11/12, 25, 29 (1991); interview with Donna Payne, Organiser, New Zealand Nurses Association, in Wellington (May 8, 1992).
7. *Hard Times: Newsletter of the Manawatu Peoples Alliance*, 1 (n.d.).
8. Interview with Maxine Gay, Organiser, Public Service Association, in Palmerston North (May 17, 1992).
9. Interview with Graeme Clarke, General Secretary Manufacturing and Construction Workers Union, at Wellington (May 5, 1992).
10. Interview with David Morgan, President, Seafarers Union, in Wellington (May 14, 1992).
11. Interview with Rosslyn Noonan, National Secretary, New Zealand Educational Institute, at Wellington (May 26, 1992).
12. Haultain.
13. *Id.*
14. *Id.*
15. *Id.*
16. Brad Tattersfield, "CTU Calls for Week of Protests," *National Business Review*, Feb. 22, 1991, at 1.
17. Gay; Mike Munro & Jason Barber, "Roundtable Job Plan Fails to Impress," *Dominion*, Feb. 19, 1991, at 2.
18. Gay; Tattersfield, "CTU Calls."
19. Payne.
20. *Auckland Area Health Board v. New Zealand Nurses Association* [1991] 1 ERNZ 795, 796.
21. *Id.*, 796.
22. *Id.*, 796.
23. Payne; "We Say IT STINKS!" *NZ Nursing Journal*, 4 (May 1991).
24. Interview with Hel Loader, Research Advocate, New Zealand Engineering Union, in Wellington (May 13, 1992).
25. *Id.*
26. *Id.*
27. Letter from Graeme Clarke (Nov. 13, 1996).
28. Clarke interview.
29. *Id.*
30. "Teachers to Stop Work Over Bill," *Dominion*, Feb. 18, 1991, at 7.
31. Jason Barber, "500,000 Workers Expected to Protest," *Dominion*, Apr. 2, 1991, at 2; Rebecca Macfie, "Protest Week Could 'Trigger Wildcat Strikes'," *National Business Review*, Apr. 2, 1991, at 1;

N.Z.P.D., 1446, 1473 (Apr. 23, 1991).
32. Barber, "500,000 Workers"; Debbie Dawson, "50,000 Education Workers Set to Strike Against Bill," *Dominion*, Apr. 4, 1991, at 1; "Much of Contracts Bill Flak 'Outrageous Lies'—Birch," *Dominion*, Apr. 4, 1991, at 2; Rebecca Macfie & Brad Tattersfield, "Govt Rules Out Action Against Teacher Strike," *National Business Review*, Apr. 4, 1991, at 2; Rebecca Macfie, "Anti-bill Protests 'Shows Need for Change'," *National Business Review*, Apr. 5, 1991, at 1, 2.
33. Erin Kennedy, "Protests Cost Over 50,000 Working Days," *Dominion*, Apr. 8, 1991, at 8.
34. Macfie, "Protest Week."
35. "Teachers To Set Appalling Example—Birch," *Dominion*, Apr. 2, 1991, at 2.
36. Jason Barber, "CTU Meets to Argue General Strike Call," *Dominion*, Apr. 18, 1991, at 11.
37. Sarah Heal, "The Struggle Over the Employment Contracts Act, 1987–1991" in *Labour, Employment and Work in New Zealand 1994*, 274, 276–77 (Philip S. Morrison, ed., 1994).
38. *Id.*, 277.
39. Jason Barber, "General Strike Call Rejected," *Dominion*, Apr. 19, 1991, at 7; Brad Tattersfield, "CTU No to General Strike," *National Business Review*, Apr. 19, 1991, at 1; Patricia Herbert, "Unions Face a Brave New World," *Dominion*, May 15, 1991, at 10.
40. Lana Le Quesne, "Unions Fighting for Survival," *Race Gender Class*, 13, 30, 32 (1992).
41. Barber, "Call Rejected"; Tattersfield, "CTU No"; Herbert, "Brave New World."
42. "South's NUPE Gathers Steam," *Labour Notes*, Dec. 1992, at 6.
43. "New Union Alliance Formed," *Labour Notes*, June 1993, at 7.
44. Sarah Boyd, "Unionism Finds New Ways in Fight to Survive," *Evening Post*, Sept. 8, 1993, at 7; Nigel Haworth, "Unions in Crisis: Deregulation and Reform of the New Zealand Union Movement" in *Organized Labor in the Asia-Pacific Region: A Comparative Study of Trade Unionism in Nine Countries*, 282, 293 (Stephen Frenkel, ed. 1993).
45. Harbridge, et al., "Unions and Union Membership in New Zealand: Annual Review for 1993," 19 N.Z. J. Ind. Rel., 175, 176 (1994).
46. Rebecca Macfie, "Mass Protests Feed On Workers' Unease," *National Business Review*, May 3, 1991, at 12.
47. "Leading from the Rear," 33.
48. Barber, "CTU Meets to Argue"; Ken Douglas, "The Employment Contracts Bill: Two Very Different Perspectives," *Examiner*, Apr. 18, 1991, at 18.
49. "Leading from the Rear," 32.
50. *Id.*, 32.

9

The Debate in Parliament

THE EMPLOYMENT CONTRACTS BILL WAS LATE IN RETURNING TO Parliament. Although no explanation was offered, this appears to have been caused by growing public opposition, including before the select committee which was holding hearings on the ECB. Efforts to sell the ECB steadily increased.

In late March, Birch sent a "Householder's Pamphlet" at a cost of $2 million to allay fears[1] and respond to misinformation and disinformation that had been "widely distributed and supported by the Opposition."[2] Although sent out while the select committee was still holding hearings, the pamphlet has detailed descriptions of the rights which would exist under the ECA.[3] During the April 4 Week of Action, Birch gave a round of television and radio interviews lobbying for passage of the ECB.[4] He asserted that, once the Bill was enacted, it would be accepted as misconceptions were brushed away.[5]

On April 3, Minister Birch announced that the ECA draft would emerge intact from the select committee.[6] However, on April 11, 1991, the select committee chair, Max Bradford, said that the Bill would be changed to require personal grievance procedures in all contracts, to improve wage and other minimum conditions, to create bargaining procedures, and to permit adding new employees to collective contracts.[7] Bradford, however, dismissed the importance of the protests as "based either on scurrilous misinformation or on emotive, worst-case scenarios."[8] One change Bradford did not intend to make was the effective date. He still intended the ECA to be law May 1, even though committee hearings were not yet finished and the bill could not be reported to Parliament until at least April 25.[9]

The select committee finally closed its hearings on April 17.[10] Birch bragged that the select committee process had led to virtually no changes from the bill:

> Despite the complexity and size of the legislation, only four technical amendments were made during the Committee stage, and only one minor supplementary order paper was introduced to make those technical amendments.[11]

This was an odd sort of pride in a democracy, yet Birch maintained that refusing to change, even in the face of testimony and submissions in opposition, was a positive aspect of the law and the process used.[12]

Bradford had rejected objections because, he said, the only people who opposed the ECB were trade union officers:

> It is not coincidental that during the Committee stage the only people, with the exception of two or three, to make a substantive comment on the legislation were former trade union secretaries. I guess that means that their contribution was a pay-off to their mates left in the trade union movement who want to carry on just as they are.[13]

This was, of course, highly inaccurate. Objections far outnumbered support, and objections came from all segments of the population, including from employers; whereas support came almost exclusively from employers or their associations. Bradford himself said that 503 persons appeared before the select committee and 62 petitions and 830 submissions were received during two and a half months of hearings. The Committee's sample analysis of 400 submissions found that 71 supported the ECB, 188 were opposed, and 141 made technical objections only.[14]

At last, on April 23, 1991, the ECB emerged from the select committee. The arithmetic on the changes also appears to have been off. Substantive changes included moving the effective date to May 15; requiring personal grievance procedures to be in all contracts; creating an Employment Court with expanded jurisdiction; allowing mid-term modifications of contracts; altering the minimum code of working conditions; creating the Employment

Tribunal; barring those with serious criminal convictions from serving as bargaining agents; allowing agents to become parties to employment contracts; allowing newly hired employees to join previously negotiated contracts; and denying unions the right to strike in support of a multi-employer agreement (essentially a replacement for awards).[15] It also eliminated a provision in the ECB which had permitted the parties to contract out of coverage by the law.

When Labour Minister Bill Birch had introduced the new legislation on December 19, 1990, his speech echoed NZEF and NZBR views. First, he lashed out at those employers who preferred the existing system:

> Some businesses have hidden behind awards and have left to others the responsibility of negotiating wages and conditions. A few large firms have been able to push through the web of regulations and restrictions to negotiate agreements that suit them and their employees.[16]

Birch contrasted the less efficient employers with the innovative employers who had been stifled by the award system.[17]

Birch then contended that the government had foreshadowed its sweeping changes with clarity and thus had a mandate for them.[18] He condemned unions as outsiders to the employment relationship[19] and claimed that the ECA would normalise New Zealand industrial legislation by allowing New Zealand to ratify ILO conventions 87 on freedom of association and 98 on the right to organise and bargain collectively.[20] Ironically, in March 1994, the ILO found that the ECA violated its conventions.[21]

Helen Clark, Deputy Leader of the Labour Party and Opposition spokesperson for labour, responded. She had received a copy of the ECA only at 6.30 p.m. that day.[22]

> The Bill comes at the end of an extraordinary 2 weeks in which the Government has systematically attacked the interests of disadvantaged New Zealanders. The Government has attacked their rights of citizenship. In the previous week, it was the turn of women, the disabled, Maori, and Pacific Islanders—anyone who might conceivably have benefited from the Employment

Equity Act—and this afternoon the Government has had a go at beneficiaries and children. The Government took away the provision for free doctors' visits. Tonight it is the turn of low-income workers.[23]

Clark called the government's actions a "scorched-earth approach" and said that "[t]he real reason behind the Bill is to get at the wages of low-income workers. The real reason is to lower wages."[24] Clark pointed out specific agreements that showed the sorts of employment contracts the government claimed it wanted could be obtained under existing legislation.[25]

National Minister of Commerce Philip Burdon echoed the NZEF-NZBR claim that New Zealand's unique industrial relations legislation had caused the country's economic troubles. He claimed that the ECB was the same legislation other industrialised countries had enacted:

> The Bill is important, and will take the country into the twentieth century. It will bring New Zealand in line with every other OECD country. It is designed specifically to ensure that New Zealand has industrial legislation similar to that which has resulted in the enormous increases in productivity, living standards, and material comforts in, for example, Western Europe. It is an anachronism that New Zealand should be the only OECD country that has compulsory unionism. In particular, the Bill is designed to ensure that New Zealand has an industrial system that will allow workers to enjoy genuine increases in living standards and that will increase productivity. It is designed to take New Zealand away from the adversarial mentality of the nineteenth century.
>
> . . . Thank heavens the Government is imitating the success of the economies in Europe and in North America.[26]

Burdon claimed that the legislation promoted freedom of choice and freedom to negotiate, and would give workers freedom to negotiate for the first time. Before this, "the union secretary has, in effect, been able to dictate the terms and conditions under which those employees work, whether or not the employees like it."[27] The legislation would establish "a much more harmonious industrial relations environment than has historically been the case."²⁸

Labour MP Elizabeth Tennet praised the LRA for making it possible for hard-to-organise clerical workers to bargain collectively and for giving them a minimum code of employment conditions through their award.²⁹ Tenant contended that New Zealand's industrial relations system had carried it through all its past growth periods and had not impeded growth then. Why, then, had it now become an impediment?³⁰

Max Bradford, a new National MP, former Director of Advocacy for the NZEF, and the man who was to chair the select committee on the ECB, responded that the ECB was appropriate for modern times. Bradford denigrated the IC & A Act as the "Industrial Constipation and Arbitration Act."³¹

> For 100 years the country has suffered under a wage-fixing and industrial relations system that was associated with that poor economic performance that has played a part in producing the shambles—the lack of growth—everything that the country is no longer prepared to put up with.³²

Bradford minimised the importance of the LRA, claiming that it covered only 40% of New Zealanders. They would be able to "enjoy benefits such as the freedom to negotiate that 60 percent of New Zealanders now enjoy. . . ."³³ No one asked Bradford this question: if New Zealand's industrial relations system was causing economic privation, why would it not have been caused by the regime affecting the majority as opposed to the minority of workers?

Labour MP Larry Sutherland argued that what was needed was legislation which protected workers who had less "muscle."

> [Bradford] failed to talk about industries such as the clerical industry, the retail industry, the clothing workers' industry, the service workers' industry—industries that matter so much and that depend on industrial legislation. I refer to industrial legislation that can protect workers and that will always ensure that, no matter what kind of ratbag employer they have to deal with—and they are not all ratbags; there are some good ones—and no

matter whether those employers refuse to consider a justifiable argument for better wages and conditions, there is a structure that has worked for many years.[34]

Sutherland insisted that the ECA was intended to make workers powerless so they would be willing to accept low pay and poor conditions from employers who could "claw back conditions such as sick pay, maternity pay, statutory holidays, smoko [break] times, and the fundamental provisions that are set in place in awards and that are so crucial for the health of workers, so crucial for the rights of workers, and so crucial for workers' having a say in their industry."[35] Sutherland claimed that the ECA would fragment the workplace by encouraging worker schism.[36]

Minister of Communications Maurice Williamson compared New Zealand's economic performance with other countries in the period 1960–1987.

> [I]n Canada real wages increased by 70 percent during that time; in Japan by 174 percent; in Denmark, Finland, and Norway by 90 percent—not terribly good; in combined Europe by 147 percent; in Mediterranean countries by a staggering 285 percent; in Australia by 70 percent; and in the United States by 70 percent. In New Zealand real wages increased by a measly 1 percent between 1960 and 1987.[37]

He asserted that in the past decade average real wages had dropped 0.5% a year and that New Zealand had fallen from third to thirtieth in terms of its standard of living.[38] His statistics were not challenged, but could have been. This disparity was, in large part, an artefact of New Zealand's very high position at the start of the period selected relative to the low position then of the other countries. In other words, the changes reflected not so much New Zealand's fall as other countries' rise.

Williamson then turned to the question of the "60 percenters" who were not covered by the LRA and asked if their wages were driven into the ground or if they were on the breadline or lying on the street. Williamson contended: "The evidence is that non-unionised labour in most countries is better paid than unionised labour."[39] In addition, the ECA would improve union representation. He claimed that prior to voluntary unionism, the workers in one factory had never seen a representative from the Engineers Union but that after the National government had enacted voluntary unionism provisions, the union representative visited every few months to help them and to "justify his existence."[40]

Labour MP Paul Swain rose to take on Williamson's economic figures.

> [Williamson] failed to understand some of the figures that he quoted. Real wages are related to economic performance and growth. For some time the real wages in New Zealand have fallen, but they would have fallen a lot further without the regulations and controls that have been in the labour market over the past few years. Is the member suggesting that the wage rates and conditions in Thailand, Sri Lanka, and Chile are the kind that prevail in this country? They will be over the next few years if the Bill is passed.[41]

Swain contended that the government planned to "hack public spending, and that will snuff out demand and strangle an economy that is already gasping."[42] Swain said:

> The question to be asked is why the Bill should be introduced? What is the need for it? Who wants it, and what is it supposed to achieve? Workers do not want it. Small and medium employers do not want it. The Opposition certainly does not want it. So who wants it? Clearly, the Business Roundtable and the Employers Federation want it. The powerful in society want it, and now the Government has delivered it to them.[43]

Swain then quoted from Westpac Banking Corporation, which, on November 30, 1990, had stated that labour market deregulation would lead to falling real wages and further lay-offs over the next couple of years and "may well have a perverse effect on growth."[44]

Swain continued:

> An award is a guaranteed legal protection for wage rates, hours of work, holiday pay, sick leave, overtime pay, redundancy, and

The Debate in Parliament 159

matters such as sexual harassment. It provides a guaranteed minimum—a floor below which certain rates and conditions cannot fall. The Bill strips away that floor and allows workers to fall into the low wage/low skill crevasse of many countries.

The present floor is already extremely low—for example, retail workers who are under 16½ years earn $3.67 an hour, and those between 18 and 18½ years earn $4.76 an hour. In the case of women workers, on whom the Bill will impact most heavily, workers in the tearoom industry are earning about $8.50 and workers in the restaurant sector are earning about $9.50. What will happen when the floor is removed under the so-called deregulated labour market? The poor will get poorer and the rich will get richer, and the State will have to pick up that tab. . . . [45]

National MP Bruce Cliffe took the debate to new realms of hyperbole. Cliffe began with the theme that National had a duty to deregulate the labour market to bring it in line with other New Zealand markets.[46] He then claimed that he had worked in Germany and the United Kingdom "under the legislation that the House is discussing" and was "proud that it has come to New Zealand."[47]

Germany was one of those states cited as supporting both sides' arguments. In the April 1991 ECA debates, Labour MP Elizabeth Tennet, for example, pointed out that Germany and Japan did not have this sort of legislation and thought that the ECA was most comparable to Chile's, but without the military to enforce it.[48] The National Party frequently claimed Germany as a model for the ECA,[49] even though those more familiar with European systems described Germany and Japan as the antithesis of the ECA regime.[50]

Cliffe then moved from comparative law to extol the benefits the ECA would bring to unions.

> Despite what I have heard from members tonight the Bill sounds no death knell for unions—far from it. Some unions, as I sincerely hope, will prosper, and others will fail and vanish. The same has already happened to farmers and to manufacturers, and it must happen to unions also. The union that makes itself

accountable and deals with the needs of its individual members, that provides a service and adapts, will become indispensable to the member who needs collective support, and there will be many who want that.[51]

He concluded by claiming that the ECA would bring New Zealand into the 1980s, not the 1990s, "because everyone else had this provision in the 1980's."[52]

Labour MP Lianne Dalziel, a new MP who had been a trade unionist, argued that, although the National Party had spoken of flexibility, the ECA would have no impact on flexibility.

> All that it will do is establish unilateral management control over the way in which labour is used rather than providing the positive measures that are needed so that the work-force can adjust and respond to the economic changes in a modern democratic society. That is the difference between the growth agreement that the former Government negotiated with the Council of Trade Unions and the complete rebuttal of that agreement that has occurred with the Bill's introduction.[53]

Dalziel contended that when the Minister of Commerce's company was offered a company agreement, he had turned it down in favour of the national award, "because his workers wanted to be paid more. The reason the Minister supports the Bill is that it provides the ability to pay less. There should be some honesty in the House. The lies should stop now."[54]

Dalziel then attacked the absence of enforcement mechanisms in the ECA, including lack of access by worker representatives and the Department of Labour to work records.[55] These had proven to be necessary even under the LRA to ensure employers did not violate award terms.

> The local union from which I come recovers more than $300,000 annually on behalf of its members. That union is a very small regional union. When that figure is multiplied across the membership of the national body it amounts to more than $2 million a year. That is the kind of recovery occurring at present under legally binding awards and agreements, and that is the

kind of money that will be ripped off from the pockets of the lowest-paid workers. How it is intended that that will achieve growth is beyond me. The issue is well known on the other side of the House, and that is why the beginnings of the benefit cuts were announced today—so that wages can fall lower than they may have done otherwise."[56]

Dalziel was the last speaker before the vote on introducing the Employment Contracts Bill was taken. The vote was fifty-one in favour and twenty-five opposed. The ECA was then given its first reading and referred to the Labour select committee for hearings.[57]

After the vote, Treasury Minister Ruth Richardson praised the changes the ECA would bring as "fresh thinking in respect of our approach to our labour market and, I guess, fresh thinking in respect of the responsibility of individuals and our determination to ensure that individuals had an incentive to stand on their own feet and get ahead."[58] It was a constant theme of the National Government that unemployment was a state within the control of the individual and that those on it were only "bludgers" who needed to be urged back into gainful employment. Richardson extolled the National Party for creating an "enterprise culture"[59] and praised the ECA as a "match between fiscal, monetary and labour market policies."[60]

The ECA passed on May 7, 1991, by a vote of 43 to 24 and became law on May 15, 1991.[61]

Notes

1. Dept. of Labour Te Tari Mahi, *The Employment Contracts Act: A Brief Guide* (1991); N.Z.P.D., Question No. 2, 898 (Mar.19–20, 1991); Richard Long, "Cook Strait Strife Boosts Birch's Contracts Bill," *Dominion*, Apr. 22, 1991, at 2; Simon Kilroy, "Publicity Campaign Backfires," *Dominion*, Mar. 14, 1991, at 1.
2. N.Z.P.D., Question No. 2, 898 (Mar. 19–20, 1991); N.Z.P.D., 1462 (Apr. 23, 1991).
3. N.Z.P.D., 913 (Mar.19–20, 1991).
4. Mike Munro, "Tempers Flare in Employment Contracts Bill Hearings," *Dominion*, Apr. 2, 1991, at 2; Mike Munro, "Birch Stands Firm in Face of Outcry," *Dominion*, Apr. 5, 1991, at 1;

Patricia Herbert, "Unions Face a Brave New World," *Dominion*, May 15, 1991, at 10.
5. Kevin O'Connor, "Shop Floor's New Broom," *Dominion Sunday Times*, Apr. 21, 1991, at 9.
6. Munro, "Tempers Flare."
7. Rebecca Macfie, "Labour Bill to Change: Bradford," *National Business Review*, Apr. 12, 1991, at 5.
8. Patricia Herbert, "Max Factor Behind the Birch Bill," *Dominion*, Apr. 17, 1991, at 14.
9. Macfie, "Bill to Change."
10. Brad Tattersfield, "Contracts Bill Unlikely to Make May 1 Debut," *National Business Review*, Apr. 19, 1991, at 2.
11. *N.Z.P.D.*, 1648 (Apr. 30, 1991).
12. Simon Kilroy, "Contracts Bill Being Rushed into Law," *Dominion*, Apr. 24, 1991, at 1; *N.Z.P.D.*, 1648 (Apr. 30, 1991).
13. *N.Z.P.D.*, 1655 (Apr. 30, 1991).
14. *N.Z.P.D.*, 1425 (Apr. 23, 1991).
15. CCH Dispatch, *New Zealand Employment Law Library Personnel Management, Employment Contracts Bill Taking Final Shape*, 1 (Apr. 24, 1991); Brad Tattersfield, "Redress Steps Open To All," *National Business Review*, Apr. 24, 1992, at 1; Rebecca Macfie, "Mass Protests Feed On Workers' Unease," *National Business Review* May 3, 1991, at 12.
16. 511 *N.Z.P.D.*, 478 (Dec. 19, 1990).
17. *Id.*, 481–82.
18. *Id.*, 478; see also *N.Z.P.D.*, 1444 (Apr. 23, 1991).
19. 511 *N.Z.P.D.*, 478 (Dec. 19, 1990).
20. *Id.*, 481.
21. International Labour Organisation, *292nd Report of the Committee on Freedom of Association*, Case No.1698 ¶¶ 724–740 (Mar. 1994).
22. 511 *N.Z.P.D.*, 483 (Dec. 19, 1990).
23. *Id.*, 482. Many commentators believed that the regime would disenfranchise Maori and women and other vulnerable groups. It was estimated that under National's regime, union membership of these groups would sink to 20%. Patricia Herbert, "Battle for Power in the Workplace," *Evening Post*, July 2, 1990, at 7.
24. 511 *N.Z.P.D.*, 482 (Dec. 19, 1990).
25. *Id.*, 482.
26. *Id.*, 484–85.
27. *Id.*, 485.
28. *Id.*, 485–86.
29. *Id.*, 486.
30. *Id.*, 487.
31. *Id.*, 488 (Dec. 19, 1990). Max Bradford was in his first term at this time. He was famous for the "Bradford statistic" based on his claim, made while he was Director of Advocacy of the NZEF, that 90% of all wage settlements in New Zealand fell within 1%

of the increase found in the Metal Trades Award. See Raymond Harbridge, "Flexibility in Collective Wage Bargaining in New Zealand: Facts and Folklore," 15 N.Z. J. Ind. Rel., 241, 244 (1990); see also New Zealand Employers Federation, "Real Wages, Inflation, Unemployment and the New Zealand Wage Determination System: Discussion Paper No.3" (1982) (details of the Bradford formula).
32. 511 N.Z.P.D., 488 (Dec. 19, 1990).
33. Id., 488.
34. Id., 489.
35. Id., 490.
36. Id., 490.
37. Id., 491.
38. Id., 491.
39. Id., 491.
40. Id., 491–92
41. Id., 492.
42. 511 N.Z.P.D., 492 (Dec. 19, 1990).
43. Id., 492.
44. Id., 492.
45. Id., 493.
46. Id., 493.
47. Id., 494.
48. 511 N.Z.P.D., 1473–74 (Apr. 23, 1991); see also 511 N.Z.P.D., 1692 (Apr. 30, 1991).
49. 511 N.Z.P.D., 1671 (Apr. 30, 1991).
50. Cf. Rebecca Macfie, "Workers of the World Take Fright Over NZ Law," National Business Review, 31 (Oct. 18, 1991).
51. 511 N.Z.P.D., 494 (Dec. 19, 1990).
52. Id., 494.
53. Id., 494–95.
54. Id., 495.
55. Id., 495.
56. Id., 496.
57. Id., 496–97.
58. Colin James, "Now for the Main Course," National Business Review, Jan. 16, 1991, at 10; cf. Frances Martin, "Jobless Accepting Lower Pay—Just to Work," National Business Review, Mar. 22, 1991, at 2.
59. For example, while in Opposition, National said it would make unemployment benefits and welfare less attractive by widening the gap between them and wages to give people an incentive to get off benefits. Rather than pursuing policies that would raise wages, it decided to lower benefits. James, "Main Course."
60. James, "Main Course."
61. Roth, "Chronicle," 16 N.Z. J. Ind. Rel., 206 (1991).

Part II
Life Under the Employment Contracts Act

10

The ECA and Its Economic and Social Impacts

So it was that, after a decade of the NZBR and NZEF's advocating labour law reform, on May 15, 1991, the ECA became the law that governed workplace relations. New Zealanders were entering a new era in which everything would be different. Or would it? Did changing this law make any difference?

Its supporters told audiences around the world that it did. For example, in 1993, NZBR spokesperson Roger Kerr told an Australian audience that in New Zealand public confidence and business optimism were at all time highs and that 74% of employees were either "satisfied or very satisfied with the outcomes of their new employment contract." He said that the improved productivity due to ECA incentives and flexibility "are the stuff from which future folklore is going to be made" and that employers and employees were working together, with trust and cooperation. Although it was a buyers' market for labour, there had been wage increases of up to 8% and productivity increases of 17%.[1]

NZEF Director General Steve Marshall visited Geneva in 1991 and reported:

> Significant interest was shown at the Geneva [ILO] Conference in New Zealand's economic and labour relations reforms—in fact, we're seen as a world leader in the reform process, particularly with our emphasis on freedom of association and choice, the non-interventionist policies of the current and previous governments, and the non-prescriptive nature of our labour relations.[2]

The first disciple appeared when, in 1992, the State of Victoria, Australia, enacted its version of the ECA.[3]

Assessing the ECA is not a simple task, even though ECA supporters suggest it is when they focus only on limited criteria.[4] Their preferred yardsticks are economic measures. Indeed, ECA supporters such as the OECD,[5] the IMF,[6] and National Party members[7] can accurately say that certain economic figures improved after the ECA's enactment. The connection, however, other than their chronological order, is not necessarily so clear.[8]

An honest assessment of the way the ECA operates in the workplace makes it less likely that the changes can actually be linked to it. Before exploring how the ECA has operated in the arena it was designed for—the relationship between an employer and its employees—it is worthwhile to pause to examine some of the claims that have been made for the ECA.

ECA supporters claim enormous improvements in workplace relations, training, and productivity, particularly when unions are not involved. Roger Kerr of the NZBR claimed in late 1995: "Remuneration has changed from pay for attendance to pay for achievement. The focus is on productivity and profit. Performance is the criterion for reward."[9] There are many variations on this statement to the same effect. What is the reality?

First, it is not clear that pay has tracked productivity,[10] as even Kerr's figures suggest. Kerr claimed 8% pay increases associated with 17% productivity increases two years after the ECA was enacted, a large gap. Second, much of the data cannot fairly be interpreted to support the claims made. For example, rather than using conventional objective methods for measuring productivity (e.g., in terms of hours of labour used to produce an output),[11] ECA proponents have relied on subjective surveys or polls that ask employers to report whether they think their productivity has risen.[12] It seems that many of those surveyed have misinterpreted productivity measurement to mean whether labour costs have declined, a popular misconception of the term. When productivity data is gathered in this way, there could be a rise because wages have been slashed. A rise could be reported, even though it takes the same or more time to produce the product, not less. In other words, this method could report a rise in productivity when there has been a decline by all standard measurements.

The scenario of wage-cutting as leading to reported improvements in productivity seems likely. The 1993 Labour Select Committee Minority Report found that some employers who were unable to reach agreement restructured so that there were fewer positions. They then offered the new positions to their workers on condition that they accept the inferior terms or be laid off. The report concluded: "We do believe that the Employment Contracts Act provides a cop-out scenario for poor management in that it can disguise its own organisational deficiencies by artificially cutting labour inputs."[13]

When they are carefully examined, many claims about the ECA suffer from this same defect. For example, ECA proponents have polled employees as to whether they think their working conditions or the economy has improved because of the ECA and then reported the results as evidence that the ECA has in fact led to these results. The problem is that the question asks people to make a complex analysis that most of us do not have the ability to make. What most will do is compare their situation today in a better economy worldwide—not just New Zealand—versus a few years ago when the New Zealand and world economies were not doing as well. In other words, what most people answering the poll are saying is that they are better off now than a few years ago. These responses cannot support the claim that it was the ECA which caused the improvements. Unfortunately, this is the nature of most polling and studies performed by or for the NZEF or NZBR.

Many ECA proponents' claims suffer from other interpretational problems. Some use the most favourable time period to report on a trend. For example, changes in unemployment starting from 1991, a time when unemployment was nearing its peak, will show that since 1993 there has been an improvement. If the starting point is 1984, when deregulation first began, the picture is less optimistic.[14]

A second problem is one of context. It is usually good news to receive a pay increase. However, if that increase came along with other cuts, new costs, or increased fees people may not be better off. If inflation is factored in, there may actually be no rise.[15] In fact, when only inflation is factored into changes in pay since the ECA was enacted, many have suffered a real decline in income though some have had large rises.[16] Add to this price increases in basic necessities, such as home rentals (13.5%), education and childcare (9.5%), and food (7.1%), which have far outstripped official 1994 inflation of 2.8%, and this means that many have seen their buying power fall.[17]

A fair assessment of the ECA's operation should pay close attention to the main changes it has led to in most workplaces. This is changing working hours and penalty rates, particularly in low-waged sectors, and particularly in retail and hospitality.[18] Only 16% of workers have contracts that deal with productivity. Of these, very few have "a *comprehensive, detailed,* arrangement."[19]

Furthermore, before attributing all economic impacts since May 15, 1991 to the ECA, it would be wise to ask if they are not better explained by global phenomena or by other laws or practices.

The Economy and Society
In the first years after the ECA was enacted, the economy's performance failed to give ECA proponents positive news. In May 1992, the targeted deficit of $1.7 billion more than doubled to $3.7 billion.[20] Government cuts caused the economy to contract,[21] leading to deficit spending that then stimulated short-term growth and was "the major source of the economic upswing" New Zealand began to experience late in 1992.[22] When June 1992 unemployment topped 253,000, Ruth Richardson explained that this was just a transition before New Zealand's economy turned around.[23] Three years after the ECA was enacted, the turning around saw a decline of unemployment only to 9.1%.[24]

In human terms this meant experienced workers seeking full-time work for $50 a week.[25] It meant that, in November 1992, 50% of employment contracts provided for a minimum adult wage of $328 a week or less, with some contracts providing a rate below the legal adult minimum of $245 a week,[26] despite the government's announcing it would block loopholes that allowed employers to pay less than minimum wage.[27] It meant that a

Christchurch cafeteria could advertise "a job for a kitchen-hand for no pay, work experience only, and [get] 73 applicants."[28]

Indeed, the ECA's proponents had argued for "training wages" or "experience only" jobs at no pay. They had implied that employees would then move on to jobs at living wages. However, many will never move away from those unskilled jobs and the sorts of wages they offered.[29] In 1996, the Department of Labour found that average minimum adult weekly pay rates among New Zealand's largest employers ranged from a low of $306 in agriculture to a high of $475 in transportation.[30]

In May 1992, the Council of Christian Social Services report, *Windows on Poverty*, called on the government to "stop making human sacrifices to its economic policy." It described a new phenomenon in New Zealand: children going to school so hungry they could not concentrate and homes infested with vermin. The Salvation Army reported an increase of 548% in the need for food assistance in 1991.[31] Even when the economy improved, it did not lift the population out of poverty. The demand for food parcels increased 1,000%.[32] Those in poverty rose from 360,000 in 1990 to 510,000 in 1993, about one-seventh of the population. ECA pay cutting meant that a family in the poorest fifth had lost 20.9% of its income.[33] Real unemployment was close to 18.4% in 1993[34] and has continued high through the present.[35] Job growth rates of 2.5%–3.5% with a gain of 27,000 jobs a year could not keep pace with New Zealand's annual 12.2% population increase.[36]

One commentator observed:

> The symbol of post-welfare state New Zealand is the food bank. It has become part of the social welfare structure; official social security clerks, accosted by the indigent, may direct them to the nearest food bank. At a typical food bank—in Cannons Creek, a state housing suburb of Wellington—the number of parcels given out per month rose from 89 in January 1992 to 1,200 in January 1993.[37]

In December 1993, three New Zealand clergymen announced that stealing could be morally justified "when society deprived people of their 'birthright' of good housing, health and adequate food, and they had previously tried every other option to survive."[38]

Workplace Conditions
During the 1990 election campaign, National denied it wanted to abolish penalty rates and overtime.[39] Once in office, it supported eliminating them.[40] Bill Birch praised companies for agreements that left the right to decide leave and overtime payments to the employer's discretion.[41] Once the ECA was in place, penalty rates for overtime, shift, and weekend work were eliminated quickly. A 1992 study found that two-thirds of sampled contracts provided straight-time payments for Saturday or weekend work and 73% extended ordinary work hours and gave no shift premium.[42] In 1993, the Department of Labour was receiving 6000 complaints a month about breaches of minimum working conditions and issuing three times as many complaints as a year earlier.[43] The rapid decrease in protective conditions together with rising violations of law suggests that employers increasingly felt it was proper to worsen working conditions, even if it meant violating the law.

It was not only the smaller employers who pressed workers. Air New Zealand urged its catering workers to take pay cuts from $53,000 for a forty-five hour week to $23,000.[44] In 1991, Wellington City Transit (WCT) demanded pay cuts of 17%–18% from its drivers, but exempted management from sharing in the cuts on the grounds that this would be "a strange little gesture" which would produce "damn all" savings.[45] In 1996, Stagecoach, the owner of WCT, had nearly 100% return on its original investment and a projected profit of $7.8 million.[46]

The 1993 Select Committee hearings opened a window on the ECA's personal impact. One worker testified that he was fired when he asked to consult his union about a demand that he take a pay cut from $190 to $110.

> Another worker was hired as a trainee manager in a fast-food outlet. Two weeks later her employer presented her with a contract to sign within half an hour.

"When I tried to negotiate, I was told to take it or leave it. He said he would hold pay owing until I did," she said.

Her punishment for being the only one of 15 workers who resisted the employer's offer was to be sacked on the spot.[47]

In October 1991, when a construction worker hired at $2.50 an hour was not paid for eight months, he tried to burn down his employer's home. The employer said he had given the employee his work tools, a bicycle, a motorcycle, and work shoes in place of pay.[48]

Coral Shaw of Air New Zealand workers explained what the ECA meant to an individual worker.

> It's all very well for a member of a major union to say "No, I won't accept that, it's wrong, unfair, or unjust", and to say that with some confidence, or to not even have to say it directly to the employer but through his agent. But now we're in a situation where workers are without their strong union backing, and are face to face eyeballing the employer. Suddenly the balance of power is weighted very much in favour of the employer.[49]

The ECA made wage-cutting an easy option when employers faced financial difficulty or wanted higher profits.[50] Most popular was eliminating premium or penal wages for overtime, weekends, or shiftwork. Workers were also doing more unpaid work, so they received less money for time worked.[51] Workers were expected to work harder or faster for no increase in pay and to cover for laid-off employees or increased workloads that, in the past, meant hiring a new worker. The average worker was experiencing an intensification of work.[52] Many of these changes that resulted in less pay for more hours worked were praised by the NZEF, NZBR and the government as positive change and as evidence of increasing workplace "flexibility."

The complex ways in which wages were cut make it difficult to track changes in wages actually received by workers. In addition, curtailing government information collecting has made reliable and informative data hard to find. For example, on May 7, 1992, the government issued data on wage rates. Although there seemed to be a fair spread of increases, the figures must be examined with caution. The figures came from contracts employers had voluntarily filed and covered only 5% or 60,400 of those workers employed at worksites of over 20 workers, so they are not necessarily representative of conditions in all workplaces and may be highly skewed towards the better contracts. In 1996, the Department of Labour posted a disclaimer related to this problem with its quarterly reports,[53] but not all used the figures with this caution in mind.[54]

The fact that the figures were based only on stated hourly or weekly wage figures also meant they did not show the impact of lost penal rates. This is significant, since most changes involved eliminating or lowering penal rates and could mean losing as much as one-third of weekly earnings. Furthermore, many new jobs were part-time and would provide less weekly pay than a full-time job. Some contract terms also could not be relied on. For example, some employers illegally refused to pay for holidays,[55] thus lowering annual pay. Thus, unless great care is taken, reported wage figures are often only the best case scenario.[56]

The lack of systematic data collection by the government made possible extravagant and unjustified claims about the ECA. Thus, in late 1992 Bill Birch claimed that wages had increased 3% since the introduction of the ECA, when Raymond Harbridge's more rigorous study found mean increases less than one-tenth as large, that is, annualised wage changes of from 0% to 0.3%.[57] Furthermore, studies of wage movements were based only on collective employment contracts. They thus revealed nothing of conditions for the large number of workers not party to collective employment contracts. Certainly, some of these are management-level employees who can secure good terms; however, the bulk are the most unskilled workers in the least secure positions. Of them, little more than anecdotes were available to draw back the curtain.

In 1993, Labour Select Committee Majority and Minority reports assessing the ECA both had disturbing news about these people. The Minority found basic rights eroded and exploitation, including cuts of as much as 50%, workers employed at no pay, and a refusal to provide written contracts.[58] The Majority found that, although raises were given to compensate for lost penal rates, workers were working longer hours for the same amount of take-home pay.[59] In February 1996, Prime Minister Bolger admitted that there had only been 0.1% average real wage growth from March 1990 to March 1995.[60]

Youths were especially vulnerable, since no minimum wage law applied to them. One employer hired students at $4.00 an hour, refused to pay them on the grounds they were on trial, then released and replaced them with new students on a trial basis.[61] Workers under twenty were paid as little as $1.50 per hour, paid less than older colleagues for the same work, or paid nothing as a training rate.[62] In 1994, this adverse publicity forced the National government to enact a minimum youth rate of $147, 60% of the adult rate. Ruth Richardson, then out of Cabinet, condemned the move as a step backwards.[63]

In 1991, an advertisement in Australia touted New Zealand as the land of cheap labour:

> The bottom of the world has just become a top proposition as a manufacturing base. Right now there are many good reasons to consider relocating your manufacturing base in New Zealand. The recent Employment Contract Act abolishes industrial awards, leaving employers free to negotiate terms of employment for a labour cost saving of up to 25%.[64]

Unions were quick to point out the incongruity of this ad with National's claims that the ECA promoted doing things better, not doing them more cheaply.[65]

Bargaining
When the ECA was enacted, the NZEF exhorted employers to take advantage of the opportunities the ECA created.

> Irrespective of when their current collective employment contract expires, employers should be focusing now on bringing their labour relations strategies into the same planning arena as sales, marketing and so on. They should be communicating with their staff so that when it comes time to meet at the negotiating table, employees know the state of the business, their part in it and their employers' business objectives.[66]

In 1993, the NZEF claimed that "the Employment Contracts Act has seen more employers than ever before talking directly to their employees, to the benefit of all parties. It has not been an overnight change but it is happening and the impetus is likely to increase."[67] Gavin Fitzgerald of the Manufacturers Industrial Relations Service Ltd. wrote in August 1992 that he had already "formulated 1447 contracts under the new Act." Bargaining took an average of three months and led to an atmosphere of trust and commonality of interest. He said that the philosophy of the ECA was that "employer and employees must get their heads together, removed from the influence of third parties, and agree jointly how best to make the enterprise prosper to the benefit of both investors and employees."[68]

Was ECA bargaining this positive? Could workplace relations be improved simply by removing third parties? Did eliminating unions mean there was real communication between employer and employee?

The fact that many contracts had no wage rates at all[69] suggests that whatever was involved in the dialogue between employer and employee it did not concern wages. A survey of students found that they had no input into their working conditions.[70] The Labour Select Committee Minority report found no real negotiation was occurring; in most cases, employers insisted and workers gave in out of fear.[71] The Majority agreed that the ECA was having a troubling impact on workplace relations.

> [E]vidence received has also shown that some employers are using the removal of compulsory unionism as a way to tell employees less than before about their rights. Witnesses said that, especially in companies where the employer has actively encouraged staff to resign from a union, employers often impose contracts without negotiations. Sometimes these contracts contain scant information about employment conditions. Many witnesses, particularly from service and retail industries, said employers do not communicate with them about their contracts and frequently intimidate employees into signing contracts with the message that they will be dismissed if they do not.[72]

The ECA and its Economic and Social Impacts

The Majority report also noted:

> A much repeated statement by employees was that the Act has given too much power to employers. Employees feel powerless to negotiate suitable conditions if employers refused to take account of their wishes. Some workers wished to see the right to strike reinstated to realign the balance.
>
> Another factor much commented upon by employees is the lack of a good faith bargaining provision in the Act. This related to the feelings of powerlessness which employees feel, to in some way ensure an employer enters into meaningful negotiations.[73]

Since the ECA did not require employers to bargain with an employee's chosen representative, some employers established company unions or chose their workers' representative.[74] Employers took unilateral control to determine who would bargain for their workers, because the law permitted it and because the environment did not constrain them.[75]

Some said the steady rise in personal grievances under the ECA was the result of employers attending seminars "about the exciting new opportunities under the act" and then applying what they had learned.[76] Employer magazines were filled with notices of conferences on workplace issues. Murray French of the Wellington Employers Association blamed exaggerations by the ECA's opponents and untrained advisers for misleading employers as to what they could do:

> For instance, an employer in Christchurch announced that he was going to employ people for a dollar an hour and that the Employment Contracts Act allowed him to do that. . . . He had taken advice from his accountant or someone that wasn't a specialist in labour relations. Apparently the employer was told it was possible to employ people for a notional amount and that they could also receive a welfare payment. This would benefit everyone concerned.
>
> He wasn't a member of ours, but we took it upon ourselves to contact that employer and say to him, 'Are you aware that you're in fact bound by the minimum wage act?' When he

became aware that he was wrong, he very quickly agreed and acknowledged that in fact he was wrong. That's an example of the sort of silliness that occurred at the very early stages of the Act.[77]

On the other hand, Cyclemakers had hired an accountant to represent its employees in contract negotiations and was pleased with the result.[78]

While the employer was satisfied with the resulting Cyclemakers contract, it seems likely that workers may have been less enthusiastic about many terms. Piece-rate work and pay rates were set by management discretion. Workers were paid only when a job was completed, so "the contract disadvantages contract employees who do not complete their work one day and are sick or otherwise absent the next when the team completes its units. Sick workers do not receive any remuneration for the partly completed units from the previous day." No pay was received until errors were removed from completed work. However, the contract resulted in 25% higher earnings for workers and a 20% reduction in labour costs, because the company was no longer paying overtime or hiring temporary employees to meet seasonal demand.[79]

In general, contracts negotiated by a union or employee organisation had better terms from the employee's point of view than those negotiated directly by workers.[80] However, from the employer's point of view better terms might be lower wages or the flexibility to do as the employer wished, essentially the reverse of what employees would want.

Of firms which had collective employment contracts (CECs) nearly half had no union or other employee representation. When no union was involved, the average time spent preparing for and negotiating a CEC was two hours. When a union was involved, negotiations involved an average of twenty-two hours preparation followed by at least eighteen hours of face-to-face meetings.[81]

> There did not tend to be much movement once management's proposed contract was put in front of employees. Only 6% of firms with new individual contracts reported that there were

"significant" modifications made to management's initial position as a result of individual negotiations with some or all employees. A majority (62%) reported making some "minor" modifications during individual negotiations, though generally these applied to only a quite small percentage of affected employees.

One out of every three firms with new individual contracts indicated that all employees accepted the individual contract terms initially proposed by management without modification.[82]

Workplace Communication
The 1993 Select Committee Majority Report found that the ECA promoted closer communications between employers and employees by removing third parties—both unions and employer representatives—resulting in workers' feeling they had co-ownership of the company.[83] In 1995 Roger Kerr said management had been transformed into "self-management. Consequently, whole layers have been removed from organisations; direct communication is enhanced; beneficial relationships develop in an atmosphere freed from institutional suspicion."[84]

The evidence was mixed. In the retail industry many employers bargained without using outside representatives—possibly indicating communication—but many did no negotiating at all and thus needed no representative.[85] Nurses said they felt less trust, felt exploited, felt that conflict still existed or had increased, and felt that employers tended to determine working conditions unilaterally.[86] In May 1995, staff at Countrywide Bank struck even after their contract was settled, as a protest over their employer's negotiation tactics.[87] Indeed, many sectors, including essential services, were experiencing first-ever strikes or other work actions beginning in 1995. Figures showed a steady increase in strikes each year, with a 36% rise in 1994–1995 over the prior year.[88]

A 1993 CTU poll found that 44% of workers wanted to leave their jobs. Many said they had less power to control their environment, and work accidents had increased by 50%. Use of stimulants and mild drugs had increased. Although not asked, 20% mentioned the ECA in a negative way. When employees were asked about changes in their work conditions, the results were mixed. They felt they were working harder, felt communication had increased and that they were learning new skills, but felt less trust and security. All other measures were mixed, including job satisfaction, cooperation with management, and promotion opportunities.[89]

Certainly, one way to reach different conclusions was to limit who you talked to. Employers and employees had widely divergent views of ECA bargaining[90] and of changes in the workplace under the ECA:

PERCEPTION OF WORKPLACE IMPROVEMENTS[91]

	Employers' View	Employees' View
Job Security	60%	14%
Job Satisfaction	51%	23%
Communication	52%	31%
Trust	42%	15%
Cooperation	61%	22%

These differences continued into 1996. Managers believed they had good workplace relations and high employee morale and satisfaction, despite high degrees of concession bargaining and very high employee turnover.[92] To the extent that staff turnover is a measure of dissatisfaction, it has been high and continues to rise. Staff turnover in the public sector, for example, had risen 17.8% for the year 1993/1994 and an additional 21.4% for the year 1994/1995.[93] Even if turnover does not measure employee dissatisfaction, managers should be less sanguine about this problem. High turnover or the risk of it inhibits employer training and tends to lead to an undertrained and thus less productive workforce.[94] This could reflect the Exit v. Voice phenomenon. When workers feel unhappy with work conditions but disempowered, the only way they can improve their situations is to leave. Leaving is what New Zealand workers wanted to do and have been doing.

The differences in the way that employers and employees saw the changes that were occurring in the workplace remind us that, in trying to assess the ECA, it is important to bear in mind its different impacts on different groups. The very changes that are seen as positive by one may not be so for the other. In addition, much of what has been advanced as research on the ECA fails to meet basic research standards. Much of it is obviously generated to give support to predetermined positions rather than to shed light.

Notes
1. Roger Kerr, "The Challenge for the '90's: Labour Reform in Australasia," Speech to the Australasian Institute of Company Directors Western Australia Division, Perth 4–5, 10–11, 15 (Feb. 19, 1993).
2. NZEF, *1991 Annual Report*,5 (1991).
3. "Push Turns to Shove," *Bulletin*, Dec. 15, 1992, at 16.
4. Doug Kidd, "National's Industrial Relations Policy," Empl. L. Bull., 3, 4 (Jan. 1996); Douglas Myers, "Why Not Full Employment by 2000?" Address to the Moving Forward Conference, Auckland (May 15, 1996). NZBR et al., "Moving Into the Fast Lane," 30 (Mar. 1996).
5. Michael Munro, "Voting for the Lash in the NZ Laboratory," *Sunday Times*, Oct. 31, 1993.
6. Peter Norman, "IMF Seeks Labour Reform to Cut Europe's Jobless," *Financial Times*, Apr. 21, 1994, at 30.
7. Doug Kidd, Speech to the Plenary Session of the International Labour Organisation, 3–4 (June 8, 1994).
8. Brian Easton, "Some Macroeconomics of the Employment Contracts Act" (Dec. 2, 1996).
9. Roger Kerr, "Bargaining Under the Employment Contracts Act," Empl. L. Bull., 97 (Sept. 1995).
10. John Dickson, "Nurses Deserve Pay Rise," *Nursing NZ*, 24 (June 1993).
11. Edward Denison, "Productivity: Data and Determinants" in *Labor Economics and Industrial Relations: Markets and Institutions*, 545 (Clark Kerr and Paul Staudohar, eds., 1994).
12. John Savage, "What Do We Know About the Economic Impacts of the ECA?" (NZ Institute of Economic Research, May 15, 1996).
13. Report of the Minority of the Labour Select Committee on the Inquiry into the Effects of the Employment Contracts Act on the New Zealand Labour Market, 9 (Sept. 21, 1993).
14. Brian Easton, "Does *Free to Work* Tell a True Story?" (Apr. 30, 1996); "What's So Wonderful About the ECA?" *Metal*, 9 (Dec. 1995).
15. Peter Harris, "Labour Market Deregulation and Economic Performance" (Oct. 6, 1995) (Australian Local Government Study

Tour); NZCTU, "The Employment Contracts Act: A Summary of its Effects" (May 1993).
16. Laila Harre, "The Alliance Party Strategy," Empl. L. Bull., 7 (Jan. 1996).
17. Jane Kelsey, *The New Zealand Experiment: A World Model for Structural Adjustment?*, 170–71 (1995).
18. This was a study by the Australian employer association, the Metal Trades Industry Association. Steve O'Neill, "Labour Market Deregulation: The New Zealand Experience," 20 (Parl. Res. Serv. Background Paper No.5 1993).
19. Raymond Harbridge & Anthony Honeybone, "The Employment Contracts Act and Collective Bargaining Patterns: A Review of the 1994/95 Year" in *Employment Contracts: Bargaining Trends & Employment Law Update 1994/95*, 18 (Raymond Harbridge & Peter Kiely, eds. 1995).
20. Denis Welch, "Welch's Week," *Listener & TV Times*, May 18, 1992, at 36.
21. Brian Easton, "State of the New Zealand Economy," 4 (Sept. 11, 1992).
22. Brian Easton, "From Rogernomics to Ruthanasia: New Right Economics in New Zealand" in *Beyond the Market: Alternative to Economic Rationalism*, 149, 159–60 (Stuart Rees et al., eds., 1993).
23. Roth, "Chronicle," 16 N.Z. J. Ind. Rel., 317 (1991).
24. Kidd, ILO Speech, 4.
25. "Situations Wanted," *Press Weekend*, May 30, 1992, at P-14.
26. Raymond Harbridge, "New Zealand's Collective Employment Contracts: Update November 1992," 18 N.Z. J. Ind. Rel., 113, 121 (1993).
27. Raymond Harbridge & Stuart McCaw, "Monitoring Collective Bargaining in New Zealand" in *Researching Management Strategies and Bargaining: Papers Presented at the Union/Tertiary Research Conference, Victoria University, Wellington*, 3, 14 (Linda Sissons, ed., 1991).
28. Russ Francis, "New Zealander Warns of Free Trade Havoc," *Vancouver Sun*, Jan. 16, 1992 at E3.
29. Brian Easton, "The Maori in the Labour Force" in *Labour, Employment and Work in New Zealand 1994*, 206, 211–12 (Philip S. Morrison, ed., 1994).
30. Contract 12 (May 1996).
31. Lynsey Morgan, "Beneficiaries 'Sacrificed' By Government," *Evening Post*, May 6, 1992, at 5; Oliver Riddell, "NZ Should Learn Lesson from Los Angeles Tumult," *Press*, May 9, 1992, at 20.
32. Munro, "Voting for the Lash."
33. Peter Walker, "What Happens When You Scrap the Welfare State?" *Independent*, Mar. 13, 1994, at 17.
34. Brian Roper, "Economic Rationalism" in *New Zealand: Impact on Employment and Industrial Relations*, 5 (Australasian Political Studies

Association Annual Conference, Monash University, Melbourne, Sept. 29–Oct. 1, 1993).
35. Kelsey, *The New Zealand Experiment*, 261.
36. Jane Kelsey, *Rolling Back the State: Privatisation of Power in Aotearoa/New Zealand*, 337 (1994).
37. Walker, "What Happens."
38. Richard Shears, "Thou Shalt Not Steal," *Daily Mail*, Dec. 21, 1993, at 12.
39. Gordon Campbell, "Bill's Act of Faith," *Listener & TV Times*, May 27, 1991, at 15, 15; 511 N.Z.P.D. 1447–48, 1466, 1472 (Apr. 23, 1991); "Bill Breaks Election Promises," *M&C Workers News*, June 1991, at 1.
40. N.Z.P.D., 1447–48 (Apr. 23, 1991).
41. *Id.*, 1467 (Apr. 23, 1991).
42. David McEwen, "Penal Rates Take Brunt Under Employment Act," *National Business Review*, Sept. 4, 1992, at 5.
43. "Flood of Complaints Under ECA," *Labour Notes*, June 1993, at 9.
44. *Unkovich v. Air New Zealand Ltd*, [1993] 1 ERNZ 526, 622.
45. Patricia Herbert, "Clipping Pay on the Buses," *Dominion*, July 16, 1991, at 6; "Firm Plans 18 More Layoffs," *Dominion*, May 7, 1992, at 16.
46. "Small Mistakes Threaten Multi-Million Profit?", *M&C Workers News*, Mar. 1996, at 2.
47. Diane Keenan, "Workers Say Contract Refusal Means Job Loss," *Press*, Feb. 11, 1993, at 8.
48. Kevin O'Connor, "Man Attacked Home of $2.50-an-Hour Employer," *Dominion*, Nov. 3, 1991, at 1.
49. Rebecca Macfie, "Air New Zealand Employs Vintage Approach," *National Business Review*, Oct. 4, 1991, at 3.
50. Rebecca Macfie, "Survey Reveals Employers Sticking to Status Quo," *National Business Review*, Apr. 16, 1992, at 27.
51. Keith Rankin, "The New Zealand Workforce: 1950–2000," 18 N.Z. J. Ind. Rel., 214, 229 (1993); National Distribution Union, *Short Changed: Retail Workers and the ECA*, 26 (1996).
52. Rankin, 230.
53. *Contract*, 3 (May 1996).
54. *Contract*, 1 (July 1992); *Contract*, 1 (October 1992); "Wages Static for 50% of Workers," *Press*, May 8, 1992, at 6; Janet Hector, Jon Hemming & Mary Hubble, "Industrial Relations Bargaining in the Retail Non-food Sector: 1991–1992," 18 N.Z. J. Ind. Rel., 326, 34 (1993); Roth, "Chronicle," 18 N.Z. J. Ind. Rel., 268 (1993); Michael Pearson & Rachell Rose, "Sign or Resign: Who Wins With Contracts?" *Management*, 57, 58 (June 1992); ECA s 24.
55. Georgina Bailey, "Three-Way Trap Catches Workers," *Evening Post*, Oct. 27, 1992, at 5.

56. Ralph Stockdill, Address to the New Zealand Employers Federation, Tables 7, 15, 17 (May 13, 1992); Alistair Pringle, "The Pursuit of Flexibility in the New Zealand Supermarket: The Employment Contracts Act, Continuities and Discontinuities," 18 N.Z. J. Ind. Rel., 306, 321 (1993).
57. Harbridge, "Update November 1992," 113, 118–20, 122–23; Bob Edlin, "Making Youth Rates Pay," *Sunday Star*, Feb. 13, 1994, at D4.
58. Report of the Minority, 3, 5.
59. Report of the Labour Committee on the Inquiry Into the Effects of the Employment Contracts Act 1991 on the New Zealand Market," 10 (1993).
60. Rasmussen, "Chronicle," 21 N.Z. J. Ind. Rel., 116 (1996).
61. Bailey, "Three-Way Trap"; Raymond Harbridge & Julia Lane, "The Effect of a Minimum Youth Wage in New Zealand," 18 N.Z. J. Ind. Rel., 275 (1993).
62. Labour Committee Report, 32.
63. Brent Edwards, "Govt Split on Minimum Youth Rates," *Evening Post*, Feb. 9, 1994, at 2.
64. Jason Barber, "NZ Touted as Land of Cheap Labour," *Dominion*, Oct. 30, 1991, at 1; Roth, "Chronicle," 16 N.Z. J. Ind. Rel., 324 (1991); "Bosses Law Exposed," *M&C Workers News*, Dec. 1991, at 1.
65. Barber, "Land of Cheap Labour."
66. "We've Arrived But the Work's Just Starting," *Employer*, June 1991, at 1.
67. NZEF, "Forward to the Past: the Labour Opposition's Industrial Relations Policy," 18 N.Z. J. Ind. Rel., 205, 205 (1993).
68. Gavin Fitzgerald, "Does the Medicine Work?" *Manufacturer*, 8 (Aug. 1992).
69. Harbridge & Honeybone, 11; Harbridge & Lane, 278.
70. Debbie Peterson, "Secondary School Students in Paid Work" in *Labour, Employment and Work in New Zealand 1994*, 189, 193 (Philip S. Morrison, ed., 1994).
71. Minority Report, 3, 5.
72. Labour Committee Report, 20.
73. *Id.*, 17.
74. Minority Report, 6–8; Pearson & Rose, 58.
75. International Labour Organisation, 292nd Report of the Committee on Freedom of Association, Case No.1698 ¶ 726 (Mar. 1994).
76. Finlay Macdonald, "You're Fired, I'm Hired," *Listener & TV Times*, Oct. 8, 1994, at 28, 29.
77. Interview with Murray French, Manger of Labour Relations Services, Wellington Employers Association, in Wellington, May 14, 1992.
78. Beverly Lord, "Innovative Contracts—Potential Benefits for Both Parties," *Chartered Accountants Journal*, 63 (June 1994).

79. Id.
80. Roth, "Chronicle," 18 N.Z. J. Ind. Rel., 267 (1993).
81. Ian McAndrew, "From Regulation to Deregulation" in *New Zealand Labour Relations: New Models of Bargaining Under the Employment Contracts Act 1991*, 6, 9–10, 12 (Jan. 5, 1993).
82. Id., 8.
83. Labour Committee Report, 19.
84. Kerr, "Bargaining Under the ECA," 97.
85. Hector, Hemming & Hubble, 337.
86. Sarah Oxenbridge, "Health Sector Collective Bargaining and the Employment Contracts Act: A Case Study of Nurses," 19 N.Z. J. Ind. Rel., 17, 18 (1994).
87. Rasmussen, "Chronicle," 20 N.Z. J. Ind. Rel., 232 (1995).
88. Rasmussen, "Chronicle," 20 N.Z. J. Ind. Rel., 227, 336 (1995).
89. Greg Jackson, "Study Finds Many Want to Quit Job," *Press*, May 21, 1993, at 1.
90. Richard Whatman et al., "Labour Market Adjustment Under the Employment Contracts Act," 19 N.Z. J. Ind Rel., 53, 69 (1994).
91. Whatman et al., 68.
92. Clive Gilson & Terry Wagar, *Employee Involvement and Human Resource Management in Australian, New Zealand, and Canadian Organisations*, 12, 13, 17 (1996); cf. Nicola Legat, "Bargain Bin Industrial Relations," *Metro*, 104, 107 (Sept. 1995) (19% annual turnover common).
93. Erling Rasmussen, "Chronicle," 21 N.Z. J. Ind. Rel., 116 (1996).
94. Paul Osterman, "Pressures and Prospects for Employment Security in the United States" in *Employment Security and Labor Market Behavior: Interdisciplinary Approaches and International Evidence*, 228, 233 (Christoph F. Beuchtmann, ed., 1993).

11

An Introduction to ECA Bargaining

IN 1992, NZBR CHAIRPERSON DOUGLAS MYERS TOLD A MELBOURNE audience that 70% of New Zealand workers had opted out of union membership and that occupational and multi-employer contracts were virtually obsolete.[1] Unions have not disappeared under the ECA, but they have not fared well and, in some industries, they have all but vanished. Unions have tended to hang on in large workplaces and where collective employment contracts (CECs) have been negotiated. There, they tend to represent 80–87% of workers covered by CECs.[2]

This, however, does not take into account the large number of workers now parties to individual employment contracts (IECs). Of this group of workers on IECs, Harbridge notes:

> There is no way of identifying at this point what bargaining, if any, has taken place for this group of workers, or whether in fact these workers have any written employment contract at all. Technically these workers have moved to individual contracts in the absence of a collective contract. The unknown variable in this move is whether the move was an "up" movement or a "down" movement. It seems likely, for example, that middle management removed from a collective settlement and placed on an individual contract may well have received additional benefits as part of that move. On the other hand, media reports over the last year or so have identified many individual workers who have received pay cuts as a result of being required to move to individual contracts. On balance it seems almost certain that there has been more "down" movement than "up" movement for individuals who have been placed on individual employment contracts.[3]

The forms of representation and the resulting documents possible under the ECA are complex. One conclusion that can be drawn is that where unions are involved in negotiations, the result will almost certainly be a CEC. Where IECs exist, a substantial number have come about with no bargaining.

FORMS OF REPRESENTATION[4]

	CEC Representation		IEC Representation	
	Public	Private	Public	Private
Trade Union	90%	67%	2%	3%
Individual	3%	9%	61%	61%
Nominated Group*	8%	17%	1%	8%
No Bargaining / No Representative	1%	6%	29%	25%
Other	3%	3%	7%	3%

*Collective representation which does not involve a union.

The existence of an IEC tends to signify a lack of negotiation. Of employers who moved their workers to IECs, 56% of the initial proposals were developed by management with no consultation with employees.[5] The balance may involve only limited to fuller consultation. Ian McAndrew found:

> There did not tend to be much movement once management's proposed contract was put in front of employees. Only 6% of firms with new individual contracts reported that there were "significant" modifications made to management's initial position as a result of individual negotiations with some or all employees. A majority (62%) reported making some "minor" modifications during individual negotiations, though generally these applied to only a quite small percentage of affected employees.
>
> One out of every three firms with new individual contracts indicated that all employees accepted the individual contract terms initially proposed by management without modification.[6]

Employees have more bargaining power when unions are involved, at least to the extent of avoiding concessions.[7] This means that knowing what has been happening to unions—and how the ECA has contributed to these results—tells us whether workers can take an active role in negotiating their workplace conditions. If unions give workers more bargaining power, the news is not good. From May 1991 when the ECA came into effect to December 1995, union density has been steadily declining. By December 1995, it was only 21.7%, a drop of approximately 30%.[8]

Losses have not been even across sectors. Most were in the wholesale, retail and hotel industries,[9] those represented primarily by the distribution unions and the SWU and those in which most workers are minorities, women, youth, and part-timers—that is, the workers who begin with the least bargaining power.

The declines are clear, but the more difficult question is what has caused the decline. The NZBR and NZEF say that unions simply cannot survive in an environment based on freedom. Once unions' statutory props were removed, workers used their freedom of association to disassociate themselves from unions. NZEF Director General Steve Marshall said that unions' retaining 50% of "market share" was very reasonable.[10] The NZEF contended, however, that the numbers did not mean workers were less represented:

> In fact many employees, both individually and collectively, are now choosing to be represented by a range of non-union people or organisations. This includes lawyers, accountants, private consultants, a parent, a friend or a workmate.
>
> The essential feature, however, is that to gain the right to represent and to keep it, the representative is being required to understand the needs and aspirations of the individual or group being represented. To understand the needs and aspirations of the employer concerned and to become a constructive part of that enterprise focused partnership.
>
> That is pretty new and radical stuff for most traditional unions and as those figures show, they have lost out in the transition.[11]

There is some truth to this, but it is more accurate to say that unions declined for reasons as complex as the roles they play in the workplace: "They act as partners and as adversaries of employers, through consent and through coercion; they insist on process, and they provide incentives. In short, they both help to guarantee the existing social order and press to modify it."[12] Unions tended to persist in worksites and to negotiate new CECs successfully where they have exerted real pressure on the employer.[13] Some employees also left unions because they had good relations with their employers or had never seen a union representative and thus saw union membership and dues as a waste of time and money.[14] Part of the reason unions declined can also be attributed to the law.

The prior system predicted what would come to be in the ECA era. Under the LRA, many employers and employees had not seen much of unions or genuine collective bargaining. That continued under the ECA, but the award's protections were lost.[15] In a sense, the ECA was not a radical shift; it simply made visible characteristics of the industrial relations that had before been restrained by law. An important part of that prior system was the way employers and unions interacted.

Steve Marshall was also correct that some unions needed legal support to survive. The SWU had predicted it would lose members, because it covered 12,000 worksites with an average of only 7.5 workers at each, many of whom worked around the clock. "Actually keeping track of and gaining access to the workforce will be a major problem for us, a problem which the Bill compounds by kindly absolving employers from any obligation to provide us with any information whatsoever about their workforce and by removing any right we had to enter employer premises." Add to this low-skilled employees who were vulnerable to employer duress to leave unions.[16] To organise workers who are mainly part-time, minority, youth and women workers, and who are employed with only a few workers at each widely dispersed worksite, there needs to be legal support for unionisation, but the ECA provided none.

A third explanation for unions' decline—and the one explored in the next chapters—is that the law, as interpreted by the courts, placed impediments in the way of organisation. In other words the law was not neutral. Members could not express their free choice by leaving; rather they were essentially forced out by law.

The Labour Select Committee Majority Report found evidence that employers were taking strong actions against union membership. Employers had forced workers to sign letters of resignation, told workers it was futile to choose a union because the employer would not deal with a union, threatened that union involvement would mean a contract with inferior terms, discriminated against union supporters in job assignments and promotions, given large payments to those who resigned their union membership, and threatened termination.[17] Much of this was not permitted by the ECA, particularly s 28, but the law as written did not always match the law as applied.

Unions also contributed to their own decline. As the number of members declined rapidly, many unions felt they had to concentrate efforts on larger employers to consolidate a base of strength. Declining memberships meant declining union resources and forced unions to make unpleasant surgical choices.[18] Unions could only hope that when the economy improved and the employer was competing for staff they would have the power to return to the smaller employers.[19]

It is important to understand that the reason the ECA has had the impact of lowering union density is not that it is anti-union. In fact, it has helped or forced unions to improve themselves. Bargaining on a regional basis rather than a national basis has led union bargaining teams to be more inclusive. Team members provided the team and workers with feedback on negotiations and worksite reactions. Workers with conflicting interests knew they had active representation within the bargaining team, and this maintained solidarity.[20] Thus, the ECA has increased worker solidarity and union communication and responsiveness in some situations.

The ECA has also not been wholly favourable to employers. Employers have had to bear the added expense of conducting their own bargaining. In addition, employers have had to sell their contracts to their employees and have not always been successful at this:

> I know instances of non-union contracts where the companies go around on a tour of the country trying to sell a contract to

its workers, receiving mixed reactions. Now it's in a situation where they've got half of them in and half of them out. So it's still not finished. And they've ended up holding a lot of stop-work meetings to discuss the contract, shipping people around to explain the contract. They could have given the workers a bloody 20% wage rise and got the thing done for the money they've spent on it, and the time it's taken them.[21]

A reporter for the New Zealand *National Business Review* came to a similar conclusion:

> Longer, slower and less formal discussions are required to sell major or controversial changes to employees. . . .
> Parties are devoting a lot of time to preliminary "courtship" matters before negotiations commence. The process of identifying who will represent employees will often be complicated and time consuming with pro and anti union factions as well as new players seeking the bargaining agency. Some employers will seek to influence this choice and even fund a bargaining agent whose involvement they wish to support.[22]

Hidden expenses for employers included more a expensive, time-consuming process for setting the terms and conditions of employment, lowering productivity. One response has been to stop negotiating contracts, at least on an annual basis. By 1993, 58% of enterprises had not negotiated a new contract in the preceding year. Smaller employers in particular seemed to have given up any renegotiation of contracts.[23]

The ECA's structure is not anti-union. Nothing in the ECA prohibits unions from doing anything. Its language and operation look scrupulously even-handed. Its goals are freedom, self-actualisation, and productivity. It is not anti-unionism but freedom of contract, neoclassical economics, and treating employers and employees as equals which are its dominant philosophy. It implements these through an even-handed treatment based on the premise that employee and employer can negotiate fairly and productively. If fairness, freedom, and equality cause New Zealand unions to decline, this is very troubling. What is there about this freedom and equality that creates a hostile environment for unions?

The answer, which will be explored in the next chapters, is that it is the unique way the ECA understands and promotes equality and freedom which are the most destructive aspects of the ECA for unions. Examining how these work provides a more useful understanding of and beyond New Zealand's specific situation. If the ECA has a profoundly detrimental impact on unions and, if it has this impact even though not anti-union, its ideology may be seriously flawed as a basis for labour law. We are then forced to ask whether unions play a sufficiently valuable role that laws should be drafted to support their existence. Other countries are currently considering enacting their own ECAs and not necessarily for anti-union reasons. Thus an analysis which focuses on how freedom of contract and the market perform as a basis for labour contracting is widely useful.

Each negative impact the ECA had on unions can be dismissed as trivial when considered in isolation. However, unions did not feel the effect of only one. Most often the law imposed many burdens at the same time. When put together, they were a heavy load to bear.

Notes
1. Roth, "Chronicle," 17 N.Z. J. Ind. Rel., 251 (1992).
2. Dept of Labour, *Contract*, 1 (May 1996); Raymond Harbridge & Anthony Honeybone, "The Employment Contracts Act and Collective Bargaining Patterns: A Review of the 1994/95 Year" in *Employment Contracts: Bargaining Trends & Employment Law Update 1994/95*, 7 (Raymond Harbridge & Peter Kiely, eds., 1995).
3. Raymond Harbridge, "New Zealand's Collective Employment Contracts: Update November 1992," 18 N.Z. J. Ind. Rel., 113, 117 (1993).
4. Richard Whatman et al., "Labour Market Adjustment Under the Employment Contracts Act," 19 N.Z. J. Ind Rel., 53, 60 (1994).
5. Ian McAndrew, "From Regulation to Deregulation in New Zealand Labour Relations: New Models of Bargaining Under the Employment Contracts Act 1991", 8 (Jan. 5, 1993).
6. Id.
7. McAndrew, "From Regulation to Deregulation," 17; Clive Gilson & Terry Wagar, *Enterprise Bargaining in Australia and New Zealand: Private Sector Comparisons* (1997).
8. Aaron Crawford et al., "Unions and Union Membership in New Zealand: Annual Review for 1995," 21 N.Z. J. Ind. Rel., 188

(1996); Raymond Harbridge et al., "Unions and Union Membership in New Zealand: Annual Review for 1993," 19 N.Z. J. Ind. Rel., 175, 176 (1994); Raymond Harbridge & Kevin Hince, "Unions and Union Membership in New Zealand 1985–1992," 18 N.Z. J. Ind. Rel., 352, 355 (1993).
9. Harbridge & Hince, 357–58.
10. Jason Barber, "Contracts Act Slashes Union Coverage," *Dominion*, Jan. 17, 1992, at 3.
11. "The 'New' Unions," Employer, 145 (Dec. 1995).
12. David Abraham, "Individual Autonomy and Collective Empowerment in Labor Law: Union Membership Resignations and Strikebreaking in the New Economy," 63 N.Y.U. L. Rev., 1268, 1274 (1988).
13. McAndrew, "From Regulation to Deregulation," 14; Gilson & Wagar.
14. *Report of the Labour Committee on the Inquiry Into the Effects of the Employment Contracts Act 1991 on the New Zealand Market*, 25–26 (1993); McAndrew, "From Regulation to Deregulation," 6, 9–10; Katherine Van Wezel Stone, "The Legacy of Industrial Pluralism: The Tension Between Individual Employment Rights and the New Deal Collective Bargaining System," 59 U. Chi. L. Rev., 575, 582–83 (1992).
15. McAndrew, "From Regulation to Deregulation," 14; John Savage, "What Do We Know About the Economic Impacts of the ECA?" 18 (NZ Institute of Economic Research, May 15, 1996).
16. Service Workers Federation of Aotearoa, "The Employment Contracts Bill: Submissions of the Service Workers Federation of Aotearoa," 9 (n.d.).
17. Labour Committee Report, 9, 27–29; NZ Nurses Organisation, "Myths and Reality: The Effect of the Employment Contracts Act on Nurses in New Zealand (1991–1993)," Paper Presented at the ICN Congress, Madrid Spain 6 (June 1993).
18. Rebecca Macfie, "Employers Set Industrial Agenda," *National Business Review*, Nov. 15, 1991, at 19.
19. *Id*.
20. Sarah Oxenbridge, "Health Sector Collective Bargaining and the Employment Contracts Act: A Case Study of Nurses," 19 N.Z. J. Ind. Rel., 17, 21–23 (1994); "The Assessors," *NZ Nursing Journal*, 13, 14 (June 1992); National Distribution Union, *Short changed: Retail Workers and the ECA*, 11, 24 (1996).
21. Interview with Hel Loader, Research Advocate, New Zealand Engineering Union, in Wellington (May 13, 1992).
22. Paul Loof, "Bargaining Style in Sudden Switch," *National Business Review*, Aug. 18, 1991, 18.
23. Whatman et al., 57–58. 61–62.

12

Bargaining and Bargaining Representatives

IN 1988, FORMER NORTHERN DISTRICT UNION RETAIL SECRETARY Owen Harvey observed that employers were being encouraged to bypass unions and go directly to their staff to negotiate workplace conditions.[1] In 1993, the NZEF was pleased to say that the ECA had employers "talking directly to their employees, to the benefit of all parties."[2] A judge observed that ECA negotiations bear no resemblance to the normal definition of that word. They may be no more than "a presentation by one intended party to the contractual relationship of a form of contract to the other and the former's refusal to deviate from its offer."[3] Seen one way, direct negotiation between employer and employee destroys unions. Seen another, employers and employees benefit by making common cause. Yet another view sees no real communication possible.

Many charged that the ECA would not permit real bargaining, because real compromise only occurs if employees are represented in a form that "is sufficiently powerful that the employer feels compelled to engage in negotiations about terms and conditions of employment."[4] The ECA required employers to recognise an employee's chosen representative but imposed no duties beyond that, just as Ralph Stockdill had predicted. In addition, nothing barred an employer from negotiating with a representative no employee had chosen. Both of these actions—not dealing with a chosen representative or imposing a representative—are likely to influence employees to join a union even though the employees might prefer a different representative.[5]

The ECA's freedom of choice and association makes it difficult to resolve issues of representation. Employees have freedom only if they can freely designate their representative. Employers can only have freedom of choice and association if they are not forced to bargain with a representative. Yet if the employer can ignore the employees' choice, their choice is meaningless. The abstract logic means that everything depends on whether the employer is willing to deal with the employees' chosen union. The ECA's language gives the same rights to authorise a representative or not and to bargain or not equally to employers and employees. The reason this does not meet the test of reality is that the theory ignored the context in which bargaining would occur. That context meant that paper equality was real inequality.

There are a number of reasons for this. Workers are more likely to want to bargain with the employer's representative, because it is the only way to get the changes they want. In all but extreme labour shortages, the employer's power over the workplace allows it to force employees to accede its wishes, whether it bargains or not.

Employers and their representatives did not hide the fact that they wanted—not codetermination—but full control. For example, Progressive Enterprises argued that if it could not control the formation of employment contracts there would be "dissension among employees as to the manner of establishing their employment contract . . . with the Company left as an affected by-stander obliged to accept whatever is put before it."[6]

The ECA's drafters knew that letting employers choose whether to recognise their employees' agent would nullify workers' freedom of association and choice.[7] Despite this, they decided to allow the employer to "have the right to refuse to negotiate with any particular person or organisation or grouping of persons or organisations" and expected workers would then "change their choice of bargaining agent in order to gain agreement to negotiate and conclude a contract."[8]

The ECA's drafters accepted the idea that the employer could legitimately select its employees' representative,[9] because choosing a representative was nothing more than a cost–benefit analysis. They denied that workers had a legitimate right to be attached to their representative and to be unwilling to "change their choice" to the employer's. As a result, employee freedom disappeared even as the ECA was being drafted, and one of the ECA's stated purposes—"To allow employees to determine who should represent their interests in relation to employment issues"—was meaningless.

The ECA is drafted to embody the view that the employment relationship is a private matter with no consequences outside the workplace. This is an odd faith, given that the ECA was supposed to play a pivotal role in the economy.

This was not the only problem ECA bargaining created. ECA negotiating is completely disaggregated from employee authorisation. It creates so many impediments to bargaining that an employer can prevent bargaining despite never directly refusing to bargain. Not all employers took advantage of these, however, because some saw union representation as advantageous for employers. Francis Wevers, a management consultant, explained:

> They are much better off to have the work force which is comfortable in terms of its relationship with the employer and in which the employer recognises that the employees have an entitlement to be represented by the union. And that the employer is relaxed about that than actively trying to separate them from their union because the negative impact of that is that people then don't trust the employer. They suspect that. They wonder about the employer's motivation.[10]

Others, however, took a different view and used the ECA to create roadblocks, starting with a simple refusal to talk about collective agreements. PSA representative Joris de Bres explained:

> We went to see the employer, said we were authorised to negotiate with you on a collective contract. They said, we don't want a collective contract. We recognise you as their representative, but we've got nothing to talk about, but we're perfectly happy for you to come along as the representative of each individual to assist in the negotiation of their individual contract.
>
> Despite the clear wish of the worker, we have no mechanism other than strike to advance the case for a collective contract.

The law does not require anything of an employer in terms of actually meeting, let alone bargaining in good faith.[11]

Refusal to recognise and bargain with authorised unions usually occurred in three ways: (1) some bypassed the union and dealt directly with employees—in effect the employer designated the workers as their own representative; (2) some employers created and recognised an entity other than the authorised union; and (3) some employers pressured employees to revoke authorisations. Often these were used together and did not violate the law. The NZEF and NZBR, for example, applauded *Alliance* as a case in which the court turned back a union's attack "on an employer's attempts to negotiate directly with its employees" and which demonstrated that the court understood that employers could "take strong industrial action in support of negotiations for a collective employment contract."[12]

1. Direct dealing: The ECA's refusal to prescribe or proscribe conduct could be characterised either as the essence of individual freedom or as creating difficult-to-overcome impediments to collective bargaining. Rick Barker of the SWU explained:

> [W]hat they were able to say to unions was not that you can't do this or can't do that. You can do whatever you like. They simply prescribe for a completely open situation and by creating a system of almost total anarchy, there's going to be the complete antithesis of organisation.[13]

Thus, the ECA's permissive individualism failed to foster collective bargaining and impeded organisation. It freed an employer to choose to negotiate with its employees' representative or not. Being able to select "or not" legitimates a wide range of behaviour.

Section 12(2) of the ECA seems to say that each side must recognise the other's chosen representative. It fails, however, to define what recognition means, so that the courts must look to other parts of the ECA for guidance. Key to deciding the legitimacy of direct dealing was s 20(3) and how the courts have interpreted it. Section 20(3) states:

Any employer may, in negotiating for a collective employment contract, negotiate with—
 (a) The employees themselves; or
 (b) If the employees so wish, any authorised representative of the employees.

Two different interpretations are possible: (1) an employer may choose whether to bargain with its employees or their representative, or (2) the employer is forbidden from bargaining with its employees, if they have chosen a representative. The courts had the burden of deciding which interpretation was correct.

ECA theory supported the first interpretation. Influential ECA proponents advocated entrusting all bargaining matters to the parties and the market. Electricorp argued: The legislation "must not be prescriptive if the freedom of association that it espouses, and that is so critical to the development of efficient labour market relationships" were to be effective.[14] Treasury advocated "bring[ing] labour market contracting firmly within the law of contract and general law."[15] In a free labour market employers (as buyers of labour) may choose not to deal with their employees' designated representative, just as any buyer can deal with one vendor and not deal with another.

In reality labour negotiations are different from commercial negotiations.[16] Buyers in the market can walk away from a seller to pursue other deals, never to meet the first seller again. However, even if an employer refuses to deal with a union, most employees will continue working but with no way to assert their own freedom of choice. Abstraction and reality were in conflict.

The drafters decided not to resolve the conflict of ECA freedoms nor to craft a provision that would take into consideration how the employment relationship works. Instead, they left these matters to be resolved by the market. What they did not intend but what should have been foreseeable was that this issue is so fundamental that a decision had to be made as to how it would be handled. By not legislating, all they did was to shift the decision to the courts. In *Alliance*,[17] the court held that the ECA required an employer to recognise a representative's authority; however, employers could communicate with their employees, even though they "undermine[d] the ability of the representative to negotiate or to negotiate effectively." As a result, Alliance violated no law when it bypassed its employee's representative to force workers to bargain individually, even though its tactics were highly coercive.

The union's counsel in *Alliance*, Robyn Haultain, explained:

> [The court] basically said that the workers could repudiate the authority that they gave the union merely by dealing directly with the employer. They took the view that it wasn't the employer that didn't recognise the union's bargaining authority, they basically said that the workers by choosing, and I use that word really advisedly, by choosing to deal directly with the employer had simply sacked us as their authorised bargaining representative and had made the decision to deal as individuals with the employer and that, if the individual workers wanted their authorised representative to be recognised by the employer, then their job was to insist that that happen.[18]

Alliance interpreted the ECA so as to give legal recognition to Stockdill's idea that the employer could choose the employees' representative. An employer could choose its employees' representation, even if what the employer preferred was no employee representation.

Alliance remained the law for the next three years until the Employment Court began to retreat from this position in *Capital Coast*[19] and other cases holding that the worker's choice had to be respected. It's difficult to say whether *Capital Coast* changed employer behaviour.[20] The Employment Court never retreated far from the position that employers had wide latitude to discuss unions and the progress of negotiations with their employees.[21] Moreover, in early 1996, the Court of Appeal issued two decisions that might signal a return to the Employment Court holding in *Alliance*.[22]

For three years, *Alliance* gave employers wide latitude to denigrate unions and deal directly with employees. This became a pervasive practice during contract negotiations and in grievance handling. Employers regularly attempted to bypass the union concerning grievances over disciplines or contract violations. Donna Payne, an Organiser for the NZ Nurses Association, observed:

> There are more attempts not to recognise the NZNA and go straight to the staff direct. . . . I've seen that happen when I've had to review service or say they have a problem with an individual over their work performance, or something like that, then instead of dealing with the NZNA, they go straight to the individual. I have one case up in Taranaki on behalf of the individual and they never responded to my letters, whereas in the past they would have done.[23]

For three crucial years, as New Zealanders adapted to the ECA, *Alliance* gave employers permission to undermine collective action. Moreover, this law did not exist in isolation. During this important period of adjustment, other doctrines, such as the partial lockout compounded the impact.

2. *Dealing with a non-authorised representative:* Stockdill had suggested that, if an employer sets up its preferred bargaining representative, workers were "obliged to change their choice of bargaining agent in order to gain agreement to negotiate and conclude a contract."[24] Employers have established their preferred representative. Alliance created a series of representatives, first designating the plant delegates as the representative, even though no employee had authorised them. It then created the Mosgiel Independent Thought Society, MITS, "an incorporated society whose constitution was drawn up by the company's lawyers and which was underwritten by the company to the tune of $10,000." Job applicants had to state whether they preferred the union or the MITS.[25]

The Engineers have had a somewhat more benign and unusual experience of having employers acknowledge it as their employees' representative in negotiating the service station multi-employer agreement. Although the Engineers could not organise that sector, employers have found it useful to have a bargaining partner to deal with and, as a result, create a level playing field, even though their chosen representative is a real union. Nonetheless, this designation was made by employers without consulting their workers as to their preferences.[26] Condoning non-representative organisations concerned the ILO's Committee on Freedom of Association in its final report on the ECA.[27]

Permitting company unions may create distortions in bargaining. Employees may believe they are getting a deal because benefits through a company union appear to be cost-free, since they may pay no dues. It is harder for them to see that the cost is in improvements not received from labour and management's joint surplus.[28] Workers are also reluctant to create problems when an employer has made it clear it prefers a particular bargaining partner and will gravitate to the company union.

Some see banning company unions as essential if worker free choice is to exist and not be subject to paternalistic nullification. Banning company unions can be seen as the linchpin to "restoring equality of bargaining power" between employees "who do not possess full freedom of association or actual liberty of contract" and "employers who are organised in the corporate or other forms of ownership" and to encourage collective bargaining.[29]

The ECA, however, sees no need to restore "equality of bargaining power," because it believes it was never lost. ECA freedom of choice prohibits eliminating any options, even ones which nullify one party's ability to make meaningful choices. It thus contains no prohibitions against recognising and bargaining with a non-representative. The problem is that, to have a voice in setting workplace conditions, employees need a representative "sufficiently powerful that the employer feels compelled to engage in negotiations about terms and conditions of employment."[30] Whether or not the law creates and enforces an obligation to recognise the workers' chosen union affects workers' willingness to join a union. When an employer can avoid dealing with a union, workers will conclude that joining or supporting a union is futile. If an employer can impose a union on its employees, they may join it despite their preferences, thus their freedom of choice is coopted by the employer.[31]

3. Pressuring employees to revoke authorisations: Another effective way an employer can eliminate obligations towards a representative is to persuade employees to withdraw their authorisations. The ECA gives employees fragile collectivity, always subject to disintegration. The ECA does not forbid employers from coercing or persuading employees to revoke authorisations, although s 8 does protect membership. This failure to protect freedom of association concerned the ILO.[32]

At first, it seems odd that the ECA fails to protect authorisations, since they seem so fundamental to the ECA processes, and actions of lesser importance are protected. Even though the employee's right to choose representation freely is the second specific goal in the Long Title to the ECA, no specific provision protects that right.

In *Alliance*, workers who authorised their union to represent them were threatened with lockout, were locked out, and were told they could not sign the employer's offered agreement until they had revoked their authorisations.[33] The union argued that this was harsh and oppressive behaviour or undue influence or duress in the procurement of a contract, which violated sections 8 and 57. The Employment Court held that the ECA's express prohibitions were directed only against pressure to join or not join an employee organisation, as distinguished from pressure to choose or not choose a representative.[34]

Although the court found that many workers who had authorised the union to represent them later changed their minds, as a result of the employer's lockouts and threats of lockouts, this did not violate the law. It also found that conditioning signing the employment contract on employees' revoking the union's authorisation to represent them, was not evidence of undue influence; rather, the court held, it showed the employer recognised the union as representative.[35] Two years later, the Court of Appeal called this

> a rather cynical argument not necessarily in accordance with the true intent, meaning, and spirit of the enactment. It would apparently mean that, although employees had authorised a union to represent them from the start, the employer need

never negotiate with the union. Certainly an employer is free not to negotiate with anyone; but if he wishes to negotiate I doubt whether he can bypass an authorised representative.[36]

How can it be that the ECA does not protect employees' choice of representative? Not protecting authorisation, interpreted literally, means that even the most extreme action to thwart authorisation is not a violation. It makes authorisation—employees' central right under the ECA—into a perilous act and freedom of association an empty right. Not protecting authorisation is more detrimental to employees under the ECA than under other regimes, not just because the employer is free to use coercion, but also because it can use more effective duress. The ECA lets the employer know who to target.

Each individual authorisation must be made known to the employer. There is no group to hide behind as with majority representation. There is no secret ballot, no being hired into a job which is already represented. When nothing forces the individual employee to reveal his or her choice to the employer, the employee is freer to exercise uncoerced choice. Even the seemingly coercive act of binding individuals to the majority's decision as to representation protects those workers who are afraid to admit they are union supporters.[37]

The ECA requires workers to disclose their preferences, not once, but continuously, each time authorisations are given.[38] The employee knows that each disclosure is potentially dangerous, in part because authorisation could be a futile act. The employer cannot refuse to recognise the employee's representative, but it can interpret recognition to frustrate bargaining. If this happens, the union may not be able to protect the employee. Thus, the ECA talks about choice but does not protect choice from coercion, aside from whatever protections the market offers.

4. *Representation authority as a procedural hurdle to bargaining:* In 1994, the government told the ILO's investigative team that, in its view, establishing authority to represent was "intended to ensure that the individual's choice of representative is respected and that the agent is genuinely representative of the employees.

It also helps to ensure that employees cannot be bound to agreements or negotiations without their knowledge and against their interests."39

Missing from this statement were crucial facts that affected whether there was real freedom of choice. The ECA did not create a regular and neutral procedure, such as a government-conducted election or confidential authorisation check to establish validity as clear and indisputable. It is up to the employer to decide whether to recognise a designated representative's authority. Unions must prove they have valid authorisations to represent; however, there is no direct legal sanction if an employer decides to bargain with an agent it knows does not represent any employee. At best, workers may refuse to ratify or sign the agreement.

The legislation says nothing about how authorisation was to be given—orally or in writing—and what authorisation meant. Many submissions—union and employer—warned that there were serious flaws concerning authorisation. Nothing was said about when authorisations had to be given and how long they lasted. No standards were set for what form of authorisation was sufficient evidence of the representative's status. The likely result was a system that would be chaotic, ponderous and frustrating.40

Failing to provide a rational way to handle representation has proved to be a serious hurdle, since a union must continually prove its representative status. At times this created barriers employers could not surmount. For example, New Zealand Rail wanted to lock out 400 employees who worked scattered throughout the country. It had to serve each personally because none had authorised anyone to receive lockout notices for them. It tried to evade this obligation by serving their union. Next, the employer gave its supervisors envelopes to distribute, and the supervisors in turn gave them to the union delegates. "Now the delegates, knowing that the last thing likely to be contained in the envelopes would be good news, but suspecting in reality from all the surrounding publicity that these would be lockout notices, refused to have anything to do with them." In the end, the employer mailed notices to each employee's home. However, by then the notices were untimely, and the employer had to change the lockout date and send notice anew.41

Most often, though, it was unions who suffered from the formidable authorisation requirements. The problem was worst in workplaces with high turnover or workers who were at different locations. Employers could and did demand fresh authorisations specific to the matter at issue. New World Supermarkets, for example, demanded proof of authorisation at each bargaining session.[42]

New situations or unanticipated events meant fresh authorisations. Rosslyn Noonan explained how this affected the NZEI-TRR, a large union with workers spread throughout the country:

> That has been terribly important because, under the ECA, as you know, there are appallingly (essentially irrelevant, but intended again to make a union's job extremely difficult)—there are technical requirements if you are to bargain for people. It's not sufficient that people are members and paying a subscription fee. We have to have separate bargaining authorities from them and then within three months of the negotiation starting, we have to get individually signed ratification forms. It is just a nightmare task. Again, we have done it, relatively speaking, incredibly well. But huge resources have had to go into achieving that and it is still far from perfect.
>
> We are in the process now of following up, so lists are going out that say "These are the members and here's our record of who signed bargaining authority. Here's our record of who has signed ratification forms, and we need to fill in the gaps." . . .
>
> Having to [get authorisations] say once, on an annual basis, is probably a good thing but when you have to do it at least twice, it's a huge effort.
>
> You have to have bargaining authorities from them. Separate from that you have to have ratification. You can do it together for people who are just joining up. But, for the others, you can't because the ratification forms can't be older than three months prior to negotiations starting. The logistics of the whole exercise mean that you need the bargaining authority forms, you need to be getting them on a continuous basis. We now get them as we join people, but like every other union, we had a

huge existing membership who had never signed specific bargaining authority forms.

The employer can decide that . . . the negotiations are taking too long and the bargaining authority forms are not valid.

The whole thing has been intended to make it as difficult as possible for unions to operate and to give employers any excuse to deny recognition of the union when they want to do, that they can do it no matter how perfect you are, because it's impossible to be absolutely perfect in those situations.

We try to make the most of it, but I have to say that the cost of the whole process—individually to every member in terms of the bargaining authority form—when you put 20,000 members. . . . let alone the envelopes, the cost of the labour for filling them and the printing and so on—that money would be better spent on members in other ways, but anyhow, we are committed to doing whatever is required and in showing that we can and we will, so the employers won't be able to use that as an excuse not to deal with us.[43]

Joris de Bres of the PSA gave examples of the difficulties created if it became necessary to strike:

They were then going to take us to court, questioning whether the authorisation form that each individual worker had to sign for us to represent them in negotiations also authorised us to give notice of strike action. As a precaution we've now had to go to all our members and say, "Will you sign a further authorisation for us to serve notice of strike action?" It becomes a huge procedural mess. . . .[44]

Requiring unions to prove they are authorised to represent individual workers takes time and effort, often at critical points, such as when preparing for a strike or a trial. According to the CTU:

This has absorbed huge amounts of resources, and thereby limited the time and money available for other forms of organising activity. It is also likely to generate administrative problems, because storage and retrieval systems will need to be able to cope with negotiations and enforcement being carried out at many and different levels—national versus regional and industry versus enterprise.[45]

Essentially, the ECA has been interpreted to create a presumption against continuity of representation.

Presuming that a union's majority or representative status continues is actually more efficient, because it raises the costs of non-productive behaviour. Behaviour is non-productive when it "threatens the success not only of current negotiations but also of future negotiations in which the other side might seek revenge."[46] The ECA has opted for inefficiency, however. Rather than having a union's legitimacy as a representative decided by an impartial body or rather than allowing a union, once recognised, to remain the representative for a reasonable period of time for the normal tasks unions perform, the ECA effectively lets individual employers make the decision. There has been little oversight to prevent employers from making the decision on grounds other than a good faith doubt as to the workers' authorisation of the union.

Requiring constant reaffirmations of authorisations means that employees must publicly reaffirm their commitment to the union. In a tight situation an employee might decide it would be safer to strike out on another course, leaving the union without support when most needed. There need be no conscious decision to leave; mere apathy or inadvertence can leave the union without valid authority.

Some unions tried unsuccessfully to use authorisations as a weapon. In *New Zealand Meat Processors, Packers, Preservers, Freezing Works and Related Trades Industrial Union of Workers v. Richmond, Ltd.*[47] the employer wanted "plant specific" CECs, while the union demanded a company-wide CEC. The union tried to reinforce its demand by getting only authority to negotiate a company-wide CEC. The Employment Court held that limiting the scope of authorisation would not limit the scope of bargaining. Instead, it meant the union had no power to negotiate with the employer because the employer was negotiating site-specific contracts. This allowed the employer to bargain directly with the employees, as Judge Palmer explained:

Confronted with this situation and the union's understandably unyielding insistence, as it impressed me, that it was authorised only to negotiate a company-wide collective employment contract, the defendant was plainly, I conclude, lawfully entitled to approach its intended workers and negotiate directly with them. What other choice, I rhetorically ask, did the company have in the material circumstances?[48]

This left the union powerless to stop its members from signing site agreements[49] and withdrawing from union membership.[50]

The Employment Court allowed an employer to ignore the workers' authorisations and to force negotiations on the employer's terms in *Design Power*.[51] Design Power was a subsidiary of Electricorp, a state-owned enterprise headed by NZBR member Rod Deane. During 1987 through 1989, NZBR members Athol Hutton, Roger Kerr, and Rod Deane had board positions at Electricorp.[52]

In submissions on the ECA, Electricorp said it saw its unions as having been imposed contrary to the wishes of employer and employee and as having "continuously placed obstacles in the Corporation's path in achieving its employee relations objectives." It argued that "any temptation to perpetuate the view that protections are required based on the comparative strengths of the parties to an employment contract should be avoided."[53]

In its first negotiations for Design Power under the ECA, the employer began by wanting its employees on individual employment contracts (IECs); however, by early 1992, the partial lockout decisions had made seeking a CEC more to its advantage. The union and members took the opposite positions for the same reasons. Those workers who had not yet signed the company's contract informed the company they had withdrawn their union's authority to engage in negotiations for a CEC.[54] Undaunted, the defendant's personnel manager, Mr M. J. Cowan, wrote its employees:

> It is the company's current preference that you be a party to the collective employment contract. *This is a legitimate right the company can exercise.* Therefore you will need to give consideration to

nominating a bargaining agent to act on your behalf, or alternatively represent yourself at those negotiations. I will advise you of the date that collective negotiations will commence and seek advice from you as to whom you wish to act as your bargaining agent.[55]

On April 6, the company warned its employees that they would be locked out unless they began negotiations for a CEC, and on April 13, it locked out those who had not signed agreements or given assurances they would negotiate.[56]

The union, the PSA, argued that the lockout transgressed employees' rights to "choose whether or not to associate with other employees for the purpose of advancing the employees' collective employment interests." The court, however, found that the employer's actions did not affect employees' rights to act or not act collectively:

> I am satisfied on an assessment of all of the evidence presented that, as the defendant asserts, it is indifferent to whether its relevant employees associate with others of them in relation to the company's desire to negotiate a collective employment contract.... I accept that Designpower is even now indifferent as to how the negotiations for a collective employment contract are to be conducted in the sense that its coercion of employees has not been for the purpose of persuading them to associate with others of them to advance their collective employment interests but has rather solely been to coerce them into negotiations for a collective employment contract.[57]

The impact of the case was immediate. The union acceded to the employer's demands.[58] The level of unionisation among Designpower employees fell to 31% after this case from 88% four and a half years earlier.[59]

If employee freedom of association should mean anything, it ought to include a right to refrain from concerted activities. Instead of permitting workers to make this decision, the court gave the employer the ability to determine the form bargaining would take. This result highlights the disaggregated nature of bargaining under the ECA, a subject that is discussed in more detail later. In addition, the ECA's decision to make the number and type of contracts in a workplace a matter for agreement by the parties increased the grounds for dispute. Indeed, a twelve-page 1994 issue of *Labour Notes* discussed six separate disputes in which the key conflict was over the form of agreement.[60]

Notes
1. Owen Harvey, "Towards a Union Strategy for the 1990's," 3 (June 1988).
2. NZEF, "Forward to the Past: the Labour Opposition's Industrial Relations Policy," 18 N.Z. J. Ind. Rel., 205, 205 (1993).
3. *Northern Distribution Union (Inc.) v. 3 Guys Ltd.* [1992] 3 ERNZ 903, 915.
4. Colin Hicks, "Submission on the Employment Contracts Bill," 7 (Feb. 18, 1991).
5. Hicks Submission, 8; Wellington Unemployed Workers Union, "Submission on the Employment Contracts Act," 1, 2 (Feb. 8, 1991).
6. Progressive Enterprises, Ltd., "Submission to the Labour Select Committee on the Employment Contracts Bill," 5–6, 8 (n.d).
7. Memorandum from R. A. Stockdill, General Manager of the Industrial Relations Service of the Department of Labour, & D. J. Martin, Assistant Commissioner of the State Services Commission, to Minister of Labour and Minister of State Services, 4–5, 9 (Nov. 12, 1990).
8. Memorandum from R. A. Stockdill, General Manager, Industrial Relations Service, Department of Labour, to Bill Birch, Minister of Labour, 2 (Nov. 29, 1990).
9. Patricia Greenfield & Robert Pleasure, "Representatives of Their Own Choosing: Finding Workers' Voice in the Legitimacy and Power of Their Unions" in *Employee Representation: Alternatives and Future Directions*, 169, 178 (Bruce Kaufman & Morris Kleiner, eds. 1993).
10. Interview with Francis Wevers, Principal of Francis Wevers and Associates, Ltd., Wellington, N.Z. (May 20, 1992).
11. Interview with Joris de Bres, Central Operations Manager of the Public Service Association, in Wellington, NZ May 7, 1992.
12. NZBR & NZEF, "A Study of the Labour–Employment Court," 36–37 (Dec. 1992).
13. Interview with Rick Barker, National Secretary, Service Workers Federation of Aotearoa, in Wellington, N.Z. (May 14, 1992).
14. Electricity Corporation, "Submission to the Labour Select Committee on the Employment Contracts Bill," 22 (Feb. 1991).

15. Memorandum from Bill Birch, Minister of Labour to the Chairman, Cabinet Strategy Committee, 4 (Nov. 1990).
16. Richard Edwards, *Rights at Work: Employment Relations in the Post-Union Era*, 56–59 (1993).
17. *Adams v. Alliance Textiles (NZ) Ltd.* [1992] 1 ERNZ 982, 986–87, appeal dis'd as moot sub nom. *Eketone v. Alliance Textiles (NZ) Ltd.* [1993] 2 ERNZ 783 (CA).
18. Interview with Robyn Haultain, lawyer, in Wellington, N.Z., (May 19, 1992).
19. *New Zealand Medical Laboratory Workers Union Inc v. Capital Coast Health Ltd.* [1994] 2 ERNZ 93. Impetus for this retreat came from the Court of Appeal decision in *Eketone*, the appeal from *Alliance*.
20. Lee Tan, "Romanos Workers Fight for Collective Bargaining Rights," *Labour Notes*, Dec. 1994, at 6.
21. *Caledonian Cleaners and Caterers Ltd v. Hetariki* [1994] 2 ERNZ 400, 403.
22. *N.Z. Fire Service Comm'n v. Ivamy* [1996] 1 ERNZ 85; *Airways Corp. of N.Z. Ltd. v. NZ Air Line Pilots Assoc. IUOW, Inc.* [1996] 1 ERNZ 126.
23. Interview with Donna Payne, Organiser, New Zealand Nurses Association, in Wellington, N.Z., (May 8, 1992).
24. Memorandum from R. A. Stockdill, General Manager, Industrial Relations Service, Department of Labour, to Bill Birch, Minister of Labour, 2 (Nov. 29, 1990).
25. [1992] 1 ERNZ 982, 999, 1001–02, 1104; "Alliance Tries Union Busting," *M&C Workers News*, Dec. 1991, at 7.
26. Interview with Suze Wilson, National Industrial Officer, NZ Engineering Printing & Manufacturing Union, in Wellington (June 14, 1996).
27. International Labour Office, 295th Report of the Committee on Freedom of Association Case no.1698 ¶ 137(h) (Nov. 1994).
28. Mark Barenberg, "Democracy and Domination in the Law of Workplace Cooperation: From Bureaucratic to Flexible Production," 94 Colum. L. Rev., 753, 805 (1994).
29. Barenberg, 776, 803, 802; Greenfield & Pleasure, 187; 29 U.S.C. s 151.
30. Hicks Submission, 7.
31. Barenberg, 781–82.
32. ILO Report, ¶ 137(f).
33. [1992] 1 ERNZ 982, 993.
34. *Id.*, 1008–09.
35. *Id.*, 1017; Walter Grills, "The Impact of the Employment Contracts Act on Labour Law: Implications for Unions," 19 N.Z. J. Ind. Rel., 85, 91 (1994).
36. *Eketone v. Alliance Textiles (NZ) Ltd.* [1993] 2 ERNZ 779, 787.
37. Maryan Street, "The New Act's Effect on Low Paid Members," 5

(Longman Professional Conference, Auckland May 7–8, 1991); interview with Maxine Gay, Organiser, Public Service Association, in Palmerston North, N.Z. (May 17, 1992).
38. ECA s 12(1).
39. ILO Report, ¶¶ 193, 221.
40. New Zealand Clerical Workers Union, "Submission to the Labour Select Committee on the Employment Contracts Bill," 17 (Feb. 1991); Carter Holt Harvey Ltd., "Submission on the Employment Contracts Bill," 13, 15–16 (n.d.).
41. *New Zealand Merchant Service Guild IUOW; New Zealand Seafarers Union v. New Zealand Rail Ltd.* [1994] 1 ERNZ 482, 486–87 488, 489.
42. ILO Report, ¶ 157(c).
43. Interview Rosslyn Noonan, National Secretary, New Zealand Educational Institute, in Wellington, N.Z. (May 26, 1992).
44. de Bres.
45. CTU, "The New Zealand Experiment," 15 (Oct. 1994).
46. Kenneth Dau-Schmidt, "A Bargaining Analysis of American Labor Law and the Search for Bargaining Equity and Industrial Peace," 91 Mich. L. Rev., 419, 504 (1992).
47. [1991] 3 ERNZ 294 (preliminary injunction); [1992] 3 ERNZ 643 (permanent injunction and declaratory judgment).
48. [1992] 3 ERNZ 643, 720–21, 724.
49. Rebecca Macfie, "Employment Act Saps Strength From Union Muscle," *National Business Review*, Oct. 18, 1991, at 24.
50. Michael Turner, "Meat Workers in Last-Ditch Stand Over Contracts," *National Business Review*, Nov. 29, 1991, at 19.
51. *NZ Public Service Association v. Design Power* [1992] 1 ERNZ 669.
52. Barry Spicer, et al., *The Power to Manage: Restructuring the New Zealand Electricity Department as a State-Owned Enterprise—The Electricorp Experience* (1991); Michael Williams, "The Political Economy of Privatization" in *The Fourth Labour Government: Politics and Policy in New Zealand*, 140, 141–144 (Martin Holland & Jonathan Boston, eds., 2d ed., 1990); Nicola Natusch, *An Analysis of the Influence of the New Zealand Business Roundtable Since Its Inception*, 68 (1990); John Deeks, "Colonising the Managerial Mind: Management and Business Ideologies in Transition" in *Business and New Zealand Society*, 106 (John Deeks & Peter Enderwick, eds., 1994).
53. Electricity Corp. Submission, 6–8.
54. [1992] 1 ERNZ 669, 673–75; Jason Barber, "Lockout Comes as Court Hears Union's Case," *Dominion*, at 3 (1992).
55. [1992] 1 ERNZ 669, 686.
56. *Id.*, 674; Barber, "Lockout"; cf. *Hawtin v. Skellerup Industrial Ltd.* [1992] 2 ERNZ 500.
57. [1992] 1 ERNZ 669, 683–84.

58. de Bres.
59. ILO Report, ¶ 154(b).
60. Tan; John Maynard, "Mobil Workers' Action Wins Right to Bargain Together," *Labour Notes*, Dec. 1994, at 7; Pat Bolster, "Drivers Thwart Push for IECs," *Labour Notes*, Dec. 1994, at 8; Grant Cairncross, "Housing Agency Fails to Purge PSA," *Labour Notes*, Dec. 1994, at 10; "Lab Staff and CHE in Court," *Labour Notes*, Dec. 1994, at 11.

13

Party Status and Workplace Access

IN 1995, THE AMALGAMATED NATIONAL DISTRIBUTION UNION (NDU) had 22,000 members,[1] down from the approximately 36,000 members of its constituent unions in May 1991.[2] By the time of the ECA's fifth anniversary, NDU membership and resources were so depleted that merger with the similarly decimated Service Workers seemed to be the only way to survive.[3]

Two years after the ECA was enacted, NDU official Peter Conway assessed the impact:

> In the retail sector there is a three level structure emerging. There are collective union-negotiated contracts covering around 20,000 workers. Although there has been some concessionary bargaining, these contracts have strong protection of rights, and involve a very democratic process. At a second level there are largely de-unionised workplaces with non-union contracts. There has been little or no negotiation. Although the contracts are often collective, this is in name only as they usually provide for individual variation and there was no collective negotiation process. There is also a number on expired awards. Many workers have no idea what is in their contract except for a pay rate. . . . At the third level there is more overt exploitative practice, and considerable fear and vulnerability.[4]

A survey of seventeen contracts in the third category found clauses which allowed employers to vary hours unilaterally, provided for pay reductions of up to 17% as a disciplinary measure, and required waiving meal breaks if the shop was busy.[5]

The NDU's main problem was being unlucky enough to represent workers in an impossible-to-organise industry. Potential members were dispersed across huge numbers of small worksites and were largely youths, part-time, short-term workers, with low attachment to the job. Such workers are unlikely to see any benefit in union representation and are all too aware of their own vulnerability.[6] Even worse, many worked in the retail industry, which had long faced intense competitive pressures.[7] Companies frequently closed down, and new ones opened before any union could get involved.[8] The industry was reacting to depressed conditions, deregulation, and the entry of overseas competitors by lowering profit margins and changing operations,[9] which increased overtime and raised labour costs. Eliminating penal wages would obviously help shave costs.

In the ECA's first month, however, things appeared hopeful. The Northern Distribution Union lost only 56 members but gained 800 new members while collecting signatures for bargaining authorisations.[10] That happy beginning was not an accurate forecast. In the first year, the NDU lost between 20% and 25% of its members, "largely as a result of hostility from employers to union involvement in contract negotiations and of continuing business closures."[11] Collective employment contracts (CECs) with retail chains such as Deka, Woolworths, Whitcoulls, and Farmers were all gained only at the cost of penal rates.[12] By 1995, retail workers' wages were the lowest of any workers at $303 a week for food retailing and $316 for other retailing, and average wage increases were also the lowest at 0.3% and 0.5%.[13]

To understand how these results were achieved, it is helpful to look at some of the difficulties the distribution unions encountered. Whitcoulls, one of New Zealand's largest book and stationery stores, seized upon the ECA as its opportunity to de-unionise. It was owned by Brierley Investments, a company with ties to the NZBR.[14] Whitcoulls at first refused to collect union dues, but pressure from the Association of University Teachers persuaded Whitcoulls to resume collecting dues in July 1991.[15]

Whitcoulls hired Rob Campbell, a former Distribution Union organiser, to campaign for an enterprise agreement.[16] As with many other management consultants, Campbell borrowed labour–management cooperation techniques to promote agreement. He represented both workers and company in what was termed a "facilitation process" and developed a base contract which he marketed "to everybody on the basis of we're all one big, happy family."[17] There was minimal union involvement.[18] The NDU was not alone in seeing increased use of management consultants. Two Victoria University staff members observed that management consultants were encouraging anti-union attitudes among employers "and openly promot[ing] union busting policies."[19] Some techniques were similar to those of US management consultants.[20]

Campbell set up a staff association called "Team Whitcoulls." Its philosophy was that the employer and employees were united, that unions disrupted this positive relationship, and that maintaining union membership would not help employees. Management held meetings at which they read employees award provisions that were irrelevant to their conditions and used this as evidence that the union was out of touch with their needs. In addition, they targeted delegates to persuade workers to leave the union. Whitcoulls distributed union resignation forms and made it clear employees were expected to sign. Eventually the union was left with about 10% of the employees prepared to authorise the union as their bargaining agent.[21]

The employer then negotiated individual employment contracts (IECs) that traded a small hourly increase in pay for penal rate payments for Saturday and Sunday work and overtime; reclassified jobs and simplified classifications; changed leave provisions; changed the definition of misconduct; established in-house grievance and dispute procedures; and let the employer schedule workers more flexibly.[22]

Events at Whitcoulls were repeated throughout the retail industry. Deka, a variety store chain, was a subsidiary of Lion Nathan, in which Douglas Myers, Chief Executive of Lion Nathan and head of the NZBR, was a substantial investor.[23] The Distribution Union received bargaining approval from 600 Deka workers, but the company refused to recognise the union since it represented less than half the workers.[24] This was not a basis for refusing to recognise a union, since the ECA had no requirement of majority representation.

The union had asked to represent those for whom it was the designated bargaining agent and also to negotiate terms that would be offered to new staff under s 21 of the ECA. It argued that current workers had an interest in the terms offered new staff and that new staff could still reject these offered terms. Considering that Deka's owner was a key mover in the NZBR and the ECA, opposition to unionisation was to be expected. Indeed, an internal company memorandum stated: "We do not want a head to head confrontation and you need to spend time with staff reminding them that Deka has already provided at no cost what the union now proposes to charge them for."[25]

The union placed newspaper advertisements calling the contract unfair and urging workers not to sign.[26] On August 7, 1991, at a time when Myers was trying to sell Deka, a two-hour strike took place at the Mount Wellington store in Auckland.[27] On August 14, Deka settled with the union for a CEC that gave a 2% raise with a lower new hire rate but union recognition. The new hire rate was $5.00, whereas the employer's offer had been $3.82.[28]

In July 1991, the union began trying to forge multiple-employer regional CECs with small retail employers within a shopping mall or a small-town community. The union believed this might be attractive to employers as requiring less employer time and money and ensuring that all competitors had the same labour costs. The union itself desperately needed multi-employer negotiations. Its finances were severely strained as a result of losing members and their dues while, at the same time, negotiating many more contracts, each of which covered relatively few workers. However, persuading employers to negotiate at all, let alone to recreate award negotiations, was difficult.[29]

The key exceptions to the general landscape of members on IECs and falling union membership were employees of Farmers and K Mart. Not only were they covered by CECs but the union was a party to them.[30] That this was so is remarkable since under the ECA it was no longer the norm to include a union as a party to an agreement it had negotiated. The ECA presumes that the natural parties to any employment agreement are the employer and employee. No one else may become party to the contract unless they agree.[31]

The party requirement is another provision that is drafted to provide equal treatment of employer and employee representative. However, that is theoretical and abstract equality only. In this situation, again, it is impossible to understand what it takes to achieve equality without considering the different positions of employer and employee and their representatives. At the most basic level, any employer which is incorporated has no other way of joining a contract than by having a representative sign it. Corporate law supports the collective nature of corporations and provides that representatives naturally perform the functions of corporations. In addition, corporations can give economic incentives to bind its components together.

In contrast, workers do not need the law to say that they are persons. Furthermore, they can join contracts without using a representative. In addition, no New Zealand law currently gives workers the sort of support corporation law gives employers. When they join a union, workers create a fragilely collective body. There will always be a split in identity between the individuals and the union which represents them. Thus, the ECA's freedom of choice puts that collectivity in constant danger of schism.

In the early days of the ECA, unions considered it important to have party status because they believed it was necessary so that they might protect their members and the bargains agreed to in the contract. Non-party unions could not sue if the employer breached the contract. Some employers opposed giving unions party status for ideological reasons, viewing the agreement as one between the real parties in interest—employee and employer— with the union acting essentially as an attorney.[32] Employer Capital Coast Health wrote to its employees to explain why it did not want their unions to be party to the contract they were then negotiating:

> The parties to the contract are Capital Coast Health and the employees who indicate they wish to become a party. . . . Unions or other employee representatives not being parties to this contract,

does not prohibit your union (or any other representative) helping you in enforcing the contract should this be necessary. In effect the choice becomes yours as to whom you want to act for you in any given situation.[33]

The NZEF urged employers and advised its advocates not to allow unions or other negotiators to have party status. Some employers were guided by the NZEF and decided that, if they did not repudiate unionisation, at least they should deny unions party status.[34]

In the 1993/1994 period, unions were parties to only 52% of contracts. This average, however, hides the enormous variation among industries. In the restaurant and hotel industry unions are parties to 2% of contracts compared to 75% in community and public services. Most industries cluster about 35%–45%.[35] Without the public sector, the 52% figure would shrink to as low as one-third. In the private sector, the majority of employers have steadily denied unions party status. In 1995, 53% of all contracts made unions parties—26% in retailing industries; and only 5% in the accommodation and cafe industry.[36] The ILO was concerned that the ECA did not provide unions with automatic party status.[37]

Although unions originally might have made concessions to secure party status, experience with the ECA has shown that party status has little value. The plain truth is that other factors severely handicapped unions when they tried to bring actions alleging ECA or contract violations, and party status does nothing to overcome these problems.[38] As a result, a union must assume that it can only sue as the expressly authorised agent of a party[39] or if given special permission by the Employment Court as being justly entitled to be heard.[40] The burden of establishing the authority to represent another rests on the person asserting it.[41] At this point the law is still so unclear as to what will allow a union to proceed and the consequences of guessing wrong are so serious that a prudent union will act in all cases as if it is not a party to an agreement.

The Distribution Union reached the K Mart and Farmers agreements before this case law had developed when it was still believed that having party status was necessary to unions. In the case of K Mart and Farmers, the union wanted party status so it could enforce the agreement that the company offer the negotiated contract terms to new employees.[42] Both the union and employer regarded the K Mart agreement as a good one, with improved terms for workers as well as union rights.[43] The K Mart contract, however, had many similarities to the Whitcoulls agreement. It too had youth rates, reduced penal rates, and increased the employer's ability to schedule workers outside traditional working hours. It was seen as far more progressive, however, because it maintained a role for the union, gave the union access to workers at the workplace, included new workers under the contract terms, and allowed union education leave.[44] This contract also demonstrated a new trend in New Zealand: the parties agreed not to disclose its terms.[45]

In the grocery industry, the union managed to achieve some contracts. CECs with Foodtown and 3 Guys supermarkets had 2% raises but traded some penal rates for additional pay. It reached other contracts covering thousands of grocery workers but faced the problem of discount grocery stores, which had captured 39% of the market in 1992. Grocery stores saw wages as key to competitiveness since the crucial element for shoppers was price. This made it harder to push employers for agreements.[46]

By late 1991, the union had begun an increasingly aggressive and public organising stance. On November 26, 1991, it picketed New World supermarkets asking customers to shop elsewhere after the employer refused the union access and attempted to bypass the union and negotiate directly with employees. The consumer boycott and information picketing forced Titirangi New World to allow the union access to the premises. In Kaikohe, on December 3, the supermarket owner was denied an injunction against the picketing. The Auckland Retail Grocers Association representative was surprised that the pickets "were not being chased out of town by people with pick handles and baseball bats."[47]

The union also borrowed from American and British unions and began a "Buy Union" campaign which listed 500 unionised retail outlets. It also enlisted support from New Zealand celebrities and politicians, including Gary McCormick, Elizabeth McRae, Bruce Kendall, Jim Anderton, Sonja Davies, Helen Clark, and Phillida Bunkle. Union General Secretary Mike Jackson explained that they had been hit with "American-style tactics" and would respond with "American-style tactics" adapted for local conditions.[48]

Other unions also tried innovative tactics during this time. Nurses Union members employed at four geriatric hospitals and rest homes run by Presbyterian Support Services in Auckland, Hamilton, and Tauranga announced a hunger strike for Sunday, May 9, 1992, to protest against the employer's offer. It proposed removing penal rates in exchange for a 10% increase. The Nurses Union estimated the net change to be a 13% cut. The union chose a hunger strike over striking to gain favourable public relations by not affecting patient care. At the same time, the Nurses Union announced it was suing the employer since fifteen nurses said they had signed the contract under duress. It also sought an interim injunction to stop Presbyterian Support Systems from changing the hours and duties of nurses who had refused to sign the contract.[49]

The hunger strike had wide public support, and as many as 650 nurses and domestic workers were expected to join the 48-hour fast beginning May 10, with the strike ready to spread to other church-run hospitals which had offered the same contract to their workers. The union also tried moral suasion. The churches had condemned the ECA when it was introduced. The Nurses Union contended that the employer was behaving more like the NZBR than a religious organisation. It asked Presbyterian leaders if they thought the hospitals were behaving as Christians. All these tactics, however, ultimately failed to move the employers.[50]

The new tactics were not cost-free. Often they meant legal expenses to fight lawsuits. On May 2, the Glen Innes Pak'n Save supermarket sued the Northern Distribution Union for over $279,000 in damages for loss of goodwill and profits, additional advertising and security guards during an unsuccessful four-month picket and boycott.[51] The store had low rates for young workers, no penal rates, 10-hour days, and no minimum hours. Winning this boycott was seen as crucial since a new Pak'n Save was due to open in Hamilton within one hundred metres of a store with a union contract.[52] Having stores operate with these sorts of terms would eventually drive union employers out of business or erode working conditions when unionised employers claimed, justifiably, that they could not compete without concessions.

The one thing missing from many of these campaigns was involvement by the workers at the targeted store. The union admitted there had been almost no contact between union officials and the workers.[53] Most of the pickets were union members who wanted to protect industry working conditions. The union's problem was that it had trouble making contact because the employer had denied it access to workers and threatened organisers with trespass.[54]

The ECA changed union access rights, and this hit New Zealand organisers hard. For generations, the law had delivered members and had also provided access to recruit and interview potential members or to collect fees or other charges. Refusal to allow entry carried a fine of up to $1000.[55] The LRA also legislated two paid 2-hour "stopwork" meetings a year during working hours.[56] As a result, unions never needed to develop organising strategies. Lawyer Robyn Haultain explained the impact denying access had on unions:

> One of the reasons that it was hard for our union and lots of other unions to respond, I think, was that for the previous 15 odd years, the unions had fairly much unrestricted access to workplaces and this tradition of running union meetings in the employers' time, when the workers were getting paid, was really well established and so it was very easy to get people to come to a union meeting when they get off the job for an hour and get paid for it. Great. Everybody loved it and rushed along to the meeting even if they are not interested in the description of the meeting or the outcome.[57]

The ECA gives "a person, group, or organisation . . . seeking to represent any employee or employees in negotiations" access to seek authorisations, but only if the employer agrees.[58] Once a union is an authorised representative, it can have access to employees to prepare for negotiations.⁵⁹ The hard part—and the crucial part—is getting access to unrepresented workers. Access for other purposes is no longer a statutory right but can be negotiated in a contract or be permitted by an employer.

Union organisers' problems were greater even than having to learn new skills. The ECA focused only on representation and negotiation. As a result, it did not consider access to be necessary for purposes other than seeking authorisations to represent or, once those were given, to negotiate. In other words, actions fundamental to representation and to the collective bargaining relationship—policing the agreement, checking on members' current conditions, and forging strong ties—are not recognised by the ECA as a basis for access. This is a serious problem, because unions act "as workers' collective monitor of managerial behaviour. The union has a greater capacity than either individual workers or company union representatives to assess managerial honesty because it can draw on information about the behaviour not only of the immediate employer, but of comparably situated employers as well."⁶⁰

The ECA does not recognise any value in fostering unions' relationships with members, in assuring workers of their union's ongoing concern, protection, and accessibility, and in demonstrating a union's presence to the employer. The importance of access as a means to these ends was underscored when, just after the ECA became effective, major unions lost important worksites precisely because they had not maintained a presence in the workplace and the employees had, as a result, become convinced they could not rely on the union.⁶¹ Early cases exacerbated unions' problems with lack of access:

> While s 14 establishes the right of access for bargaining representatives, employers appear to have considerable control over the actual terms of the access, and can frustrate the bargaining process. For example, in the *Alliance Textiles* case the employer granted access at 6 a.m., and then only after trying to convince their employees to rescind the authority they had given to the representative. Similarly, in the *Argyle Hospital* case the employer

only allowed the union representative the opportunity to speak to an employee in the corridor amidst the general flurry of workplace activity.[62]

A union denied access might not learn that it needs to take action. If it learns of a violation, the union cannot be present in the workplace to support employees' resolve. If it must resort to the courts to gain access, this makes it less likely individual employees would be brave enough to come forward to assert their rights. Workers are less likely to trust their fates to a representative who cannot demonstrate its competence and ability to promote their interests.[63]

All these barriers to effective representation resulted from the ECA's limited focus on authorisations and contract negotiations as the purpose of representation. In the view of ECA supporters, it was merely a way for unions to compete for "market share".[64] The ECA failed to support actions which made representation meaningful, because it failed to comprehend employment as an ongoing relationship with a continuing need for representation and negotiation once a contract was signed.

With these barriers, it should be no surprise that, despite all the NDU's efforts, successes were at best partial victories. Many workers in the industry were not union members, and many members found themselves working under contracts with inferior terms. Non-members' terms were normally set with no bargaining:

> The bargaining process in these cases varies but generally takes the form of the employer preparing a contract, putting it to the staff and then persuading them to sign. It is rare for there to be any negotiation leading to the alteration of the employer-drafted contract. Existing workers find it hard to get overtime, access to additional hours (there is severe underemployment in the retail sector), and promotion if they refuse to sign.
>
> This is not a genuine negotiating process. It is a perversion of the term "negotiation". In the retail sector there are workers of 14 and 15 years of age working weekends or evenings. Now that the award system is abolished, and there are no minimum rates for young workers, these young people are extremely

vulnerable. Their first taste of employment can be extremely bitter. We have had reported cases of $1.50 and $2.00 an hour being paid to such workers.

Is it fair to have a labour law that says "If a young worker and an employer reach agreement on such a contract this is an entirely private arrangement and it is not anybody else's business to interfere?"[65]

Two years after the ECA was enacted, changed employment terms allowed employers to deploy full and part-time workers at will. Overtime pay was virtually eliminated. There was increased employer discretion and less worker freedom as the result of new terms, such as ones eliminating the notice required for changes in scheduling.[66] The increase in two-tier wages meant lower terms for future workers, with wage trade-offs of as much as 40% just to maintain a union presence and collective representation.[67]

No better could be achieved when the union was in a constant fight for its life. The industry's natural turnover meant constantly having to recruit new members to replace those who had left. Recruitment was important, but the union was stretched thin just to complete negotiations. In 1993, the NDU negotiated 500 contracts as opposed to its pre-ECA bargaining obligations for 40 awards and 30 agreements. Each negotiation meant securing bargaining authorisations, settling ratification procedures, and communicating with each group of workers concerning the progress of negotiations.[68]

Defectors formed their own groups, merged with other groups, such as the Engineers, or formed new unions, such as the Amalgamated Workers Union of New Zealand.[69] One aspect of the instability unions experienced was the impact the ECA had on career union organisers. As they saw their memberships decline, they worried about the security of their own jobs. The series of mergers taking place meant that organisers had to understand the needs of new types of workers and potentially affected their understanding of and commitment to the membership. It is no wonder that organisers tended to experience the ECA environment as full of stress and themselves as powerless to meet its challenges.[70]

As of 1995, the reality for unions representing the sorts of workforces the Distribution Union did was so desperate that it is hard to fault them for weak agreements. They had few alternatives. Refusing to agree to these sorts of terms meant that no CFC could be reached and the workers would finally agree to IECs and leave the union.[71] Bad as many of these agreements were, what makes it even worse is that it may not have been the unions' power which secured them. Alistair Pringle argued:

> Indeed there is some evidence to suggest that the union's present involvement in collective agreements has been the consequence of employer policy decisions, rather than the result of the so-called "countervailing power" of an organised workforce. This invites the question, will organised labour continue to have a role in the setting of conditions of employment in this industry; and if so, who will it organise and to what purpose?[72]

Sarah Oxenbridge observed: "Employer cooperation is the major determinant of success in contract campaigns, and it has been suggested that successful union involvement in contract negotiations to date has been largely dependent on employer policy rather than the industrial strength of the union."[73]

Notes
1. Sarah Oxenbridge, "Organising the Secondary Labour Force" in *The New Zealand Experience, Proceedings of 9th AIRAANZ Conference*, 347, 350 (Larry Sonder, ed., 1995).
2. Raymond Harbridge & Kevin Hince, *A Sourcebook of New Zealand Trade Unions and Employee Organisations*, 28 (1994). The NDU was composed of several unions which merged and restructured during this period. Sorting out the genealogy here could distract from the main focus, so they are all referred to here generically as the NDU or the Distribution Union.
3. Alastair Duncan, "CEW Collapse Highlights Pitfalls of Merger Mania," *Labour Notes*, 1 (Dec. 1995).
4. Peter Conway, "Stayin' Alive," *Political Review*, 8, 9 (July–Aug. 1993).
5. Conway, "Stayin' Alive," 8.
6. Janet Hector, Jon Hemming & Mary Hubble, "Industrial Relations Bargaining in the Retail Non-food Sector: 1991–1992," 18 N.Z. J. Ind. Rel., 326, 331 (1993).

7. Alistair Pringle, "The Pursuit of Flexibility in the New Zealand Supermarket: The Employment Contracts Act, Continuities and Discontinuities," 18 N.Z. J. Ind. Rel., 306, 308, 311 (1993).
8. National Distribution Union, *Short Changed: Retail Workers and the ECA* (1996); Peter Conway, "National's Blitz: Labour Market Reform," *Race Gender Class*, 11/12, 2, 4 (1991).
9. Hector, Hemming & Hubble, 328–29.
10. Patricia Herbert, "Workers Stick Close to Union's Petticoats," *Dominion*, June 19, 1991, at 12.
11. Hector, Hemming & Hubble, 330; Rebecca Macfie, "Employers Set Industrial Agenda," *National Business Review*, Nov. 15, 1991, at 19.
12. Macfie, "Employers Set Industrial Agenda."
13. Raymond Harbridge & Anthony Honeybone, "The Employment Contracts Act and Collective Bargaining Patterns: A Review of the 1994/95 Year" in *Employment Contracts: Bargaining Trends & Employment Law Update 1995/95*, 14 (Raymond Harbridge & Peter Keily, eds. 1995); Rasmussen, Chronicle v.21, 114.
14. David Steele, *The Business Roundtable*, 37 (1989).
15. Roth, "Chronicle," 16 N.Z. J. Ind. Rel., 318 (1991).
16. *Id.*, 208.
17. Interview with Paul Kimble, Organiser, Distribution Workers Union, in Wellington (May 12, 1992).
18. Hector, Hemming & Hubble, 333.
19. Gordon Anderson & Pat Walsh, "Labour's New Deal: A Bargaining Framework for a New Century?" 18 N.Z. J. Ind. Rel., 163, 172 (1993).
20. Martin J. Levitt, *Confessions of a Union Buster* (1994).
21. Kimble.
22. Hector, Hemming & Hubble, 333.
23. Steele, 39.
24. Rebecca Macfie, "Deka, Unions on Collision Course," *National Business Review*, June 26, 1991, at 3.
25. Macfie, "Deka, Unions"; Roth, "Chronicle," 16 N.Z. J. Ind. Rel., 208 (1991); NDU, *Short Changed*.
26. Roth, "Chronicle," 16 N.Z. J. Ind. Rel., 320 (1991).
27. Karen Ruka, "Wine and Spirits Deal Earns $61M for Lion," *National Business Review*, Sept. 3, 1991, at 3.
28. Roth, "Chronicle," 16 N.Z. J. Ind. Rel., 320 (1991); Rebecca Macfie, "CTU Leads Last Ditch Award Fight," *National Business Review*, Aug. 29, 1991, at 2.
29. Hector, Hemming & Hubble, 331; Rebecca Macfie, "Union Bids for 'Umbrella Pacts'," *National Business Review*, July 10, 1991, at 3.
30. Macfie, "Umbrella Pacts."
31. ECA s 17.
32. Interview with Francis Wevers, Principal, Francis Wevers &

Associates, in Wellington, May 20, 1992.
33. *New Zealand Medical Laboratory Workers Union Inc. v. Capital Coast Health Ltd.* [1994] 2 ERNZ 93, 113.
34. NZEF, Employment Contracts Bill 1991: Submission A-3 (Jan. 30, 1991); interview with Rick Barker, National Secretary, Service Workers Federation of Aotearoa, in Wellington, N.Z. (May 14, 1992).
35. Harbridge & Honeybone, 25.
36. *Id.*, 7.
37. International Labour Office, 295th Report of the Committee on Freedom of Association Case no.1698 ¶ 258 (Nov. 1994).
38. *NZ Nurses Union v. Argyle Hospital Ltd.* [1992] 2 ERNZ 314, 344 (Empl. Trib.); *Northern Distribution Union (Inc.) v. 3 Guys Ltd.*, [1992] 3 ERNZ 903, 916–18.
39. ECA ss 45, 123 (1) (c); but see *Airline Pilots v. Mt. Cook* [1992] 3 ERNZ 355.
40. ECA s 123(3). *Prendergast v. Associated Stevedores Ltd.* [1992] 1 ERNZ 737; *NZ Air Line Pilots Assn IUOW v. Air New Zealand Ltd.* [1992] 1 ERNZ 880, 884–88.
41. ECA ss 12, 59.
42. Macfie, "Umbrella Pacts."
43. David Munro, Letter to the Editor, *Dominion*, May 11, 1992, at 8.
44. Hector, Hemming & Hubble, 333.
45. Macfie, "Umbrella Pacts."
46. Peter Conway, "Pak'n Slave Picket Hangs In for Fundamental Union Demands," *Labour Notes*, Sept. 1992, at 5; National Distribution Workers Union, *Under Contract: A Brief Report on the Use of the Employment Contracts Act in the Retail Sector*, 1 (n.d.); Roth, "Chronicle," 17 N.Z. J. Ind. Rel., 125 (1992).
47. Roth, "Chronicle," 17 N.Z. J. Ind. Rel., 124, 250 (1992); Conway, "Pak'n Slave"; Conway, "Stayin' Alive," 9; "Supermarket Picketed," *N.Z. Herald*, May 4, 1992, at 3.
48. Roth, "Chronicle," 17 N.Z. J. Ind. Rel., 250 (1992); Conway, "Pak'n Slave"; "NDU Launches 'Buy Union' List," *Labour Notes*, 4 (Dec. 1992).
49. "Support Grows for Hospital Workers' Protest Fast," *Dominion*, May 9, 1992, at 3; Jason Barber, "Nurses at Church-run Hospitals to Hunger Strike," *Dominion*, May 7, 1992, at 8; "Nurses Protest," *Press*, May 6, 1992, at 8; Roth, "Chronicle," 17 N.Z. J. Ind. Rel., 255 (1992).
50. Roth, "Chronicle," 17 N.Z. J. Ind. Rel., 256–57 (1992); "Support Grows"; "Church Home Staff Plan 48-Hour Fast," *Press*, May 9, 1992, at 8; Barber, "Hunger Strike."
51. Roth, "Chronicle," 17 N.Z. J. Ind. Rel., 256 (1992).
52. Conway, "Pak'n Slave."
53. *Id.*

54. Pringle, 322.
55. LRA s 56.
56. LRA s 57.
57. Interview with Robyn Haultain, lawyer, in Wellington, N.Z. (May 19, 1992).
58. ECA s 13.
59. ECA s 14(1); *National Distribution Union Inc. v. Foodstuffs (Auckland) Inc.*, [1994] 1 ERNZ 653, 660.
60. Mark Barenberg, "The Political Economy of the Wagner Act: Power, Symbol, and Workplace Cooperation," 106 Harv. L. Rev., 1379, 1470 (1993).
61. Haultain.
62. Lorraine Skiffington, "The Renaissance of the Duty to Bargain in Good Faith," Empl. L. Bull., 92, 93 (Sept. 1995).
63. Michael Gottesman, "In Despair, Starting Over: Imagining a Labor Law for Unorganized Workers" in *The Legal Future of Employee Representation*, 57, 66 (Matthew Finkin, ed., 1994).
64. Wolfgang Kaspar, *Free to Work* (1995).
65. NDU, *Under Contract*, 3.
66. Pringle, 317.
67. Macfie, "Employers Set Industrial Agenda"; Roth, "Chronicle," 17 N.Z. J. Ind. Rel., 253 (1992).
68. Conway, "Stayin' Alive," 8.
69. Raymond Harbridge & Kevin Hince, "Unions and Union Membership in New Zealand 1985–1992," 18 N.Z. J. Ind. Rel., 352, 359 (1993).
70. Grant Michelson, "New Zealand Under the Employment Contracts Act 1991: Career Attitudes," 5 Lab. & Ind. 137, 143–44 (1993).
71. Macfie, "Employers Set Industrial Agenda."
72. Pringle, 321.
73. Oxenbridge, 350.

14

Contracting and Duress

ON MAY 14, ONE DAY BEFORE THE ECA WAS TO BECOME EFFECTIVE, the Service Workers Union of Aotearoa (SWU) became the last union to be registered under the LRA. It was a merger of hotel, hospital, restaurant, cleaners and caretakers unions which represented 70,498 members. In 1995, only 24,900 members remained.[1] How is it possible that a union like the SWU, one which had tried to prepare for change, was so ravaged? The SWU's main problem was that it represented the wrong sorts of workers in the ECA environment. Its potential members were mostly unskilled, young, part-timers, women, new immigrants, or minorities, and worked in small numbers in thousands of workplaces.[2] Many worked in tourism, a $2.24 billion industry employing 80,000 people. These industries were labour-intensive, so employers had an incentive to try to save on labour costs.

In 1990, Ian Wearing of the NZBR said: "Moreover, even within an industry such as accommodation, there is such a broad range of enterprises—from international hotels, to motels, to caravan parks, to camping grounds, to youth hostels and farm/homes—that it is quite absurd to subject them to the same industrial 'rules'."[3] These factors translated into a radical change in employer behaviour under the ECA. About 4%–5% remained friendly and continued to want a collective agreement to avoid fragmentation and the inconsistent agreements they feared the ECA promoted. Some found it useful to have a credible bargaining agent representing their workers as a way to achieve their business goals. The rest to a greater or lesser degree, wanted to use the new law to their benefit, including eliminating the union.[4]

Once change was upon it, the SWU found itself so hard-pressed that it was 1993 before it was able to use the organising model it had investigated before the ECA. The amalgamation, which was intended to strengthen the union, instead drained strength as it demanded attention and time. While it was locked in a battle for survival, the SWU had no time or energy to pursue new and untried strategies.[5]

The SWU and other New Zealand unions had problems in addition to hostile employers, hard-to-organise industries, and the difficulties so far described. The ECA operates in ways that are not obvious from the legislation. In addition to the problems already discussed which stem from the way it treats employee representatives, the ECA's language as to individual or collective contracts presented peculiar stumbling blocks. It is obvious that the language of the ECA does not support or promote collectivity. What is not so obvious is that it not only promotes individual contracting and individual employment contracts (IECs), but it also actually places barriers in the way of collective action and collective employment contracts (CECs).

A good example of its bias in favour of IECs can be found in the operation of s 19(4). When an award or CEC expires before a successor contract is agreed to, its terms continue, but s 19(4) transforms the contracts into IECs. Section 63(a) makes it illegal to strike before the current CEC has expired. By the time workers can strike, they will be on IECs and any terms relating only to the collective nature of the expired agreement—those which cannot be performed as individual obligations—will have dropped out. In other words, when there is an impasse, the parties start negotiating from an IEC. There is no logical reason why the status quo of collectivity should not continue. That status quo at least is one both parties once agreed to, rather than conditions neither has agreed to but which are likely to favour the employer and give it additional leverage.[6]

A second way in which the ECA is biased against collective negotiations is in the way it treats its two forms of employment contracts—the IEC[7] and the CEC[8]—and the negotiations leading to them. Individual or collective negotiations do not predict—indeed, they have no bearing on—whether the result is an IEC or CEC. The only significant distinction between an IEC and a CEC is the number of employees who have signed the document. An IEC is "an employment contract that is binding on only one employer and one employee."[9] A CEC is "an employment contract that is binding on one or more employers and 2 or more employees."[10]

The terms "collective" and "individual" must be used with caution and precision, because they may refer to nothing more meaningful than the number of names at the end of the contract. Employees can sign and have signed CECs one by one. When this happens, the agreement came about without the power and processes of collective negotiation. IECs can be collective in the sense that all employees in the workplaces have identical IECs, with not one individual term. An IEC can arise from collective negotiations. These can either be for the purpose of achieving an IEC or, by default, when a collectively negotiated CEC expires and its terms are incorporated into an individual contract by s 19(4).

Employers quickly learned that the form of ECA negotiations and the resulting contract are totally disaggregated. In the ECA's first year, employer attorney Christopher Toogood argued that negotiations for CECs did not require collective negotiations, either theoretically or practically, and the judge agreed.[11] To workers there would often be little difference between being offered a CEC or an IEC if the conditions were the same and there were no collective negotiations leading up to either agreement.[12] As a result, if the employer preferred IECs, the wise employee might prefer them too.

Given these built-in biases toward IECs, it should be no surprise that, during the ECA's first three years, as many as 34% of employees worked under IECs whose terms arose from expired awards by the operation of s 19(4).[13] In 1996, 45% of employers surveyed had IECs as the predominant contract form.[14] These were not just the smaller employers. In 1995, 33% of employers employing over 50 workers were seeking IECs.[15] This would seem counter-intuitive and inefficient, if they actually had to negotiate each one of those agreements. The fact that so many of the largest corporations are moving in this direction casts doubt on the existence of workplace co-determination.

Even less obvious is how this disconnection of contract from process and the definition of CEC gives employers the power to control workplace conditions with minimal effort. An employer can enter into a CEC "with any or all of the employees employed by the employer."[16] When a CEC exists, "each employee and the employer may negotiate terms and conditions on an individual basis that are not inconsistent with any terms and conditions of the applicable collective employment contract."[17] Thus, an employer can enter into an agreement with two employees—the minimum for a CEC—and then use the CEC to control all other employees' terms.[18] Wellington management consultant Francis Wevers used three layers of CECs and IECs with different expiry dates so at least one was always in force to remove the right to strike or lockout.[19]

An employer can have CECs with differing terms and then use them to play workers off against each other. For example, if a union is unable to attain a "new employees" clause under s 21—that is, an agreement that requires the employer to offer the CEC to new employees—the employer can offer new hires different terms and then try to compel existing workers to accept the new-hires' CEC.[20] There is almost no end to the ways employers can use combinations of IECs and CECs as leverage to set working conditions.[21] The fact that new employee clauses are not in most contracts suggests that employers are opposed to maintaining uniform conditions. This is a particular problem for the service industry. While across all industries, 51% of CECs provide either no new-hire clause (10%) or extension of terms at the employer's discretion (41%), in the industries represented by the SWU those figures are 42% no new hire clause and 35% discretionary extension.[22]

Having inferior terms for new-hires occurred widely. Harbridge argues that tiered employment "has only disadvantages" for unions, particularly if the union agreed to those terms.

> New hires engaged on an inferior employment contract are unlikely to unionise as the union is very much caught between a rock and a hard place: If the union is to settle an inclusive

contract covering all employees then it is dealing with an employer who is most unlikely to want to raise the cost of benefits for new hires. Accordingly, the union either has to reduce the benefits available to existing employees (an unpopular move guaranteed to lead to de-unionization) or to accept a tiered contract with different conditions applying to staff undertaking the same functions (sure to be unpopular with new hires as they receive nothing more than the employer was offering anyway).[23]

Anti-union employers could effectively split their workplaces four ways—between union and non-union, and between existing staff and new staff.[24] For example, in the hotel industry, it became common for an employer to hire workers for a three-month trial period at a lower wage and then terminate the worker at the end of that time. During the employee's retention, however, he or she might be given more favourable shifts and conditions than those with higher pay under the CEC.[25]

One of the boldest uses of IECs to control workplace conditions occurred at Tiwai Point and involved the Engineers and New Zealand Aluminium Smelters (NZAS). Tiwai Point is a large South Island aluminium plant owned by Comalco Aluminium, a subsidiary of CRA Ltd, a Melbourne-based company. Prior to the ECA, the Engineers represented 75% of Tiwai's 1200 workers and had 760 members; the rest were represented by other unions. When the dust cleared about November 1991, the Engineers was left with but 200 members, none regarded as firmly in the union's camp.[26]

The Engineers contributed to its problems. Union–management relationships were poor, and some job delegates had been undermining and discrediting the union in the eyes of its members. Few workers identified with the union. One Engineers' organiser said that many workers "thought their union stretched no further than the smelter gates."[27]

In contrast, the company was prepared to use the ECA and IECs to achieve its economic goals. Company official George Mark said that the ECA provided "a visionary approach which allowed people the opportunity for choice and a more appropriate means of being rewarded in accordance with their work effort."

Mark felt it was in the company's and the workers' interests to have direct negotiations. He prepared an education package for workers and had company managers meet with all employees. "During the discussions considerable interest was expressed in the possibilities surrounding individual contracts of employment."[28]

The company then sent a personal letter to each employee's home. "This letter was personalised with the use of the employee's first name (or indeed nickname in some cases) and dealt with the issue of union membership, the state of the aluminium industry and the Company's wish to pursue the option of individual contracts of employment."[29] The IECs were a letter with all terms standard except pay. Negotiating individual salaries took from fifteen minutes to two hours each, with all agreements concluded after three months. Mark says that results have been uniformly positive, with workers pleased and the company able to start twelve-hour shifts, something he says workers wanted but which was opposed by the union.[30]

In addition to pay increases of from $5000 to $9000, the agreement also extended the management superannuation scheme to all workers and provided medical insurance, reimbursement of telephone costs, subsidies for children's education, fifteen days sick leave, four weeks vacation leave to be paid at the rate of five or six weeks, and thirteen weeks long service leave after fifteen years.[31] In exchange, workers were put on salary and lost penal rates. Wages were to be reviewed annually, but no increases were guaranteed. The company eliminated job demarcations and other restrictions and says these have resulted in productivity gains.[32]

Workers were motivated to sign the IECs not only by these carrots, but also by the stick. When the company announced that it planned to make 150 workers redundant, workers felt pressured to sign or face lay-off.[33]

> They timed it beautifully to coincide with the lay-off of 3000 freezing workers in the Southland area, so there was considerable fear for job protection. I'm not saying it was orchestrated, but it certainly would have helped their case. They put a substantial

pay rise into the document at a time when people were signing documents with nil rights. . . .

It's going to be a nightmare for them to administer. There's several thousand individual contracts, all varying pay rates and God knows whatever else. A lot of them for all intents and purposes are identical and there are certain groups that have the same rates and the rest of it. But as it grows, various workers may say their productivity is better than someone else's and try a pay rise. All sorts of things can happen and for them to keep control on that amount of bargaining is just phenomenal. So I think they've bought a big headache for themselves. They saw it as a way to get the kind of flexibility, cross-skilling they wanted that they were having difficulty getting through multi-union negotiations.[34]

It was the option of being able to offer IECs and settle terms one by one that gave the employer this leverage.

Some Engineers' members at Tiwai did sign a CEC but lost any pay increase as a result. Furthermore, the union found it difficult to keep in contact with this small outpost of members. The Engineers tried to maintain a presence by visiting the plant and tried to encourage workers to rejoin the union. However, five years later, the union had to admit that Tiwai is lost for the foreseeable future.[35]

Although ECA proponents had argued that workers needed individual terms, the Tiwai IECs were identical in every respect, with the exception of the wage clause. IECs do not mean the individualised contracts ECA proponents had promoted. Even worse, although collective in their terms, workers had no collectivity to give them strength in negotiations. All contracts were offered to workers on a take-it-or-leave-it basis.[36] Thus, workers at Tiwai had no real involvement in the process of governing their work lives. In New Zealand, workers who ask to negotiate find that their employer shows "displeasure at being challenged, and the employee is made to feel powerless to achieve any real negotiated changes, but is often made to feel that he/she is putting his/her future with the employer in jeopardy by continuing to stand up for the right to negotiate."[37]

Losing Tiwai created problems for the Engineers beyond the losing members. It set a precedent of IECs in the aluminium industry and was taken as a model campaign by some companies, including CRA's Weipa plant in Australia.[38] Even had the Engineers been able to consummate a CEC, the ECA changed the parties' statuses in fundamental ways. All employment contracts—individual or collective—were only between the individual employees and the employer. The contract bore the signature of the employer. Each employee who wished to be covered by its terms had to sign the document. The union was placed in the role of outsider.

This legal framework and the general economic malaise formed the environment the SWU and other New Zealand unions faced in negotiations. As a result, assuming a union was able to negotiate an agreement, it was legally binding only between an employer and each individual worker who signed it. Signature pages could be longer than the substantive parts of the document. This created an odd dissonance between negotiation and being bound to an agreement.[39]

Of course, there is not always a document to sign. Unless the employee asks, IECs do not have to be in writing.[40] This means that, for many workers, an employment contract arises from a process that most would not recognise as negotiating.[41] At Pacific Steel, workers represented by the Engineers were given company-drafted IECs they were expected to sign. New hires are asked to sign employment documents, including tax forms and their employment contract. In many places the employee was told that if he or she enjoyed working there or working at all, the only options were either to sign or quit. Workers who had little employment security tended to sign.[42]

A hotel offered a contract that was a half-page cover memorandum to "All Staff" which stated that a copy of the Hotel's employment contract was attached and would take effect over the next two weeks. Nothing was individual, except potentially the pay rate. The contract set out no pay rate and told employees to call "Carol" to "discuss your personal rate . . . Failure to contact Carol by the above date will result in your rate being set without negotiation." Many written IECs are nothing more than pre-printed forms with no space for individualisation. "[O]rganiser, Judy Sheppard, says the Employment Contracts Act is nonsense in many cases: small employers do not draw up contracts with workers. They just tell workers 'these are the conditions' and they can take it or leave it."[43]

> It's "Take the job or leave it. This is all we offer, and that's it." I mean, if you are unemployed or you're between jobs there is no bargaining. This is an incredible environment.
>
> See, what people get is the misimpression that collective bargaining presupposes collective contracts. Well, they are not collective contracts in the sense that you would believe in internationally or in an American sense. They are, in effect, individual contracts which happen to coincide with other individuals and so the individuals all came in, put their pen to the paper on the same document. We have a number of contracts that we have signed as an organisation on behalf of those who we represent and what we have to supply to the employers is a list of names and a copy of the authorisation they have signed with us to make us the agent, so it is administratively very complicated and is almost as difficult as you can get.[44]

The existence of so many contracts that do not provide more than the most basic terms and which do not deal with the actual conditions under which work will be performed, such as lighting, ventilation, temperature and attitude of the supervisor suggests that those who had contended that the employer–employee relationship is no more than a contract misunderstood the complexity of the relationship. The more current view is that the complex conditions under which work is performed and the length of the relationship means that it cannot be captured by contract.[45] By promoting a regime which encouraged IECs, the ECA created the conditions for employers to eliminate these details. The silence of IECs on most terms tended to give employers broad discretion over working hours, the right to dismiss the employee, and the right to change working conditions.[46]

The SWU, other unions, and individual employees also encountered outright anti-union employers. When employers were firmly opposed to unions, the SWU has felt it must make hard choices about whether it could feasibly represent the group. Workers in very small worksites whose employer refused to negotiate a contract were the most likely to lose union representation. The SWU told those members that they could retain their membership and the union would offer whatever services it could. However, the union explained, there would be no real negotiations, and they would be on IECs. Even under these terms, a number of members decided to retain their membership.[47] Even if they received no union representation in negotiations, they would be able to call upon the union's legal and financial resources if they were terminated and wanted to file a personal grievance.

Knowing where and whether to draw the line was no easy decision. Although the SWU's decision was practical, it had potential negatives beyond just losing members at the site. Abandoned members might persuade others not to trust the SWU or unions in general and would make organising other sites more difficult. On the other hand, workers in small sites were most likely to be a drain on the union's already overtaxed resources. The SWU's experience in trying to retain recognition was not unique. Other unions, such as the Distribution Union, made the same decisions.

It would be unfair to assume that just because employers did not want unions that they all simply cut their workers' wages to the bone. However, even when they did not aim to lower wages, the changes employers wanted often decreased workers' total pay. The most common targets were terms that limited employer hegemony or which were seen as being inflexible. These included restrictions on hours worked and penalty wages. Penalty rates were designed to limit hours of work or times of work by making the employer decide whether the extra hours were worth the higher labour costs. Employers often traded these restrictions for a higher base pay—usually 2%. These were "equalisation payments" which were used to "wean" workers from their existing conditions.[48]

A four-day work week quickly became standard in the hotel industry as a trade-off for a 5% wage increase.[49] Such an exchange was attractive to workers who saw penalty rates only as a way of increasing take-home pay, rather than as a way to prevent overwork. Making a trade allowed employers to see themselves as being fair and certainly not as brutal as the law permitted them to be. As more employers made these changes, it was easier to excuse these actions as necessary to compete in the new economic environment.

Whatever the intention, workers lost pay as a result of these trade-offs. Penalty wages had come to make up such a large percentage of wages that even very large increases in base pay in lieu of lost penalty pay resulted in a lower weekly income. From 1991 to 1993, there was a 40% reduction in hours paid as overtime for all employees and a corresponding increase in hours paid as regular time. Even penal rates could be apples and oranges. Sometimes penal rates remained but were lower than before the ECA.[50]

These changes occurred so quickly and so dramatically altered the way pay was earned that it was difficult to calculate their impact. The Department of Labour, for example, studied only base pay rates rather than the total take-home wage and found that pay had increased in the ECA's first year. For workers who tended to receive large portions of their pay from penalty rates, this missed the impact these changes had on workers:

> Hourly rates are going up, but income is going down. We may be getting a 2 to 5% pay increase, but there was one in Wanganui where workers sold off their time and half and double time and received an extra dollar an hour to do that. So for them initially it looked like another $40 a week. But at $8 a hour, they would not have to work very much overtime in order to recoup that, and they are now working a lot more overtime. So the actual income for hours worked has gone down. Overtime used to be calculated on a daily basis, not just on a weekly wage, and in many instances it's now back to just a straight 40-hour week. You get paid overtime after you've done 40 hours, but you might do 40 hours in four 10-hours slots in which case your income would be lesser because under the old system you would have been paid overtime for the hours each day.[51]

Cutting penalty rates, even if there was a rise in base rates, could result in substantially reduced labour costs.[52]

This was the environment which the SWU faced as it began to negotiate in the ECA environment. Nonetheless, the SWU had some important successes in its first year, even against powerful employers. Two months after the ECA was enacted, in July 1991, Kentucky Fried Chicken offered two-tiered IECs which reduced new hires' pay by more than a dollar an hour and lowered their weekend penal rates. The SWU responded with radio advertisements telling members not to sign the IECs. It also asked Labour MPs and community leaders to make public statements and to put pressure on KFC. KFC soon withdrew its contracts, began to negotiate with the union, and eventually agreed to a CEC. The August 9 CEC was a victory, but it contained the standard formula of trading a small wage increase for reduced weekend penal rates and inflicting the pain on new hires.[53]

Other agreements came closer to being successes. In November 1991, the SWU negotiated a one-year CEC for Pizza Hut workers with a 2% raise, no concessions, and an agreement to discuss a new wage structure based on training and competency.[54] In February 1992, it reached a multi-employer agreement with all major companies in the commercial cleaning industry, an agreement that preserved some features of the award system. However, it preserved current hourly rates only by cutting weekend penal rates to time and a quarter for the first year and then ending them in 1993. The SWU said that this would affect few cleaners since they mainly worked weekdays only.[55] It also reached a multi-employer agreement with the seven employers who employed two-thirds of the workers in the security industry. The CEC abolished penal rates only for Saturday morning.[56]

In March 1992, McDonald's signed a two-tiered CEC covering 4000 employees in 54 restaurants. The union traded a 2% pay rise on a base rate of $7.55 for no weekend penal rates for new hires only.[57] This was followed by a series of concessionary contracts. In one, the parties agreed that personal grievances would be heard by company-paid arbitrators rather than the Employment Tribunal.[58]

The positives of these resolutions existed as islands in a sea of troubles. By August 1991, it was clear that the Tearooms and Restaurants Award would not be replaced and that all SWU members not employed by McDonald's, Kentucky Fried Chicken, and contract caterers would be on IECs.[59] In April 1992, the Salvation Army proposed a 10% base pay rise but with an effective 27% pay cut from lost penal rates, leave and other benefits.[60] In February 1995, McDonald's announced it no longer wanted CECs. Three weeks later, after refusing to deal with the SWU, all of McDonald's 5000 workers were on IECs.[61]

As 1991 wore on, the SWU tried more confrontational tactics. On December 18, the union protested Lion Nathan's attempts to cut Hancock Hotel workers' wages while the parent company had a $71 million profit. It picketed Lion Nathan's general meeting, while outside a member dressed in a lion suit handed out pamphlets condemning the company. Hancock said that prices at its restaurants had already been reduced because it was certain pay would be cut. The SWU urged Hancock workers not to sign because those who regularly worked Saturdays would be 6% worse off and those who worked weekends would earn 16% less.[62]

In June 1992, the SWU rejected a multi-employer CEC offered by the Hotel Association that provided for a flat rate of $8.25 with no penal rates. The Hotel Association argued that the contract reflected "the harsh economic reality and the state of the industry." In the end, the SWU gave up trying to hold a multi-employer agreement together and decided to try to negotiate CECs with individual employers. Employers began hiring new workers at $6.80 and then discharging them at the end of their three-month trial period. While employed, the new hires were given the preferred shifts as a way to persuade workers to negotiate away their award conditions. By October 1992, this influx of inexperienced, very low-waged workers meant that wages in the hotel industry had plummeted, from the old award minimum of $8.49 an hour to an average of $7.00.

The NZEF said that the drop in wages did not mean that employers were being harsh. Instead it was the inevitable result of a weak economy and businesses' need to remain viable.[63] Furthermore, the NZEF contended, workers who felt exploited could seek legal redress. The Labour Inspectorate manager, however, said many workers did not know government assistance was available or were "far more keen to hold on to their jobs, whatever the level of apparent exploitation."[64]

Section 57 forbids harsh and oppressive behaviour, undue influence and duress in procuring an employment contract. The difficult question is what conduct these terms forbid. To interpret them, it is necessary to consider the real and ideological context in which the ECA was enacted. NZBR economist Penelope Brook had argued that employment contracts should not be set aside as being harsh, unconscionable or unjust. Brook was influenced by American torts and contracts professor Richard Epstein, who would limit only contracts made using force or fraud or which take advantage of the "young, feeble-minded, and the insane." They argue that duress does not include economic duress. Rather, it is economic constraint and economic consequences that make the system work. Protecting people from the natural results of their choices restrains their freedom of choice.[65] Accordingly, s 57 does not hinder people from using whatever bargaining power they have.

The ECA was enacted in the midst of serious economic trouble. High unemployment meant that many workers were vulnerable to coercion, particularly long-term workers with either low skills or only firm-specific skills. These were the sort of workers who came before the Employment Court claiming to have signed their IECs under duress from their employer, Alliance Textiles:

> [M]any of the people who signed the contract first and who subsequently came to court and gave evidence in support of the employer position in the court were people who had had experience of being made redundant from two and three jobs, three times from that plant in the past when it had been owned by other owners. So they had worked there, been made redundant, suffered periods of unemployment of up to ten months in some cases, hadn't been able to find any other work and had been rehired in the Mosgiel plant only to then be nitpicked by the last-on first-off rule when the next round of redundancies came around.

And something that was very important to those workers was the fact that the redundancy rules were changed under the new contract where the employer had 100% right to select who went and who stayed in the event of any company restructuring or downsizing or redundancy. So those people frankly said, in the case, that they had signed the contract because they thought that if they worked hard and showed willing, then their employment would be protected and assured in the future and that the union couldn't do that for them, that the union hadn't done it for them in the past, and the union wouldn't be able to do it for them in the future. And there is a certain kind of sad logic in that.[66]

Parliament believed that nothing about the normal employer–employee relationship is an impediment to bargaining. There is no reason to believe that Parliament was unaware of the employee's normal dependence on and subservience to the employer and the employer's control of the workplace. This subservience can mean that employees are afraid to negotiate individually with their employers. The Public Service Association (PSA) decided to push the government, to face the expense and inefficiency of negotiating on an individual basis with all its employees. The PSA proposed to members that they negotiate IECs one by one, working through the entire workplace:

> Yes, we would bargain on one [individual contract] until we got it right. Then we would go on to the next one. That was really an attempt to persuade the employer that they either saw us seven hundred times or they saw us once. What we couldn't find was a person willing to do that. And I think what you've got there is an element of fear.
> ... We couldn't find one person who wanted to be at the front.[67]

Worker fear meant that the union was never able to put this strategy into action.

Key to defining illegal duress must be the employment relationship Parliament knew would affect negotiations. When the ECA was enacted, New Zealand was in a severe economic crisis with high unemployment. Parliament must have known that this would give most employers more power in bargaining with individual workers. Parliament must also not have intended to define the normal employment relationship as illegal duress. As a result of what was the norm at the time the ECA was enacted, an employee has a heavy burden to prove illegal coercion. The Employment Court agreed:

> Many people who enter into contracts are under some pressure to do so arising from a need, real or perceived, to enter into the particular contract or from an irresistible desire to do so. . . . Usually where parties enter into contracts with their eyes open as to the consequences of doing so and conscious of their right to refuse there is not only no reason for the courts to intervene but it would be wrong for them to do so.[68]

Judge Palmer pointed out that the ECA allows employers to negotiate contracts directly with their employees; thus it contemplated each side would seek its own advantage.[69] This means that the employer and employee must be prepared to use every weapon available. The ECA offers nothing to protect parties if they refuse to use the power they have or if, when they use it, they are unsuccessful.

Even if a worker can prove a violation of s 57 its coverage is so limited as to be of little practical use. Section 57 only applies if a contract comes into existence as a result of coercive conduct. If a worker is treated harshly but holds out and does not agree to a contract, there is no violation.

Even more fundamental, Parliament and the Brook and Epstein models failed to take into account the substantial protections custom, government regulations and laws provide employers, particularly those who are incorporated. Laws on limited liability and corporate ownership mean that those who make the decisions need not suffer the full consequences of their decisions. Even if the corporation loses money, this may not be reflected in the pockets of its managers. As a result corporate managers can afford to be ruthless and may even be rewarded for having the courage to make hard decisions. No law shields workers from bearing the full burden of any decisions they make.

Of all the unions in New Zealand, the SWU was one whose members were least likely to have much in the way of economic weapons to use against their employers and the most vulnerable to adverse consequences. For example, the Social Welfare Department denied unemployment benefits to a rest-home worker for two and one-half months after her employer locked her out for refusing to accept a pay cut. The worker described the impact this had on her ability to negotiate: "If I didn't have relatives here and, if the Housing Corp hadn't been so good, I would have probably gone back to work and accepted the lower conditions. There wouldn't have been anything else I could have done."[70] This was just economic coercion, a core part of the ECA.

Exploitation was greatest for young workers:

> A delicatessen had a practice of taking on students, offering $4 an hour. After three or four weeks, when they asked for wages, they would be told they were on trial so would not be paid. Then they would be paid for two or three weeks and sacked, while more students were taken on trial.[71]

Wages were a major target of employers but so too was gaining unilateral control over working conditions. One contract provided that employment was "hour to hour" as long as the company had work, but with a minimum of forty-four hours a week expected from employees. In exchange, no statutorily required payments were to be paid, since, according to the contract, they were included in the rate of $8.00 an hour for a painter's labourer.[72]

Even contracts that were more benign nevertheless gave employers unilateral control. The Hospitality Association of New Zealand created a ten-page standard industry document complete with three pages at the end for employee signatures. The only place for a variation of terms is the wages and qualifications provision. Section 12.1 gives the employer the right to vary rules and policies unilaterally.

As workers lost ground, so too did the union. The SWU lost approximately 30% of its members in the first year after the enactment of the ECA. Although grim, it was not as bad as the SWU's worst-case scenario. That the loss was lower than expected was due to several factors. First, the severely depressed New Zealand economy and workers' feelings of insecurity made people nervous about their jobs. Aggressive employer tactics frightened these people into staying with the union for protection. Second, staff turnover was lower than normal, so the union did not have to organise new workers.[73]

At its fifth anniversary, the June 1996 *Service Worker* portrays a union experiencing mixed successes. A few court decisions favourable to unions prevented one hotel from being able to use direct approaches to union members to sign the company's contract. This helped the union achieve an offer of a 4% pay rise.[74] On the other hand, the Quality Hotel chain had profits during 1993–1995 of $9 million, $18 million, and $21 million, was increasing directors' fees by 21% to $165,000, but paid workers an increase of only 2.5% in October 1995 and 1% in January 1996.[75] On one page, workers were gaining their first raises under CECs since the ECA was enacted. On the next page were workers with no raises, cuts in pay, increased work, and job insecurity.

Worse could have been expected of the SWU, especially when it had to deal with employers who could use IECs and CECs to play workers off against one another and as long as there were no real limits to the coercion employers could exert.

Notes
1. Raymond Harbridge & Kevin Hince, *A Sourcebook of New Zealand Trade Unions and Employee Organisations*, 67 (1994); Sarah Oxenbridge, "Organising the Secondary Labour Force" in *The New Zealand Experience, Proceedings of 9th AIRAANZ Conference*, 347, 350 (Larry Sonder, ed., 1995); Roth, "Chronicle," 16 N.Z. J. Ind. Rel., 207 (1991).
2. Mark Gosche, "The Impact of Enterprise Bargaining on New Zealand Workers" in *Enterprise Bargaining: Experiences from New Zealand Workplaces: Papers from a Conference Organized by ACIRRT*, 36, 37 (University of Sydney, Australian Centre for Industrial Relations Research and Teaching, 1993).
3. Ian Wearing, "Labour Relations in the Tourist Industry in Sustaining Economic Reform," 113, 113–15 (NZBR, ed. 1990).
4. Interview with Rick Barker, National Secretary, Service Workers

Federation of Aotearoa, in Wellington (May 14, 1992).
5. Sarah Oxenbridge, "New Zealand Unions and the Organization of the Low-wage Service Sector" (AFL-CIO/Cornell Organizing Research Conference, Washington, DC, Mar.31–Apr.2, 1996); Sarah Oxenbridge, "Organising in the Service Sector: New Zealand Unions Since the Employment Contracts Act" (Unionism in Australia and New Zealand: Roads to Recovery Conference, University of Queensland, Brisbane Sept. 18, 1995); Oxenbridge, "Organizing the Secondary Labour Force," 351.
6. "160,000 on Individual Contracts from 1 July," *PSA Journal*, June, 1992, at 1.
7. ECA s 19.
8. ECA s 20.
9. ECA s 2.
10. ECA s 2.
11. *NZ Public Service Assn Inc. v. Designpower NZ Ltd* [1992] 1 ERNZ 669, 682, 684.
12. Peter Conway, "National's Blitz: Labour Market Reform," 11/12 *Race Gender Class*, 2, 7 (1991).
13. John Deeks, et al., *Labour and Employment Relations in New Zealand*, 518–19 (2d ed., 1994).
14. John Savage, "What Do We Know About the Economic Impacts of the ECA?" 14 (May 15, 1996).
15. Clive Gilson & Terry Wagar, "Employee Involvement and Human Resource Management in Australian, New Zealand and Canadian Organisations," 14 (June 1996).
16. ECA s 20(1).
17. ECA s 19(2).
18. Ian McAndrew, "From Regulation to Deregulation in New Zealand Labour Relations: New Models of Bargaining Under the Employment Contracts Act 1991," 6, 9–10, 12 (Jan. 5, 1993).
19. Interview with Francis Wevers, Consultant, in Wellington (May 20, 1992).
20. Peter Conway, "Stayin' Alive," *Political Review*, 8, 10 (Jul.–Aug. 1993); Mark Gosche, 38.
21. "Honda Aims for Company Union," *M&C Workers News*, Mar. 1996, at 5.
22. Raymond Harbridge & Anthony Honeybone, "The Employment Contracts Act and Collective Bargaining Patterns: A Review of the 1994/95 Year" in *Employment Contracts: Bargaining Trends & Employment Law Update 1994/95*, 8 (Raymond Harbridge & Peter Kiely, eds. 1995).
23. Raymond Harbridge, "External Legitimacy of Unions: Trends in New Zealand," 17 J. Lab. Res., 425, 438 (1996).
24. Barker.
25. Georgina Bailey, "Three-Way Trap Catches Workers," *Evening Post*, Oct. 27, 1992, at 5.

26. George Mark, Principal Industrial Advisor, New Zealand Aluminium Smelters, Address to the NZEF, 2 (May 13, 1992); Patricia Herbert, "Democracy Versus Fringe Benefits," *Dominion*, Nov. 28, 1991, at 6; Roger Kerr, "Bargaining Under the Employment Contracts Act," Empl. L. Bull., 97 (Sept. 1995); "ACTU Wins Battle Against Comalco," *Labour Notes*, Dec. 1995, at 8.
27. Owen Johnstone, "Tiwai—A Case in Point," *Metal*, Dec./Jan. 1991/2, at 6.
28. Mark, 3, 4, 6.
29. *Id.*, 7.
30. *Id.*, 9.
31. Herbert, "Democracy."
32. *Id.*
33. Johnstone.
34. Interview with Hel Loader, Research Advocate, New Zealand Engineering Union, in Wellington (May 13, 1992); see also Edmund Byrne, *Work, Inc.: A Philosophical Inquiry*, 128 (1990).
35. Interview with Suze Wilson, Organiser, Engineers Union, in Wellington (June 15, 1996).
36. Herbert, "Democracy."
37. "Individual contracts—Not Negotiable!" *Local Body Language*, 6 (Mar. 1995).
38. Bruce Mackinnon, "The Struggle for Managerial Prerogative: Ramifications of the CRA Weipa Dispute" in *Proceedings of 1996 AIRAANZ Annual Meeting*, 287, 288 (1996); Nikki Tait, "Australian Firm Rewrites Labor Rules: Mining Group Replaces Union Negotiations with Individual Staff Contracts," *Financial Post*, Oct. 5, 1995, at 58; Nikki Tait, "Mining a Seam of Controversy—CRA's Approach to Hierarchy and Pay Upset Australia's Highly Politicised Industrial Relations," *Financial Times*, Sept. 29, 1995, at 13.
39. Barker.
40. ECA s 19(5), (6).
41. Debbie Peterson, "Secondary School Students in Paid Work" in *Labour, Employment and Work in New Zealand 1994*, 189, 193–94 (Philip S. Morrison, ed., 1994).
42. Barker; Gosche, 45.
43. Bailey.
44. Barker.
45. W. Rosenberg, *New Zealand Can Be Different and Better: Why Deregulation Does Not Work*, 80–81 (1993); Peter Linzer, "The Decline of Assent: At-Will Employment as a Case Study of the Breakdown of Private Law Theory," 20 Ga. L. Rev., 323, 392–93 (1986).
46. "Individual contracts—Not Negotiable!" *Local Body Language*, 6, 7 (Mar. 1995).

47. Barker.
48. Michael Quigg, "Employment Act Revisited," *Manufacturer*, 9 (Aug. 1992).
49. Raymond Harbridge, "New Zealand's Collective Employment Contracts: Update November 1992," 18 N.Z. J. Ind. Rel., 113, 121 (1993).
50. Janet Hector, Jon Hemming & Mary Hubble, "Industrial Relations Bargaining in the Retail Non-food Sector: 1991–1992," 18 N.Z. J. Ind. Rel., 326, 334 (1993); Barker.
51. Interview with Maxine Gay, Organiser, Public Service Association, Palmerston North, May 17, 1992; Alex Bruce, "The Employment Contracts Act—Good News for Women Workers, Not!!!" *Broadsheet*, 26 (Summer 1993).
52. Ken Johnson, "Private Hospitals Face Closure," *Nursing NZ*, 25, 27 (Apr. 1994).
53. Roth, "Chronicle," 16 N.Z. J. Ind. Rel., 318, 320 (1991); Barker.
54. Roth, "Chronicle," 17 N.Z. J. Ind. Rel., 120 (1992).
55. *Id.*, 128.
56. *Id.*, 251–52.
57. *Id.*, 248.
58. "Back to the Future," *Labour Notes*, Mar. 1995, at 2.
59. Rebecca Macfie, "CTU Leads Last Ditch Award Fight," *National Business Review*, Aug. 29, 1991, at 2.
60. Roth, "Chronicle," 17 N.Z. J. Ind. Rel., 252 (1992).
61. N.Z.P.D. 6436 (Mar. 22, 1995); "Big Mac Puts the Bite on Staff," *Labour Notes*, Mar. 1995, at 1.
62. "Lion Wage Protest," *Dominion*, Dec. 19, 1991, at 16; Roth, "Chronicle," 17 N.Z. J. Ind. Rel., 123–24 (1992).
63. Bailey; Roth, "Chronicle," 17 N.Z. J. Ind. Rel., 247, 258 (1992).
64. Bailey.
65. Penelope Brook, *Freedom at Work*, 103, 104 (1990); Richard Epstein, "In Defense of the Contract at Will," 51 U. Chi. L. Rev., 947, 955 (1984).
66. Interview with Robyn Haultain, Lawyer, Wellington, May 19, 1992.
67. Interview with Joris de Bres, Public Service Association Central Operations Manager, in Wellington (May 7, 1992).
68. [1992] 1 ERNZ 982, 1039.
69. *Id.*, 1083–85.
70. Jason Barber, "Locked-Out Worker 10 Weeks Without Dole," *Dominion Sunday-Times*, Oct. 20, 1991, at 3.
71. Bailey.
72. "'Model' Contracts That Don't Hit the Headlines," *PSA Journal*, Mar. 1992, at 8.
73. Barker; Raymond Harbridge, "Collective Employment Contracts: A Content Analysis" in *Employment Contracts: New Zealand Experiences*, 70 (Raymond Harbridge, ed., 1993); Raymond

Harbridge, "Bargaining and the Employment Contracts Act: An Overview" in *id.*, 31.
74. "Hyatt Staff Settle on 4%," *Service Worker*, 1 (June 1996).
75. "Quality Hotels Drags Heels on Promised Grading Review," *Service Worker*, 1 (June 1996).

15

Impasse and Partial Lockouts

ALL INDUSTRIAL RELATIONS SYSTEMS MUST HAVE SOME WAY TO DEAL with bargaining deadlocks. Some may tolerate them and simply rely on the parties to break them, while others may intervene to end the impasse quickly. Some may have formal procedures, while others have mere customary practices. The second is not what we usually think of as impasse procedures, but it is still a method of dealing with impasse. The absence of a statutory impasse procedure does not mean that none exists. Deciding to provide no assistance to the parties to resolve a stalemate, as is the case with the ECA, is just one of many ways of dealing with impasse.

Different consequences, however, flow from choosing different systems—in particular, a system with a written process as opposed to one with an unwritten, informal procedure. The ECA's drafters did not mandate how bargaining impasses should be resolved, because they wanted to let the market and the parties determine the outcome. The problem with giving no guidance was that it simply made the courts responsible for resolving questions that arose in connection with impasses.

Impasse resolution caused unions serious suffering. Within the first four years of the ECA, the Employment Court went through wide swings in its interpretation. Most damaging to unions and workers, within the ECA's first year and for several years thereafter, the court held that impasses were to be resolved by letting employers impose the terms they wanted. The court has since swung away from this interpretation, but having this be the method for resolving impasses in the first formative years of the ECA took its toll on unions.

Allowing employers to impose their terms did not occur immediately. At first, the Employment Court held that employers could not change the pay and working conditions in an IEC unless the worker agreed to the changes.[1] This was a relief to unions and workers who had feared that employers would impose their terms once the ECA was enacted. Murray French of the Wellington Employers Association blamed opponents of the ECA for these beliefs:

> The problem that we encountered was that the opponents of the Act very much created an environment where it was suggested that employers would be doing all sorts of horrible things to employees, simply taking conditions off them, unilaterally reducing wage rates, the whole lot. Now, unfortunately, that created some misconceptions out there in terms of what employers could actually do and the more hard-nosed employers sometimes believed that propaganda and in some cases they were as much a problem to us as they were to the employees that they employed. Quite simply because they believed what they were reading in the newspapers and therefore acted accordingly.[2]

Bill Birch applauded the Employment Court decision, because, he said, the government had not intended that employment contracts could be changed unilaterally.[3] After this case unions had a brief burst of confidence that workers could not be forced to sign inferior contracts.[4] John Hughes of the University of Canterbury pointed out that these reactions were "a sad reminder of just how far away from anything approaching a balance in bargaining the new legislation has led us" and that the decision "simply asserted a fundamental principle of contract law."[5]

During this early period, the court solidly supported the invulnerability of IECs from attack.[6] The problem was that, although the decisions might follow normal contract law, they failed to address employer desires for changed conditions. Employers grew frustrated because they believed that the economic and legal conditions meant they could have the upper hand in bargaining. Thus, employers who wanted changes had several options: they could bargain; they could leave workers on IECs and let terms stay in status quo; they could terminate recalcitrant employees and replace them with new ones willing to agree to the employer's terms; they could use the mix of carrots and sticks that Alliance Textiles and Tiwai Point had found effective; or they could press the courts to interpret the law in a way that let employers set the terms.

Each of these potentially had negative consequences for employers, depending on the skill level of their current workers, the strength of the employer's desire for new terms, the employer's ability to litigate to create new precedent, or the employer's willingness to let workers and unions co-determine workplace conditions. Most employers apparently wanted a system that let them keep their current employees but on different terms and with a minimum of force. This meant that employers continued to press the court to let the employer change employment terms unilaterally.[7]

The court began sending strong signals that it was sympathetic to the employers' arguments and problems. Decisions hinted that the court was having difficulty reconciling employees' right to refuse to change their employment conditions with employers' claims of economic necessity.[8] The more employers pressed the court, the more the court was faced with a dilemma and no clear way to resolve it. All the statute said was that, once impasse occurred, there was no way to resolve it other than agreement, strike or lockout—and these were not appealing for either employers or employees. Employers had been promised that the ECA would remove conflict as it removed unions. It was therefore hard to understand the reality of irresolvable conflict.

Stalemate demonstrated a flaw in ECA theory, since it revealed that conflict still existed. Stalemate interfered with the idea of promoting an efficient labour market, since it insulated employees from market forces. Absolute freedom of choice for one party meant none for the other, unless both agreed, and conflict showed they were not agreeing. When they disagreed, there was no way to reconcile their rights. All these conflicting theoretical and practical issues put pressure on the judges to find a way through the morass created by Parliament.

Within one year, employees' rights to remain on IECs were interpreted away. At first, the court refused to let employers unilaterally change employment terms, either explicitly or by ignoring them.[9] The Court was firm in rejecting employers' claims of economic necessity.

> Such an approach, if accepted, would enable almost any contractual obligation to be evaded. . . . By and large, however, the time for the exercise of the management prerogative is when entering into employment contracts and not at the time of their performance. If an obligation has been assumed then it must be discharged and a party to an employment contract which fails to discharge an obligation is always at risk of being ordered to comply with the contract. It is quite fallacious to regard some obligations under an employment contract (for example, to pay wages) as being important and others . . . as being in some way subsidiary and requiring to be complied with only if the party on whom the obligation rests sees fit. The cardinal rule is that employment contracts create enforceable rights and obligations and it is not for the Court or the Tribunal to decide which obligations should be enforced and which need not be; the parties have already decided that for themselves by entering into the contract, and it is not open to the Tribunal to exempt any party from the obligations assumed.[10]

The court explicitly rejected arguments that an employer had "wider responsibilities."

> If by that he meant wider than its contractual obligations and so wide as to relieve the respondent from performing those obligations, I must firmly reject that submission out of hand as being without foundation in law or reason. As I indicated in the course of argument, the fact that the respondent could make a large saving by altering the contractual environment did not authorise it to do so any more than a similar consideration would authorise it to stop paying its taxes or its rates.[11]

This outcome was compelled by common law contract doctrine as well as ECA s 43, which protected sanctity of contract. ECA supporters attacked the court for deciding that employers were held to the bargains they had made. One employer argued that protecting sanctity of contract when the parties reached impasse was wrong, because "the ruling, if unchallenged, would allow workers' terms and conditions to survive indefinitely in conflict with the employer's desire to rearrange its business more effectively."[12] The NZEF blasted the court's decision as "retrograde" and continuing "the old rigidities" of prior law.[13]

The irony was that s 43 was only included in the ECA because the same groups which now complained about it had been demanding sanctity of labour contract terms for at least a decade. The NZBR had argued that prior law was defective because it lacked such a provision and that this omission was "a major reason why unions are encouraged to behave irresponsibly, why the relationship between unions and employers often becomes sour and confrontational, and why the opportunities for productivity-enhancing cooperative behaviour are severely restricted." It continued:

> One of the employers' most common complaints concerns (the absence of) sanctity of agreement. Agreements have come to be broken with impunity, sometimes because the cost of insisting on adherence is greater than the immediately discernible benefits of preventing the erosion of legally acceptable behaviour. What gradually develops is the industrial habits of the swamp. Agreements should have the standing of contracts. If one party breaches the contract the other party should have access to remedies within the law. It should also be the basic responsibility of the parties to a contract to ensure it is enforced.[14]

As the ECA's enactment drew near, however, the NZEF realised that impasse could be a problem. It proposed resolving impasses by letting employers establish terms of employment unilaterally.[15] In fact, their concern was well-founded. The post-ECA reality was that many employers were having difficulty convincing their employees that the employer's terms were in everyone's best interest. The only alternative to remaining at impasse for ever seemed to be to let employers impose terms unilaterally. At least this would allow economic change to flow quickly—if not efficiently, as economists use the term—through the economy.

The problem with this was that the NZEF could not erase what it had earlier argued with regard to sanctity of contract. It had been very clear in arguing that labour agreements "should be contractual. This would give them greater sanctity because the parties would be bound by agreements which they themselves had fashioned and had to enforce."[16] If an employer can decree workplace terms, this would not only conflict with sanctity of contract, it would undermine the ECA's premise that contract terms be set by market forces through party negotiations.[17] It would also make sanctity of contract a nullity, violate free market ideology, and undercut claims that employers and employees could peaceably resolve workplace terms without intervention. Allowing employers to impose their terms was not a happy solution.

Impasses meant that, if there was a labour market, it was more complex than ECA theory had envisioned. Employees did not seem to realise that their interests were one with their employers. Employers did not seem able to bring themselves to share information so a win–win solution could be reached. Where employers had employees they deemed to be overpaid and who would not agree to the rate of pay their employers offered them, the employers should have terminated the relationship and retained new workers willing to accept the offered rate. Employers should have been bidding against each other for workers.[18] None of this happened.

Economic and social factors showed that the reality of the employment relationship was far more complex than the rudimentary version of economics described by ECA proponents.[19]

> The theory relies on crude and irrelevant hypotheses about the employment relationship, which have been rejected by recent theories of capital–labor relations. Labor market flexibility is optimal for employment and welfare only if labor can be assimilated to its services and if labor is hired in a spot market where no adverse selection problems occur or commitment and loyalty issues are at stake. By contrast, when we recognize the separation of contracting labor from its actual utilization, the long-term character of most modern employment relationships, and the key importance of work effort and loyalty to the firm,

then the basic neoclassical model collapses. New and more sophisticated models provide evidence of numerous contradictory effects that the impact of employment security can no longer be assessed on a priori grounds.[20]

The ECA, unfortunately, was drafted according to these "crude and irrelevant hypotheses" and thus provided the court with no guidance for resolving conflicts. When employers argued ever more vigorously that they should have the right to control the workplace because of economic exigency, this created an intellectual and practical conflict which profoundly troubled the Employment Court. A new trend became visible, a trend towards giving employers absolute control over their businesses.

The key to overturning employees' rights to remain indefinitely on IECs and to giving employers the right to unilaterally modify IECs was to expand the interpretation of ECA provisions on lockouts involving CECs. Section 64 defines as lawful a lockout if it "relates to the negotiation of a collective employment contract for the employees concerned." ECA s 62 defines as a lockout either an employer's discontinuing employees' employment wholly or partially or breaking some or all of the employment contracts to compel compliance.

In *Prendergast II*[21] when negotiations broke down, the employer wrote the employees that negotiations for a CEC were at an impasse and that it would no longer observe the terms of their IECs on the deadlocked issues. The employer stated that the company's "breach" of the IECs' terms would continue until employees agreed to the terms and that it expected its workers to perform their work as usual, except for these changes.[22]

The union charged that this was an unlawful lockout and a breach of the workers' contracts.[23] The unions could not have asked for a more favourable set of circumstances in this case. The employer's actions were blatant and in defiance of an earlier court decision, so it could be found in contempt. Instead of finding a violation or contempt, the court held that the company had not breached the worker's contracts and that this was actually a legal lockout. This was a lockout that involved the breaking of some or all of the employment contracts with the purpose of compelling the employees to accept the employer's proposed terms or demands in relation to the negotiation of a CEC for the employees concerned. Thus, it did not violate the law.[24] This was not a unilateral alteration of IECs, because now the employer's purpose was not just to alter the IECs but to consummate a CEC.[25]

On January 15, 1992, the Employment Court issued *Paul v. New Zealand Society for the Intellectually Handicapped (IHC)*.[26] IHC told its employees it was cutting their wages by a third, not as a unilateral change but as a lockout from some contract terms. Even though their wages were being cut, IHC told its employees that they must continue "to perform all the work specified in your Contract of Employment. . . . The action by IHC as your employer in breaching some of your terms of employment is taken with the view to having you accept employment on the foregoing terms."[27] From the employees' point of view, everything about their work remained the same. The only change was that their pay had been cut—and cut substantially. Plaintiff Evelyn Paul's pay was reduced from $30,555 to $20,650.

The logic of the partial lockout was fragile. If an employer breached a contract by imposing new terms, it violated the ECA.[28] If the employer breached a contract by imposing new terms because the employer said it wanted the workers to accept the changes, the employer did not violate the ECA; the cuts were transformed into a lawful partial lockout.[29] In each case, the breach of contract and the employer's demands were identical. The crucial difference was what the employer intended. In the former case, workers can enforce the original contract terms. In the latter, they have no such right. An employer who can make changes this way has no incentive to end a partial lockout, especially since the ECA places no onus on an employer who refuses to bargain. As a result, once imposed, a partial lockout could last a very long time indeed.

Judge Colgan explained that partial lockouts were necessary because there was no other way to resolve a situation when one party would not agree to the other side's terms. "Such a proposition does not permit of any legitimate attempt to vary a contract of employment and could, if taken to its logical conclusion, mean that either an employer or its employees could indefinitely frustrate the other from ever being able to move from the existing terms and conditions of an inherited employment relationship."³⁰ When pressed, the judges were hard put to explain why the courts should give this power to an employer who had made an offer its workers did not find attractive. Judge Castle stated: "[T]he only relevant issue is whether negotiations are in fact being conducted, not quality or bargaining strength of them or the parties. The allegation that IHC has been unreasonable or inflexible, if found to be so, is therefore of no avail to the [union]."³¹

Rudd Watts & Stone, a firm of barristers and solicitors, advised clients that these cases likely meant that an employee could not respond to a partial lockout by refusing to work, unless a legal strike could be taken, because this would then allow the employer to cancel the employee's contract. The employer would then be free to replace the employee with a new employee under a new IEC. "This highlights a difference in rights reserved to employers under the Act as compared to the corresponding rights of an employee. An employer may suspend employees on strike— that is, to effectively suspend the operation of the employer's obligations to the employees. However, an employee subjected to a lawful lockout may not suspend the employee's obligations to the employer."³²

Trade unionists criticised these cases and the court's holdings as evidence that the ECA's purpose was to give employers unilateral control over employment conditions. Anne Knowles of the NZEF claimed that the doctrine was but a simple and limited endorsement of the rights of strike and lockout under the ECA.³³ Labour relations reporter Rebecca Macfie savaged the court's treatment of the issue:

> Any employer looking for concessions in wage bargaining from his workforce should be swotting up on the Employment Court's decision on the recent IHC dispute with the Community Services Union. It's a step by step guide to how to enforce immediate pay cuts on an unwilling workforce without falling foul of the law.
>
> All he needs to do is follow the protocols established in the IHC case:

- First, ensure the collective employment contract with his workers has expired.
- Tell his workers that he wants a new collective contract(s), listing the changed conditions he wants included in that new contract.
- When the workers resist the proposals in negotiations, notify them the changes will be imposed on them regardless, being careful to specify that this measure takes the form of a lockout under section 62 of the Act, and that the lockout action is taken with the intention of compelling them to accept the proposed new terms of employment.
- Let them know they are expected to front up for normal work regardless of the lockout. (Remember, a lockout doesn't necessarily involve literally locking the factory gates. As the IHC case shows, non-observance of selected provisions of workers' contracts can constitute a lockout.)

Voilà! Immediate cost savings have been achieved without having to laboriously extract agreement from an intransigent union.

True, having taken this course of action the employer does not yet have a new contract with his workers, but the terms and conditions he was seeking are in place, and there is no compulsion to end the state of lockout.[34]

It is no exaggeration to say that making this tactic legal transformed the ECA into a non-bargaining regime. Indeed, a study of bargaining outcomes and behaviour during this period confirmed Macfie's observations. It found that in non-union workplaces (the majority situation), no bargaining was taking place, regardless of the form of contract.[35]

Michael Quigg, an employment lawyer, included as negative effects of the ECA:

- a greater exposure of the lower paid, less articulate workers to abuse, particularly where employed in isolated positions
- discord caused by the greater use of lockouts by employers, even against a single worker
- the long term effects on employers who unilaterally change

terms and conditions to the employees disadvantage
- the absence of any sunset provision on existing terms and conditions[36]

In each case that followed, the Employment Court rapidly expanded the partial lockout doctrine. In *Petricevich v. Transportation Auckland Corporation Ltd*,[37] the Northern Local Government Officers Union wanted a CEC for 154 salaried employees, while the employer wanted IECs. When the employer unilaterally changed the terms in employees' IECs, the court held that this was not an illegal modification of IECs but, rather, was a legal partial lockout, because one of the parties—here, the union—had been pursuing CECs. The court denied that it was permitting the employer to impose a new contract unilaterally:

> There can on the facts placed before me be no issue about that. The employer on the facts is clearly proposing to reduce its compliance with its obligations under the subsisting contracts. It proposes not to pay as it had before. It proposes no other interference with the terms of the present contracts. It does not propose to bring in any terms of any new contract.[38]

In other words, there was no new contract; the workers were simply working indefinitely under the terms that would have been in a new contract if the employer could have got its way.

The only difference between partial lockouts and breaches of contract was some connection with a CEC. Given the slim distinctions between IECs and CECs, a connection was usually not difficult to find. The only time there could be no possibility of a CEC—and thus no possibility of a legal lockout—would be if an employer imposed a partial lockout against a single employee. It was not long, however, before the court found itself upholding a partial lockout in precisely that situation.[39] When the employee refused to agree to the employer's proposed concessionary IEC, the employer notified him he would be locked out.[40] The notice of lockout came before the employee had even seen the contract. The employer next compiled all its separate IECs into a document which it called a "CEC which incorporated all IECs in its workplace".[41] Although there was no collective contract or bargaining at any point, the Court upheld the imposed terms since the "individual workers were made aware by management—and no doubt through discussion with each other—that their IECs essentially reflected the same terms and conditions which were to apply through the work force."[42]

To be lawful, a lockout must relate to "the negotiation of a collective employment contract." In *Hawtin v. Skellerup Industrial Ltd.* the court eliminated the need for negotiation.

> The phrase, within its particular context, "relates to the negotiation of a collective employment contract", enables an employer, I hold, to peremptorily and *without any prior process of negotiation* with its affected work force, to present an otherwise lawful collective employment contract to its particular employees and to uncompromisingly insist that unless they accept the collective contract terms within a prescribed time, they will then be locked out. Mr Weston [employer's counsel], I conclude, has correctly submitted that:
>
> > An employer . . . can, theoretically, set its bottom line as from day one. If that bottom line is not acceptable to the employees then it can lock them out.[43]

This was true even though it was "significantly removed from the primary meaning of ' negotiations', contemplating a process of 'conferring with another with a view to compromise or agreement'".[44]

The court took other routes to expand the employer's power to impose terms. Normally, the common law requires that a change in contract or a new contract have an exchange; that is, a trade that will induce the other party to agree to the contract. The thing exchanged is called "consideration." The court expanded the meaning of consideration by holding that the changed terms themselves might constitute such consideration, even though the changed terms "superficially appear to be one-sided." Although the court did not say so, it appeared willing to find that terms the employee had rejected as undesirable could be adequate consideration. Indeed, the court said, the court should find consideration where it could.[45]

After three years of expanding the doctrine of partial lockout, the Employment Court began to reverse itself. In early 1994, it held that a lockout was not lawful when there had been no negotiation.[46] In June 1994, the full Employment Court explicitly repudiated the partial lockout doctrine and its intellectual underpinnings.[47] It rejected as tortured logic that an employer's coercive motive can justify its unilateral variation of terms as a distinction that was "circular, unhelpful, and spurious."[48] The Court explained that, in New Zealand, it had always been understood that a lockout meant that an employer lost production but could withhold wages. The court reasoned: "We find it unthinkable that parliament ever intended that employers could withhold wages without suffering any halt in production."[49] The court said that partial lockouts violated natural justice and common law values so deeply held that even Parliament could not destroy them. To require employees to work under a partial lockout was to force the employees to become serfs instead of free people, making the more accurate term a "lock in."[50]

Although the court at last abandoned the partial lockout concept, it cannot undo the impact of those three crucial years when it was good law. Partial lockouts and other early court decisions led to an atmosphere in which employers have been willing to engage in "a combination of a new mood of daring and the eyeball-to-eyeball nature of bargaining under the ECA."[51] Equally worrying, the very pressures that led the court to create the partial lockout doctrine are still there. Impasses still occur and need to be resolved. Unless Parliament is willing to act, the court will find itself forced to approve other actions, including subcontracting work or threats to subcontract, that will have the same impact as partial lockouts.

Notes

1. *Lyn Grant v. Superstrike Bowling Centres Ltd.* [1992] 1 ERNZ 727; Diane Keenan, "Landmark Contracts Act Ruling Pleases CTU," *Press*, July 16, 1991, at 1.
2. Interview with Murray French, Wellington Regional Employers Association, in Wellington (May 14, 1992).
3. Rebecca Macfie, "Cook Strait Ferry Row Charts Way for Future," *National Business Review*, Sept. 13, 1991, at 15.

4. Keenan.
5. John Hughes, "Changing Contracts," *Indust. L. Bull.*, 74 (Nov. 1991).
6. *Northern Local Government Officers Union, Inc. v. Auckland City* [1992] 1 ERNZ 1109, 1123.
7. *New Zealand Resident Doctors Association v. Otago Area Health Board* [1991] 1 ERNZ 1206; *Northern Local Government Officers Union, Inc. v. Auckland City* [1992] 1 ERNZ 1109; *Beazley v. City of Auckland* [1992] 2 ERNZ 716, 721–22.
8. [1992] 1 ERNZ 727, 736.
9. *Prendergast v. Associated Stevedores* [1991] 1 ERNZ 737, 753; Rebecca Macfie, "Labour Court Stops Move to Dilute Work Contracts," *National Business Review*, July 31, 1991, at 12.
10. *Northern Local Government Officers Union, Inc. v. Auckland City* [1992] 1 ERNZ 1109, 1127–28; *Northern Distribution Union (Inc) v. 3 Guys Ltd* [1992] ERNZ 903, 921–22.
11. *NZ Merchant Service Guild Industrial Union of Workers, Inc. v. NZ Rail, Ltd.* [1991] 2 ERNZ 587, 601.
12. Keenan.
13. "Retrograde Decision Under Appeal," *Employer*, Sept. 1991, at 1; Anne Knowles, "Four Months Down the Track: Is the Employment Contracts Act Working?" *Examiner*, Sept. 5, 1991, at 19.
14. NZBR, "New Zealand Labour Market Reform: A Submission in Response to the Green Paper," 38 (Apr. 1986). (Parenthesis in the original.)
15. Rebecca Macfie, "Opinion," *National Business Review*, Sept. 20, 1991, at 8; NZEF, "Submission on the Employment Contracts Bill 1991," Part A, p.3 (Jan. 30, 1991).
16. "Employers Federation Submissions on Industrial Relations Green Paper," *Employer*, June 1985, at 3.
17. NZBR, Green Paper Submission, 40; "The Labour Relations Bill," *Employer*, April 1987, at 5.
18. Paul Weiler, *Governing the Workplace: The Future of Labor and Employment Law*, 125–26 (1990).
19. Christoph Beuchtmann, "Introduction: Employment Security and Labor Markets" in *Employment Security and Labor Market Behavior: Interdisciplinary Approaches and International Evidence*, 3, 47 (Christoph F. Beuchtmann, ed., 1993); Robert Boyer, "The Economics of Job Protection and Emerging New Capital–Labor Relations" in *id*.
20. Boyer, 117.
21. *Prendergast v. Associated Stevedores Ltd.* [1991] 2 ERNZ 728; Rebecca Macfie, "Watersiders Fail in Bid for Lockout Injunction," *National Business Review*, Sept. 6, 1991, at 3.
22. *Prendergast II*, 732.
23. *Prendergast II*, 732–33.

24. *Prendergast II*, 734, 741; ECA s 64(1)(b).
25. *Prendergast II*, 741.
26. [1992] 1 ERNZ 65; Jason Barber, "Employment Court Ruling Angers Unions," *Dominion*, Jan. 15, 1992, at 1.
27. [1992] 1 ERNZ 65, 67, 76–77 81–82; Jason Barber, "IHC Parties Plan Talks Under Threat of Action," *Dominion*, Dec. 5, 1991, at 9; Roth, "Chronicle," 17 N.Z. J. Ind. Rel., 123 (1992).
28. *Prendergast II*; *NZ Dairy Food and Textile Workers' Union v. Cavalier Bremworth, Ltd.* [1991] 2 ERNZ 519.
29. Roth, "Chronicle," 17 N.Z. J. Ind. Rel., 125 (1992).
30. *Hyndman v. Air New Zealand Ltd.* [1992] 1 ERNZ 820, 835.
31. [1992] 1 ERNZ 65, 85.
32. Rudd Watts & Stone, "Employment Law Letter," 2 (May 1992).
33. Rebecca Macfie, "Employers Exercise Muscle Under Contracts Act," *National Business Review*, Mar. 6, 1992, at 39.
34. Macfie, "Employers Exercise Muscle."
35. Ian McAndrew & Matt Ballard, "Negotiation and Dictation in Employment Contract Formation in New Zealand," 20 N.Z. J. Ind. Rel., 119 (1995).
36. Michael Quigg, "Employment Act Revisited," *Manufacturer*, 9 (Aug. 1992).
37. [1992] 3 ERNZ 807.
38. *Id.*, 812.
39. *O'Malley v. Vision Aluminium Ltd* (I) [1992] 2 ERNZ 368; *O'Malley v. Vision Aluminium Ltd* (II) [1992] 2 ERNZ 660.
40. [1992] 2 ERNZ 368, 369.
41. *Id.*, 369, 370.
42. [1992] 2 ERNZ 660, 677.
43. *Hawtin v. Skellerup Industrial Ltd.* [1992] 2 ERNZ 500, 536 (emphasis added).
44. *Id.*, 537; *Northern Distribution Union (Inc) v. 3 Guys Ltd* [1992] ERNZ 903, 915 (negotiations may be only presentation of contract to other party with refusal to deviate).
45. *United Food and Chemical Workers Union of New Zealand v. Talley* [1992] 3 ERNZ 423, 439.
46. *Mineworkers Union of NZ Inc v. Dunollie Coal Mines Ltd.* [1994] 1 ERNZ 78.
47. *Witehira v. Presbyterian Support Services (Northern)* [1994] 1 ERNZ 578 (1994).
48. *Id.*, 585–86.
49. *Id.*, 592.
50. *Id.*, 597, 601.
51. Rebecca Macfie, "An End to Equity," *Political Review*, 20, 24 (June 1992).

16

Collectivity, Free Choice, and Schism

Collectivity
Fundamental to the ECA is the individual's right to freedom of association. The ECA evenhandedly allows an employee or an employer to select a representative to perform any acts related to negotiating or enforcing employment contracts or prosecuting statutory violations.[1] The other party then must "recognise the authority of that person, group, or organisation to represent the employee or employer in those negotiations."[2] Authorisation was supposed to be a business decision by the employee or the employer. As Penelope Brook described it, this

> decision to delegate bargaining to an agent, whether by employers, or by employees or by both, will similarly depend on an analysis of costs and benefits. The benefits associated with the use of specialists to process information and carry out negotiations will be set against the costs of an agent failing to represent the true interests of his or her party. The balance may be tipped in favour of unionism if the unions are able to supply other services, such as education, pension schemes or medical centres.[3]

Although this sounds logical, it fails to appreciate and account for significant differences between employees and employers. Laws which apply equally but which fail to account for relevant differences may not be equal in impact or effect.[4] Thus the ECA legislates for equality while it ignores background inequality.

Are there differences in employers and employees that affect the ECA's impact on them? Employees will invariably be people, while many, if not most, employers will be corporations. The

ECA assumes that the difference is not significant. Adherents of neoclassical economics often conflate individuals and corporations. This "ignores a vast literature in history, sociology, and other disciplines that shows beyond doubt that organisations do not usually behave as individuals do and that groups of varying sizes have different patterns of behavior."[5]

Corporations can depend on other laws, such as corporation or partnership law, to provide special supports to maintain their collective nature. In addition, the employer-corporations' fictional personhood means they naturally exist only through representatives. If they want to speak, they must designate parts of their corporate anatomies to be mouths. They cannot interact with the world except through agents and would need representatives whether the ECA existed or not. Equally important, corporations do not have consciences or learn cause and effect, because the law limits their liability and permits those who make decisions for the corporation (the brain) to escape personal consequences.

Employees, on the other hand, face constant obstacles to collectivity, even when their employer is not opposed. Worker collective action is interpreted as negative or even antisocial, whereas incorporation is seen as promoting important social goals. Worse, workers who are already a part of their employer's collectivity must act in ways that may seem harmful to the employer when workers want to promote their own ends. When employees act together, this usurps workplace hierarchy. It cuts against requirements that workers obey their employers and act for their employer's well-being.

When collective action is not protected, employees are at a disadvantage because they are not fictional or collective persons. Unlike corporations, people can exist whether or not they unite. They can speak without needing to appoint a "mouthpiece". Furthermore, often they can only speak with a collective mouth if they shut their individual mouths. Workers have consciences. They feel cause and effect all too keenly. They know organising may have unpleasant consequences and may leave them unable to support their families. When employees appoint a representative, this takes an act of will, whereas it is natural for a corporation.

PSA representative Joris de Bres explained that under the ECA

> any collective democratic decision is broken down into individual choice. It sounds attractive, but at the beginning of the process of bargaining it breaks people up. They have to determine to come back together. Once they've determined to come back together there is actually a collection of individual choices to be individually represented together and any of them can pull out of that again. It makes it very difficult for a union to have a role on a more mature basis in terms of people accepting majority decisions and then entering into bargains or agreements with the employer. Because it's always actually no more than a collection of individuals.
>
> The law now defines each worker as an individual.[6]

A second way in which the ECA burdens workers more than employers is that it ignores the different reactions each is likely to have to the other's representative. A union (as employee representative) or employer's representative can act only if the agent meets its burden of providing authorisation that is satisfactory to the other party.[7] This literal equality leads to actual inequality, because many employers will react to the employees' representative in ways which are profoundly different from employees' reaction to the employer's representative.

An employer can gain power by separating a representative and employee. Work will still be done, and it may then have greater bargaining strength. Even more, the ECA requires no more than that the employer recognise the representative; it can still refuse to bargain. "[T]he law is the employer has to recognise the union. Recognition is like walking down the street, and I recognise a friend and you just have to say hello and that is the end of it. It doesn't mean that you have to do any more about it."[8] In other words, an employer can recognise a union, not bargain, and continue to run its business.

In contrast, employees usually want bargaining to move ahead. Employees realise they can only secure improved working conditions if the employer can meet and negotiate and that to do this it must have a representative. Thus, authorisation requirements have vastly different consequences for employers and employees.

The ECA separates joining a union from authorising a union to act as a representative. When the ECA came before New Zealand's parliament, among the amendments unsuccessfully proposed was one by NewLabour Party MP Jim Anderton:

> Where an employee is a member of an employees' organisation, and the rules of that organisation provide that membership of that organisation shall authorise the organisation to represent its members in negotiations, such membership shall prima facie be evidence of the authority of that organisation to represent that employee.[9]

This would not be necessary under most labor relations systems, because membership and representation are intertwined. The ECA does not permit this automatic connection.

What is elsewhere a single act of joining and then being represented by a union in bargaining, grievance processing, and legal actions is a diffused, complex, and legalistic process in New Zealand. Unions could not even condition membership on employees' agreeing to relink the two. In early 1992, the PSA was attempting to do just this by changing its rules to provide that membership meant that the PSA would negotiate on the worker's behalf.[10] The Dairy Workers Union found themselves in court for trying to do this very thing, requiring broad authorisation as a condition of membership. The Employment Court commented:

> Employees are free to choose their bargaining representatives. It is contrary to the philosophy of the legislation for an association of employees (a union) or anyone else to seek to restrict them in that choice by requiring such employees to accept the union as their bargaining agent as a necessary consequence of membership. . . . Across the spectrum of unions it is now well recognised that employees may be union members and may remain so but without having given a bargaining authority or having withdrawn or revoked the same. Although negotiation

of employment contracts is a clearly important function of a union, benefits such as representation in disputes in personal grievances and actions for the recovery of wages underpaid are simply some common examples of the range of benefits available to employees because of union membership in circumstances where they may wish either to bargain individually or collectively for themselves or to have another representative do so. In its rejection of the applications for union membership of Hautapu employees other than those where full bargaining and other representative authority was given, the union acted wrongly.[11]

Union representation in bargaining does not automatically allow the union to advance the cause of those it bargains for, including taking strike action. Negotiating a contract does not mean a union can sue to enforce contract violations or to protect its members. Each step is conditioned on the representative's proving it has been authorised by its principal to perform the specified act. The problem of having proper authorisations was a serious one for a large union like the PSA. It had to negotiate 83 separate agreements between February and November 1992[12] and had 62,000 members.[13] Getting authorisations just for these negotiations from each member was a major undertaking.

Free Choice
Individual freedom, self-determination, and choice are important values. Again, they operate differently for unions and employers. Corporations, bodies which actually engage in market transactions, do not have absolute freedom in their existence or in relations with their representatives. The law recognises that values other than absolute freedom may sometimes be paramount. Although worker representation too cannot be effective without some limits to protect organisation, the ECA recognised none. "[T]he 'Freedom of Association' embodied in Part 1 of the act is not the traditional protection for collective action but a freedom to disassociate."[14]

The ECA allowed an employee to use a union as a representative if the employee saw them as offering a worthwhile service. If a union does no more than deliver a service, then there is no reason not to allow the buyer (employees) to select or discard the service provider at will. NZBR Board Member Alan Jones said that "unions need to provide services which are valuable, affordable, and relevant. If their customers think they are worthwhile they'll survive; if not, they won't, and we'll see more groups of employees seeking advice from other agencies in the market."[15] National Party member Bruce Cliffe declared that under the ECA:

> Unions must now work for and earn their members. They must provide a service, they must deliver agreements, and they must want to protect their members. In other words, unions must provide the service that is usual in a normal competitive business. Any successful enterprise understands the importance of competition and I believe that the unions will now realise that competition is the way it should be in labour relations.[16]

The NZEF faulted "unions [as] not market driven; rather, an artificial market has been created for them." The NZEF's solution was that unions "should be exposed to the same competitive environment other providers of goods and service must face."[17] After the ECA was enacted, Alan Jones argued:

> As unions shrink and are, therefore, less ubiquitous, they will want to focus. No one believes compulsory unionism will return. Therefore unions will want to market themselves where they can be afforded. That is not amongst the lowest paid. . . . Thus unions will have made at least one major, if historically perverse, adjustment to the new environment: by ignoring those who were their roots they will be able to ensure their own viability.[18]

Voluntary unionism would force unions to improve their services and workplace productivity. Penelope Brook asked if there was any benefit to be gained by giving unions an exclusive right to negotiate on behalf of a group of workers and suggested that unions might benefit from greater freedom to "define the range and price of their activities (subject to their ability to attract members). . . ."[19]

Others, including unions and employers, were concerned that this unfettered choice would be harmful. The Engineers criticised the ECA for not providing procedures to select or remove a bargaining agent, for allowing an employer to dominate the determination of who could become a bargaining agent, and for allowing individual rights to override the collective good of the enterprise and of the "wider body of people working within it."[20] Labour Party spokesperson for Labour, Helen Clark argued that allowing a worker to change authority to represent during bargaining would create instability: "The Minister of Labour is so obsessed with choice that he cannot understand that in some of those matters choice could lead to anarchy and instability."[21] Ken Douglas of the CTU worried that the law lacked ways of selecting bargaining representatives other than the parties' muscle and willingness to use it:

> There is no stability of representation required in the bill. The bargaining agents can be changed as often as workers like during the course of negotiating a contract, they can be changed at contract renewal time, and the agencies for bargaining need not be the same as those for administration or enforcement of the contract.[22]

Union concerns were obvious: unstable coalitions could lead to unpredictable resources in terms of people and dues. Employers, too, were uneasy about the instability created by unhindered choice. Telecom worried that there would be multiple bargaining representatives and negotiations, which would threaten industrial relations within the company.[23] Carter Holt Harvey was concerned by workers' being able to retract authorisations, even late in bargaining and by splits when workers saw the settlement their agent had bargained.[24]

Peter Carroll, Chief of the Auckland Employers Association, stated:

> As a private opinion, I think that it's going to be freedom at the expense of stability, which will be found undesirable by employers and responsible unions and it may be confusing for workers too.
>
> At some stage in this act, or in some later legislation, the possibility for introducing procedures for the recognition of

bargaining agents may be necessary. One has to have some procedures for recognising how an agent gets his authority.

I think this is where there is most trepidation by the larger employers, that we could be buying freedom at the cost of stability.[25]

McDonald's shared these concerns and argued for majority decision by employees rather than individual choice.[26]

Minister of Labour Bill Birch dismissed the employers' concerns. He argued that allowing individuals to choose whether to belong to a union and whether to bargain individually or collectively left parties free to make their own choices. This freedom, he felt, necessarily would benefit business.[27] Employer concerns were also belittled by management consultant Rob Campbell, a former union representative.

> Some of the less far-sighted and competent employer representatives have been seen in action at the Select Committee bemoaning the difficulties [that making strategic plans about labour relations] will cause them. The same employers are clearly fearful that they may face a number of bargaining agents from within their workforce. This is an interesting case from an economist's point of view as it presents the prospect of a buyer being concerned at facing too many sellers! Certainly in situations where the employer has no clear strategy and lacks skills the prospect is daunting, but no labour relations system structured around the needs of the poorly prepared or incompetent employer has much of a future.[28]

This argument of choice versus stability demonstrates that the ECA must be understood as legislation that is naively doctrinaire and cannot be explained solely as an anti-union statute. Soon after its enactment it was possible to see the impact of the ECA's freedom of choice on stability. Joris de Bres explained how limitlessly freedom of association operated:

> Our problem now is that you've really got total individualisation. There's no legal recognition of that step in the process that says once you've made a democratic decision, you stick

with it for the term of the contract. That would have made a big difference.

It's in those little technical difficulties of getting the process going on a collective basis that I think we see our greatest challenges. Anytime there's a sort of dip in the negotiation, if we get that far, or in trying to establish how to bargain because the employer might want 24 contracts and we want 3 or the like, there are huge administrative obstacles, like getting individual authorisations, the ability for any group to withdraw those authorisations at any time in the process. And while in theory it empowers the individual, it weakens the collective.

That's at the heart of it for us. There are going to be some pluses and minuses, for instance, in any settlement that you reach with an employer if you get that far. And if there's any hint of that before a settlement, before the ratification process is over, any group can, and some groups have, withdrawn their authorisation. Because they don't want any variation in their conditions. So . . . the Act is premised on . . . the individual having an absolute power, vis-à-vis the collective. But the reality beyond that is that the employer then has the additional power of being able to deal essentially with individuals.[29]

The ECA made it more difficult for unions to counsel patience in volatile situations. Workers could not depend on the continued existence of the collective. As a result, in 1992, negotiations came to the brink of shutting off electrical power around the country.

Because we have no way left . . . because normally when things settle down, they say, "Oh well, that was O.K. That was reasonable advice." Now they told us three weeks ago, "If you don't serve that notice we will leave and serve it ourselves." And so, there is much less room for a union to present a bit of a longer term view or a broader strategic analysis of proposals for industrial action for instance. It's basically "If you don't do it, if you don't serve the notice, we'll go." And we are constantly now bargaining with our own members about strategies and so on. So yes, it's had that effect.

> ... There's no doubt, the Employment Contracts Act has both empowered and disempowered workers. It's empowered them individually. It's disempowered them collectively. So, it doesn't matter ... the chief executive of the Department of Conservation might want one union to deal with and an orderly system, but if we had, as we did a couple of weeks ago, one bad meeting, where people disagreed with something an organiser was saying—you get people saying, "If this doesn't improve we'll leave." I don't think it's affected the majority of workers yet, but it's sort of divided off anybody who wants to divide off. And the employer can't do anything about that either. He might refuse to negotiate with them, but then in turn they would have their rights. It's a pseudo-power of workers based on division.[30]

In other words, the ECA's emphasis on the individual encourages employees not to see their well-being in democratic values of solidarity, compromise, patience, and the long term but in demanding that individual desires be absolutely and immediately satisfied. This makes enduring relationships and, ultimately, democracies difficult to maintain. Work is no longer a place in which individuals can learn to be citizens of a democracy by practising seemingly insignificant routines which build habits for action as individuals within society.[31] This was certainly the experience of unions under the ECA.

> You've got to get all sorts of written authorisation. For instance, when we went back to people to say, "Will you sign individual authorities for us to serve notice of industrial action?" the whole issue's being relitigated. Some people ... had voted against and they happened to be, in our terms, quite a small minority. But the votes were all carried significantly. The people who voted against, who would normally accept a majority vote, were saying, "Well, I voted against it. I'm not going to authorise you to serve that notice."[32]

Economist Richard Freeman and law professor Joel Rogers have observed that individual voice "does not promote deliberation among employees about shared preferences, leaving management with conflicting signals from disagreeing workers."[33] The easy exit which the ECA makes possible, and which is even attractive compared to the compromises necessary to achieve a collective voice, exemplifies this problem.

In the past, workers would have been unable to leave the union in protest when it took an action they did not like or to exercise this degree of pressure after they lost a vote.[34] Now they could and did. In May 1991, there were 80 unions with a total membership of 603,118. By December 1994, there were 82 unions representing a total membership of 375,906.[35] In other words, there were roughly the same number of unions in December 1994 as in May 1991, but they were representing only half as many members. Fifteen new unions came into existence between 1993 and 1994. Some of the increase is the result of unions leaving the amalgamations they were compelled to enter to meet the LRA's requirement to have more than 1000 members.[36] However, other unions are the result of fracture.

As employers feared, the proliferation of unions means that some workplaces have had more than one union representing the same classification of workers. For example, some Air New Zealand's pilots were covered by a CEC negotiated by their traditional union, others were represented by another union, and the rest were on IECs.[37] Accompanying this increase in the number of unions and the drop in members was an increase in negotiations. The National Distribution Union moved from 55 negotiations before the ECA to 700 after its enactment, even though its membership had been nearly cut in half.[38]

The PSA had real difficulty maintaining collectivity under the ECA, because it was and is a very large and very diverse union. The PSA primarily represents employees who perform core services for the central government throughout the country in jobs ranging from administration through health care. Its 1991 membership of 61,892 had grown to 71,858 in 1993, primarily through affiliations.[39] Its size and diversity have been a source of both strength and weakness. Even more complex has been its relationship with its members' main employer, the author of the ECA. This created the possibility that the government might see negotiations as an opportunity to set an example for other employers.

Even though it was a very large union, the PSA faced a number of the same problems that smaller, weaker unions did. Just as with other unions, the PSA had trouble convincing some employers to bargain with it.[40] Even though it was able to negotiate many agreements just as the ECA was coming into effect, it also entered the ECA era with expired awards. This meant that many PSA members were on IECs based on the award terms. The government used this situation by trading pay increases for reduced severance packages which then allowed it to spend less when it downsized an agency. In one case, a worker agreed to a 3% increase in exchange for a 50% cut in redundancy pay. Two days later, he was made redundant and received $20,000 less than he would have been entitled to under the old terms.[41]

The PSA attempted to meet these crises and also tried to hold its diverse membership together by finding a way to be all things for all its constituents. It tried to demonstrate that it was a leader by having its voice heard on the issues of the day and also to show that it was listening attentively to its members.

As part of these efforts, the PSA polled its members and other workers as to their feelings about the union. The information it got must have made setting policy even more difficult. It got good marks for communication but was scolded for being bureaucratic, slow to act, invisible, out of touch, and "weak and ineffective; a soft touch for the employers." It got mixed advice on how militant to be: "It was difficult to pin them down on this. Members wanted their union to be both democratic, dynamic and fearless in representing its members and professional and responsible. When forced to a choice many insisted that a union should take a balanced approach." Some said they would only remain a member if the union was responsible and non-militant.[42]

The PSA seemed to be trying to follow the NZEF's advice to entice workers to take up PSA membership by offering an array of benefits. Its health and superannuation (retirement) plans capture the diverse forces it was trying to hold together. On the one hand, it promised to oversee its health plan to ensure that it provided good service. On the other hand the health plan was a potential source of revenues, whose surpluses would be returned to the union.[43] It offered superannuation to assist those who suffered from government cutbacks.[44]

The PSA saw that the ECA put it in competition with employers for the hearts and minds of its members and responded by saying: "We have to sell the union as never before."[45] At the same time, the union wanted to make itself an appealing partner to employers:

> We've also been nudged more firmly to understand business practices so that we can talk on equal terms with employers. We can make a positive contribution to the way enterprises are run and of course we also have to know about their finances so that we can negotiate in full knowledge of the employer's circumstances.[46]

The PSA planned to seek new members in both the private and public sectors, something the government's massive and ongoing privatisation of public services necessitated. It also began to reach out to professional organisations to join a cooperative partnership.[47] Outreach, in particular to professional organisations whose members had not been interested in unionism, had special dangers. It risked increasing the PSA's heterogeneity and making representation more difficult. It meant bringing in new members who did not understand unionism and who might prevent the union from undertaking core union functions. It also meant moving into the jurisdiction of other unions, which might be seen as poaching.

As it was reaching out for new members, the PSA had to battle with the government if it was to retain its current members. The government demanded that public sector workers be on IECs and would only agree to a CEC in exchange for a pay cut. When no agreement was reached and the contract expired, the government was able to get its way, because s 19 put the workers on IECs. As of July 1, 1992, 160,000 public sector workers were automatically on IECs.[48] As a union, the PSA could not promote IECs, yet it also could not just abandon this growing body of workers—members and potential members.

In April 1992, the PSA responded to this challenge by creating a consultancy to help workers on IECs. The consultancy offered negotiating and legal services to members who otherwise would have had no advice or would have had to seek outside legal advice. It thus pre-empted the problem of workers who then would see no reason to maintain PSA membership. The consultancy also ensured some consistency across agreements. To keep the consultancy from undermining union efforts for CECs, it was limited to providing services to workers on IECs only "where collective activity is inappropriate."[49] In fact many workers maintained membership in unions even though they were not covered by a CEC. In 1994/1995, there were 100,000 more union members than workers covered by CECs.[50]

Schism
The CTU summed up life under the ECA as: "Overall, the picture is one of contrived instability, rivalry, fragmentation and bureaucratic obstruction of unions. Freedom of association has been implemented in a form that tries to limit the amount of actual unionisation, and to keep the unit of organisation as small as possible."[51] In May 1991, 5% of New Zealand unions had fewer than 1000 members. By December 1991, 46% of unions had 100 or fewer members. Some of these were very small unions, since the number of members in those unions had increased only from 2,954 to 13,385.[52] The key to these changes was the absolute freedom the ECA gives workers to choose representatives and to associate with other workers. Schism has been easy under the ECA. An employee could join a new union or get a new representative simply by authorising a new bargaining representative at any time.

In the early days of the ECA, it seemed as if representing employees would be a growth industry for lawyers or others who wanted to expand their businesses. Joris de Bres of the PSA described that period:

> [W]e're facing competition from non-union bargaining agents, lawyers, consultants and so on. We're facing some degree of

competition from other unions, some of them not in the Council of Trade Unions who have set up separately. We are facing competition from new organisations set up as staff associations, either with employer support or because they're not satisfied with the service we give them. So we've got that sort of flank to be mindful of.53

In 1994, 35 CECs covering 10,400 workers were negotiated by staff associations, rather than unions.54

The growth market for workers' representatives has not occurred. Far more destructive to unions than competition from lawyers or consultants has been the tendency to schism. The PSA's diversity, size, and geographic coverage made it particularly vulnerable to schism. Schism can arise through inter-union rivalry and raiding. An example of this was the ongoing dispute between the Engineers and the Manufacturing and Construction Workers Union (MCWU). Since the enactment of the ECA, the two have traded members at plants such as Mitsubishi and Honda.55 While the ECA did not create the conflict, it fanned it by allowing each union to lure members who were now free to go where they wished when they wished.

Where no conflict had previously existed, the ECA created incentives for inter-union rivalry and raiding other unions to make up for losses in membership. In some cases, employers assisted raiding. Skellerup Industrial told the court that it "made it clear to workers [who were] addressed at the series of meetings held on 17 December that the company would prefer to deal with the engineer's union only 'because that made it all much simpler for us to deal with the one union'. . . .".56

The same forces that lead to raiding also promote schism. Philosophical or other disputes have led to fragmentation. In early 1992, over 1,000 Canterbury and Nelson psychiatric health sector members resigned from the PSA and formed the National Union of Public Employees (NUPE). The causes of the schism covered the whole range of fears and grievances present in most unions.

Part of it was a residue from the failure to call a general strike against the ECA. NUPE members accused the PSA of overriding their wishes to oppose the ECA actively. They criticised unions, such as the PSA, who might be tempted to enter sweetheart deals as the price for recognition. The PSA had broken from a national bargaining coalition for the 1992 public health sector negotiations and entered an agreement with the Otago Area Health Board. Dissenters argued that the agreement recognised the PSA without the PSA's having to obtain workers' authorisation to represent them or to negotiate for them. Part of the dispute concerned issues of how the union could best be organised to meet members' needs. They felt that the PSA's new representational structure reduced effective member participation. The Canterbury members felt they had been neglected as the union pursued new members.[57]

NUPE was not the PSA's only defection. In December 1991, 300 Auckland Customs workers left the PSA to form the Customs Officers Association because they felt they could negotiate a better deal.[58] Prison officers said they were dissatisfied with the PSA but would not decide whether to follow NUPE's course until after the coming negotiations. Barry Noakes, a prison officer and PSA delegate, said: "If we feel sold down the river, then some serious questions would be asked." Other PSA members were watching NUPE to see if it was more successful in representing its members than the PSA had been.[59]

Schism could result from racial or ethnic divisions just as easily as from disagreements over bargaining strategy or organisation. Some Maori set up their own trade union as a result of grievances that mainstream labour had long been insensitive to Maori self-determination and rights under the Treaty of Waitangi.[60]

Schism, raiding, and union collapse showed no likelihood of settling down, even after the ECA had been in place for five years. In late 1995, the 18,000-member Communication and Energy Workers Union (CEWU) collapsed. Some former members set up their own independent union or considered federating with the pre-existing unions of Auckland and Christchurch posties who had left the CEWU in 1992. Other former CEWU members planned to join the Engineers, the National Distribution Union, and FinSec, the finance workers' union.[61]

ECA proponents had long claimed that the free market would increase competition for members and lead to improved member services. Anne Knowles of the NZEF said: "We have been saying: 'Well, if the unions are actually providing a good service, then they have nothing to fear with the removal of the compulsory requirement for people to be a member of theirs.'"[62] They also claimed that eradicating unions' monopoly privileges would enhance the community's opinion of trade unions and lead to unions which attracted member allegiance and loyalty without compulsion.

They were at least partially correct. The ECA has led to inter-union competition; however, it is far from clear that this competition has been benign. Authorisation and schism have had complex effects. On the one hand, where workers felt aggrieved, they now can opt out and seek more effective representation. Once members can leave, they can use this power to discipline unions and force a moribund union to be responsive.

However, benefits such as this do not outweigh the problems. Real and effective employee choice is undercut by the ECA so that it is only illusory. As long as employers have the power to refuse to bargain with an employee's designated representative and to frustrate the employee's efforts to be a partner in workplace governance, the worker is likely to direct frustration at the union and to walk out, force a schism and ultimately weaken all unions. Experience with ECA freedom demonstrates the value of stability and a clear procedure for choosing a representative. Merely permitting unions to exist in a regime of unfettered freedom of choice cannot empower workers to achieve their ultimate goals.

Notes
1. ECA s 10.
2. ECA s 12(2).
3. Penelope Brook, "Reform of the Labour Market" in *Rogernomics: Reshaping New Zealand's Economy*, 182, 194 (Simon Walker, ed., 1989).
4. Martha Minow, *Making All the Difference: Inclusion, Exclusion, and American Law* (1990); Robert Monks & Nell Minow, *Power and Accountability* (1991).
5. Thomas McCraw, "The Trouble with Adam Smith," *American*

Scholar, 353, 371 (Summer 1992).
6. Interview with Joris de Bres, Central Operations Manager of the Public Service Association, in Wellington (May 7, 1992).
7. ECA ss 12, 13, 59.
8. Interview with Rick Barker, National Secretary, Service Workers Federation of Aotearoa, in Wellington (May 14, 1992).
9. N.Z.P.D., 1580 (Apr. 30, 1991); N.Z.P.D., 1582 (Apr. 30, 1991) (Sutherland amendment).
10. "Your Rights Under the New Laws," *PSA Journal*, Feb. 1992, at 9.
11. *NZ Dairy Workers Inc. v. Hautapu Whey Transport Ltd.* [1994] 2 ERNZ 549, 570.
12. "Negotiating Timetable," *PSA Journal*, Feb,. 1992, at 9.
13. "Your Rights."
14. Peter Churchman & Walter Grills, "Employment Contract Act Revisited," 4 (1992).
15. Alan Jones, "What Were We Afraid Of? The Employment Contracts Act—The Past—The Present—And the Future," 19 (1992).
16. N.Z.P.D., 1659 (Apr. 30, 1991).
17. NZEF, Employment Contracts Bill 1991: Submission B-5 (Jan. 30, 1991).
18. Jones, 14-15; cf. Timothy McConville, "Monopoly Unionism Under the National Labor Relations Act: An Abrogation of Common Law Agency Doctrine," 46 Lab. L.J., 469 (1995).
19. Brook, "Reform of the Labour Market," 194, 196.
20. Rex Jones, "A Private Union's Perspective," 9 (Longman Professional Conference, Auckland, May 7–8, 1991).
21. N.Z.P.D., 1428 (Apr. 23, 1991).
22. Ken Douglas, "The Employment Contracts Bill: Two Very Different Perspectives," *Examiner*, Apr. 18, 1991, at 18.
23. N.Z.P.D., 1480 (Apr. 23, 1991).
24. Carter Holt Harvey Ltd., Submission on the Employment Contracts Bill 16 (n.d.). The difficulties CHH predicted did, in fact, trouble real negotiations. See, e.g., "The Perils of Being First," *NZ Nursing Journal*, 13, 14 (Aug. 1992).
25. Rebecca Macfie, "Buying Freedom at the Cost of Stability?," *National Business Review*, Feb. 18, 1991, at 1.
26. McDonald's System of New Zealand Ltd, Submission on the Employment Contracts Bill, 3, 4 (Mar. 29, 1991).
27. N.Z.P.D., 1429 (Apr. 23, 1991).
28. Rob Campbell, "The Employment Contracts Bill: Two Very Different Perspectives," *Examiner*, Apr. 18, 1991, at 18, 19.
29. de Bres.
30. *Id.*
31. Thomas Kohler, "The Overlooked Middle" in *The Legal Future of Employee Representation*, 224, 226-29 (Matthew Finkin, ed., 1994).
32. de Bres.

33. Richard Freeman & Joel Rogers, "Who Speaks for Us? Employee Representation in a Nonunion Labor Market" in *Employee Representation: Alternatives and Future Directions*, 13, 27 (Bruce Kaufman & Morris Kleiner, eds. 1993).
34. Rebecca Macfie, "An End to Equity," *Political Review*, 20, 20-21 (June 1992).
35. Raymond Harbridge et al., "Unions and Union Membership in New Zealand: Annual Review for 1993," 19 N.Z. J. Ind. Rel., 175, 176 (1994); Raymond Harbridge & Kevin Hince, "Unions and Union Membership in New Zealand 1985–1992," 18 N.Z. J. Ind. Rel., 352, 355 (1993); Georgina Bailey, "Nation's Workers Walk Out on Unions," *Evening Post*, July 15, 1995, at 1.
36. Raymond Harbridge & Anthony Honeybone, "External Legitimacy of Unions: Trends in New Zealand," 17 J. Lab. Res., 425, 436 (1996).
37. Tim Hazeldine, "Employment in New Zealand: Then and Now" in *Labour, Employment and Work in New Zealand 1994*, 19, 24 (Philip S. Morrison, ed., 1994).
38. International Labour Office, 295th Report of the Committee on Freedom of Association Case No.1698 ¶ 154(c) (Nov. 1994).
39. Raymond Harbridge & Kevin Hince, *A Sourcebook of New Zealand Trade Unions and Employee Organisations*, 60 (1994).
40. "Pay Cuts Follow Contracts Act," *PSA Journal*, Aug. 1991, at 1.
41. "Signed Up and Kicked Out," *PSA Journal*, July 1991, at 3; Harbridge & Honeybone, "External Legitimacy," 433.
42. "What People Had to Say," *PSA Journal*, Nov. 1992, at 2, 3.
43. "PSA Health Plan," *PSA Journal Supplement*, Oct. 1991.
44. "Retirement Income Planning," *PSA Journal Supplement*, Oct. 1991.
45. "Thorp Heralds Major Changes for PSA," *PSA Journal*, Oct. 1991, at 1.
46. *Id.*
47. "Who Does the PSA Serve?," *PSA Journal Supplement*, Oct. 1991.
48. "160,000 on Individual Contracts from 1 July," *PSA Journal*, June, 1992, at 1.
49. "Service Offered for Individual Contracts," *PSA Journal*, Apr. 1992, at 7.
50. Harbridge & Honeybone, "External Legitimacy," 440.
51. CTU, "The New Zealand Experiment," 15 (Oct. 1994).
52. Aaron Crawford et al., "Unions and Union Membership in New Zealand: Annual Review for 1995," 21 N.Z. J. Ind. Rel., 188, 190 (1996)
53. de Bres.
54. Harbridge & Honeybone, "External Legitimacy," 436.
55. "Honda Schemes Our End," *M&C Workers News*, Dec. 1991, at 12; interview with Graeme Clarke, General Secretary MCWU, at Wellington (May 5, 1992); interview with Hel Loader, Research Advocate, New Zealand Engineering Union, in Wellington (May

13, 1992).
56. *Hawtin v. Skellerup Industrial Ltd.* [1992] 2 ERNZ 500, 511.
57. "PSA Resignations Raise Fundamental Issues," *PSA Journal*, May 1992, at 8; Christopher Moore, "John McKenzie: Always a Fighter But Never Blind," *Press*, May 7, 1992, at 13; interview with Graeme Clarke; "South's NUPE Gathers Steam," *Labour Notes*, Dec. 1992, at 6–7; "Regional Contracts in Health Only Way Forward," *PSA Journal*, Apr. 1992, at 7.
58. Roth, "Chronicle," 17 N.Z. J. Ind. Rel., 124 (1992).
59. "PSA Resignations," 9.
60. Syd Jackson, "Te Ropu Kaimaki Maori o Aotearoa," *Race Gender Class*, 13, 16 (1992).
61. Mathew Dearnley, "Postal Staff to Form Breakaway Union," *N.Z. Herald*, Dec. 6, 1992, at 1; "Posties Will Set Up Own Union," *Evening Post*, Dec. 6, 1995, at 11.
62. Interview with Anne Knowles, Labor Market Manager, New Zealand Employers Federation, at Wellington (May 21, 1992).

17

Multi-Employer Bargaining

THE NZEF WAS OPPOSED TO MULTI-EMPLOYER AGREEMENTS, BECAUSE it was worried that they might recreate awards. Private sector unions had relied heavily on multi-employer bargaining and awards that set terms across an occupation before the ECA era. In the bargaining round for 1989–1990, 93% of private sector employees were covered by multi-employer agreements. Five years later, only 14% of private sector employees were covered by multi-employer agreements.[1] The collapse of multi-employer negotiations meant that unions, such as the Clerical Workers Union, which were especially dependent on award bargaining quickly became defunct.[2]

Multi-employer bargaining agreements, however, hung on for a variety of reasons. Many employers continue to say they like awards because they lower the cost of negotiation, they maintain industry standards or conditions, and they create a level playing field. Some employer associations have written model industry agreements that recreate awards but without unions. Forty-nine percent of employees in the hospitality industry are covered by a non-union multi-employer contract produced by their association.[3] Employers are assisted in setting wages by the agreement's schedule of minimum hourly rates payable for eighteen job classifications and three grades of workers. The actual wage is to be based on the employer's assessment of the worker's skills. There are no penalty wages.

The New Zealand Dairy Industry Employers Association has a multi-employer agreement negotiated with a union. In this case the association negotiated a contract which was essentially a successor to the award with its corresponding union. Only after it had agreement on the contract terms did the association ask industry employers for bargaining and ratification authority.[4] Although backwards, this was not illegal. The advantages to the union in negotiating such an agreement is that it might eventually induce employers to recognise and negotiate with it.

Multi-employer agreements also continued to be found where unions were able to make the case for them, either through logic or through force of organisation. The Engineers waged a serious and sometimes successful campaign for maintaining multi-employer structures. It was successful because the Engineers promoted multi-employer bargaining as a means of fostering industry training, productivity, and workplace reform. It argued that productivity and profits under the ECA were more likely to come from cooperation with unions than confrontation[5] and that the union was useful to employers and members.[6]

Not so far under the surface of the Engineers' promotion of multi-employer agreements was its judgement that employers, if left to themselves, could not properly manage their own workplaces and would trade off long-term social needs for short-term gains:

> The result has been an unusual situation in which the Engineers have implored management to restructure their work organization and bargaining structures in line with the demands of a high-technology, high value-added economy. Clouding employers' responses to these initiatives have been a combination of factors: skepticism about the motives of the unions, uncertainty about the ability of the unions to deliver on productivity, and an unwillingness to recognise unions as partners in the restructuring process.[7]

The Engineers' views about employers and their motivations existed long before the ECA. Its agreements were tailored for the new environment, by having moved from occupational to industry bargaining.[8] From 1987 to 1991, half of its 123 documents had been reformed.[9] Once the ECA was in place, the Engineers tried to persuade employers not to seek concessions but to continue down this road of reforms, particularly worker training.[10]

Multi-employer support is essential for industry training. A single employer cannot bear the expense of training and will be reluctant to train workers who might leave and take their skills and the employer's investment with them.[11] Enterprise agreements and IECs logically would decrease training. These insights received empirical support in a case study involving the State of Utah's repeal of legislation which had promoted industry training and ensured an adequate supply of qualified workers in the construction industry. When training became available only on an individual basis, it quickly disappeared as employers refused to pay for it and employees were unable to make the investment themselves. In a short time the state lost its qualified construction workers.[12]

An Australian employer association, the Metal Trades Industry Association, concluded that under the ECA New Zealand employers had begun paying less attention to training, quality, and service than to working hours and pay. It found a "dramatic decline in apprenticeships" and a shortage in skills.[13] A 1995 survey found that serious shortages in skills were affecting most of the businesses contacted and that many employers felt it was not their responsibility to train even though the shortage meant paying a premium to workers with the necessary skills.[14]

> [T]he contemporary New Zealand industry is characterised by intense competition and structural instability which is reshaping the organisation of work, and reducing pay and the quality of work for most shop assistants. Many retail employers have gone into "survival mode" and their emphasis is almost solely on the return on investments. Thus training is being neglected throughout most of the industry. This compares to related industries such as motor parts where there is a strong emphasis on training. Emphasis in the retail sector is on newer technologies, and centralised purchasing and marketing. There is no place in most managers['] thinking for training, job enrichment or worker motivation.[15]

The heavy industry experience was duplicated in the retail sector, where employers reduced labour costs by reducing staff and pay rates but not increasing training.[16] Accompanying this deskilling and exacerbating the problems retail workers experienced was the deskilling of managerial jobs.[17]

Although there were exceptions,[18] the Engineers were not the only union to claim that the unions, not the employers, were proposing training.[19] A study of New Zealand Nurses Association bargaining with area health boards found that management proposals all focused on lowering wages and eliminating penal rates. Issues such as training, workplace design and reform, and fostering improved employer–employee communication were found only in the union's proposals.[20] Management rejected them on the ground that they were not part of the negotiations, that management's focus was on short-term issues, and that "issues relating to consultation with employees are outside this document."[21]

The Engineers' Hel Loader observed: "The ECA effectively stops full lasting reform. Employers can take the short side of cost-cutting approach instead of investing in growth and creating a framework for increasing skill and productivity. They can just slash and burn for short term gain."[22] The easiest way to short-term profits was wage-cutting. "Leaked board minutes of a medium-sized Auckland manufacturer reveal[ed] directors deciding, as a matter of policy, to use the act to reduce workers' employment conditions. They estimate savings of several hundred thousands of dollars, which will enhance company profitability. There is no suggestion of expansion, reinvestment or productivity-based bargaining."[23] Despite the lack of skills, the government increased education costs and cut student allowances, thus making it more difficult to acquire the skills Treasury saw as necessary for New Zealand's recovery.[24]

Not only did anecdotal evidence suggest a long-term problem, there was statistical evidence as well. Credible studies have consistently found no evidence of bargaining reforms to enhance productivity or training.[25] If anything the problem has been growing worse. In 1993, 51% of enterprises employing 48% of workers had failed to take on training, quality improvement, or other workplace reforms, compared to 41% of enterprises and 33% of employees the year before. In 1993, only 24% of enterprises employing 29% of employees had increased training.[26] In only

44 of 1053 contracts studied was there any linkage of improved productivity with pay.[27]

Those studies which find increased productivity and a linkage of it to the ECA are not based on an examination of contracts, nor do they measure productivity in a conventional way. Rather, they simply ask employers or workers for their impressions as to whether productivity has improved.[28] In other words, there is little solid evidence to support Birch's claim that the ECA had led to "implementation of a new remuneration package, which includes innovations such as performance related wage or salary reviews."[29]

The way training is analysed and discussed captures the debate on the ECA's impact. The NZEF favours training, job enrichment, and multi-skilling in nearly the same terms as does the Engineers.[30] There is anecdotal evidence that employers have personally found it easier to use apprentices because the ECA allows more "flexibility in the employment of apprentices."[31] However, it is not always clear that apprenticeships and training have the same meaning for all people. The Canterbury Manufacturers Association said that training included basic worker attitudes,[32] rather than teaching skills. Much of what is talked about as training may be no more than programs designed to improve worker loyalty and attitudes towards their employers. Labour–management cooperation has come into increasing use in New Zealand since the ECA.[33] Indeed, most of the NZEF discussion of best practice concerns improving worker attitudes.[34] Good worker attitudes are important to employers, but they do not improve workforce skills.

The NZBR had a different view about training. In 1994, Roger Kerr stated that too much emphasis was being put on training, that there were still a large number of unskilled jobs in the economy that did not require training and warned that too much training for jobs available would only lead to "credentials creep." He suggested that the statistics on training were failing to pick up many "important training experiences, particularly in small firms, such as co-workers 'sitting next to Nelly' and keeping their eyes and ears open." Finally, he argued that appropriate levels of training and skills were only likely to be achieved when markets are open to competition.[35]

In the depressed economy of the 1990s New Zealand employers found that it served their short-term interests to lower pay even though it was easy to see that this was likely to harm their and society's long-term needs, such as modernising industry, preventing the decline of skills, and ensuring a trained workforce. Indeed, it has not take long to see that New Zealand employers' long-term interests are suffering as skills decline and trained workers become a rarer commodity. Or, to put this into the sort of language preferred by the ECA's proponents, micro-rationality is leading to macro-irrationality. The Engineers saw this as endangering high skill industries and worried that whole industries might be lost as a result. Only multi-employer agreements could overcome individual employer fears. The Engineers thus tried to talk past the Act to employers. It took the position that, although the Act let them do what they wanted, employers should think about their industries and how the union could help them and also help their members.[36]

The Engineers' strategy left them open to attack and suspicion from both unionists and employers. In June 1991, the Engineers launched a publicity campaign that described unions as positive forces which offered support and services to their members. When Bill Birch praised the campaign, this did nothing to remove other unions' suspicions about the Engineers. Critics saw the Engineers as pursuing a strategy of appeasement when it tried to persuade management to let it participate in decision-making or promoted workplace reform.[37]

The Engineers' strategy also did not make it immune from losses under the ECA. Within a month of its enactment, the Engineers lost more membership than it had gained.[38] In May 1991, it had 43,000 members; by December 1993, it was down to 32,000,[39] the loss being due both to the recession and to the ECA. On April 1, 1996, it merged with the Printing, Packaging and Media Union to cover 14 industries and grew to 60,000 members.[40]

On the other hand, it had successes in promoting multi-employer bargaining and workplace reform. It was one of only six unions able to recreate award conditions by negotiating more than one multi-employer agreement. These included the Engineers (17), Service Workers Union (16), the National Distribution Union

(8), the New Zealand Educational Institute Te Riu Roa (4), the New Zealand Post Primary Teachers Association (3), and the Nurses Organisation (3).[41]

Within the ECA's first year, the Engineers negotiated its automotive industry multi-employer agreement without the involvement of the Employers Association. During the same time, it also became party to the Metal Trades, the Motor Trades, and the National Service Station multi-employer agreements. These were large documents which covered nearly as many workers as the awards had. Achieving a multi-employer replacement for the Metal Trades Award was no small accomplishment, given both the nature of the ECA and the fact that the Metal Trades Award had been a particular target. MP Max Bradford (formerly employed by Treasury, the NZEF, and the National Party)[42] and others regarded it as the pattern setter for other negotiations.

> [T]he Employers Association took the view that if they could break the Metal Trades Award then they would break the back of the industry unions, break the back of industry awards and be able to get company bargaining off to the right start. So they put up a massive campaign against us getting the Metal Trades Award renegotiated.[43]

The process of negotiating these agreements was very different from awards. Negotiations took place with only a small group of employers. Afterwards, the Engineers marketed the document to other companies.[44] The LRA had provided government support for employer collective activity. Multi-employer agreements required recreating collectivity by promoting the formation of multi-employer industry groups to bargain with. Persuading employers to agree to a multi-employer contract was also more difficult under the ECA, since s 63(e) made it illegal to strike for a multi-employer CEC.[45] The Engineers sent organisers out to promote it as a simplified document tailored to the industry and as a way for employers to save time and money, to coordinate training, and to create standard qualifications in the industry.[46] The Engineers also urged union members to tell their employers they wanted to be covered by the industry contract.[47]

Agreement to the multi-employer Metals document took place in the face of NZEF opposition.[48] The NZEF's official view of employers' agreeing to multi-employer agreements was that the "Federation's prime concern has been that [employers] are doing so consciously and for the right reason—not because the option to change was too hard, too disruptive or too time-consuming."[49] If employer-clients wanted to be party to multi-employer agreements, employers association advocates did represent them.[50]

Having a multi-employer agreement helped continue New Zealand's tradition of a level playing field and industry training. By April 1992, 120 employers had signed the multi-employer Northern Metal Industries Contract (which covered the North Island); by the end of June, 153 had signed. Southern Metal (which covered the South Island) had more than 47 signatory employers by the end of June 1991. The Engineers multi-employer plastic industry contract had more than 100 employer signatories by then.[51]

In May 1992, the Engineers consummated two multi-employer contracts covering 5000 workers employed by more than 1000 members of the Motor Trades Association and the Engine Reconditioners Association. The Motor Trades Award covered 97% of service stations. The Engineers believed that the Motor Trades Association had agreed to negotiate because it saw the union as prepared to play a constructive role in their industry's problems, and it attributed the association's change of attitude to the experience of direct bargaining. The Motor Trades Association explained that it saw the contracts as a way for companies to compete based on skill and quality, rather than by undercutting wages. However, as a trade-off for the agreement, the Engineers negotiated a no-increase agreement.[52]

The Engineers' successes in achieving multi-employer agreements must be assessed—not alone—but against the economy and the ECA which gave employers the power to force contracts on many workers. Hel Loader of the Engineers observed:

> They've got the power. A lot of them take the point of view that during the '70s you guys used to whack us around and get extremely high pay rounds. Now the boot's on the other foot,

and it's our turn to have a bit of fun. And we expected that. That happens, and nobody's perfect. Unions have had a history of being greedy, in cases. We acknowledge that. That doesn't mean to say that during this period we're going to go back and revert to a very confrontational style of not giving an inch and protecting everything. Because I think that would be very unproductive in the end. I think we would end up cracking under that kind of strain. So we've continued with the positive attitude where we can and we necessarily have a lot of industrial action when we need to resolve the contract.[53]

In some of these cases, bargaining strategy and the cohesiveness of the workforce have enabled them to hold out for terms they want. At Pacific Steel, when the company presented the workers with IECs, the workers held out for a CEC and party status for their union. Workers printed stickers with the words "Collective Contract" and wore them on their helmets at a company open house. When one manager threatened to discharge a group of workers unless they signed the contract and took off the stickers, the workers struck. At another Pacific Steel plant, one manager responded by putting a dinosaur tag over the collective contract sticker he had been given. The strike ended within a couple of hours when a senior manager agreed to negotiate a CEC with the union.[54]

The more normal case, however, has been crisis after crisis. Multi-employer contracts may be a passing phenomenon. In May 1994, 18.4% of workers surveyed were covered by multi-employer contracts.[55] Two years later, in May 1996, only 12% of employees in the same survey or 2.4% of total employees in the workforce were covered by multi-employer contracts.[56]

Multi-employer agreements may have little directly to do with the desires of workers covered by them. The Service Station multi-employer agreement continues to exist, more because employers want it than as a result of the Engineers' ability to organise this sector. The station attendants are similar to SWU and Distribution Union members—transients, part-timers, and youth. The Engineers admit that, even with all their resources, they cannot maintain such workers as a cohesive group. However, employer desires for stability and uniform conditions, mean that these workers have higher pay and terms than they otherwise would.[57]

One little-explored aspect of multi-employer contracts is the role the regional employer associations have played. Part of their opposition may be rooted in a calculation as to which form of bargaining is in their best interest. Multi-employer negotiations are cost-effective for the parties but mean less need overall for bargaining representation and advice. Ironically then, the ECA presented a dangerous situation for some of its major proponents. The situation may become more precarious over time. Many employers have become or are becoming experienced bargainers or are developing their own bargaining resources. Nearly three-quarters of employers who engaged in collective bargaining are doing so without professional assistance.[58] As a consequence, the regional employer associations and the NZEF are in danger of losing a hold on employer bargaining policy.[59]

As a response to the enactment of the ECA a legion of employment lawyers and labour consultants grew up to assist employers in grappling with the greater complexity of the law and the greater legalism of the bargaining process. By early 1992, it was estimated that there were between 50 to 100 labour consultants[60] competing for representation work. Management consultant Rob Campbell praised the ECA for "providing a market to sort out the most efficient bargaining agents."[61] Some thought this would also extend to employee representation.

Roger Kerr, Executive Director of the NZBR, summed up the effect of the ECA on unions:

> Trade unions, having enjoyed monopoly rights for more than fifty years, were typically in poor shape to meet the EC Act's challenges. They were understaffed, and often ill-equipped, for commercial negotiations. Their focus had previously been on politically-motivated intervention. Some union officials acting as bargaining agents in workplace negotiations have turned out to be ineffectual. While unions continue to represent workers in the majority of collective contracts, there has been a significant shift to the employment of non-union agents, and to employees

representing themselves. In the largest, traditionally unionised sites, the inertia is greatest. There are geographical variations; the north of the country, where Marxist influences were previously strongest, is the most reactionary, while the south is often the most innovative.[62]

ECA proponents had long contended that the free market would have a benign impact on unions by increasing competition for members, which would lead to improved member services. They also claimed that eradicating unions' monopoly privileges would enhance the community's opinion of trade unions and lead to unions which attracted member allegiance and loyalty without compulsion.

Consultants came from a variety of backgrounds. Some had gained experience as employer negotiators, often for the NZEA or one of its affiliates. One prominent consultant, Mike Hanson of Teesdale-Meuli, made the easy transition from work as a management representative to that of being a consultant. He had been a negotiator for the Wellington Employers Association and in 1985 was accused by Labour Prime Minister David Lange of "being prone to some of the most extravagant excesses of socialist philanthropy" when he negotiated a 15.5% pay raise.[63]

Some prominent consultants received their training as union representatives. Francis Wevers, for example, was Wellington Regional Secretary for the PSA from 1981 to 1990. In fact, Wevers said, many of his management clients hired him because of his union background. Those with a union staff felt he could sell management's position more effectively. Wevers discouraged de-unionising, because he felt having a union would give the workers a security blanket and the process of de-unionising would create a rift with management. Wevers found as he continued in this new role that, while he thought the ECA was an unbalanced piece of legislation in practice, he had become a convert to its philosophy.[64] Rob Campbell, also once a union representative, embraced his new role with ardour.[65]

Although some of these new consultants once sat on opposite sides of the table, by the time the ECA came into existence, their views and modes of operation were similar. They tended to regard themselves as facilitators, although they mainly worked for employers. They said they tried to involve themselves in a process that went beyond just negotiating a contract. Hanson also said he was not anti-union; however, what this meant in practice was not necessarily positive for unions. Hanson explained: "If a union is part of the picture and if it will accept change, that's great. But if it won't, I will shift on to other options." These options included dealing directly with the employees until at least two signed a CEC, which then set the terms for the workplace. If this didn't work, Hanson was ready to use partial lockouts to impose the employer's conditions.[66]

Some, such as the CTU's Ken Douglas, condemned consultants in no uncertain terms:

> Having raped and wrecked finance, forex, share and property markets, yuppiedom is turning to the labour market as a new source of plunder. I don't think they will be a big influence in the longer term. The work is too hard and there really isn't the money-for-nothing opportunity that these parasites seem to need.[67]

However, others in the union movement felt they provided expertise to employers without the ideological rigidity of the NZEF.[68]

The NZEF and NZBR had argued that individual workers would turn to management consultant services or lawyers rather than unions. The reality was that neither lawyers nor management consultants tended to represent workers. Theory had to yield to the reality of workers, most of whom were like Harry Harris. Harris worked for Farmers grocery in Palmerston North and had two children ages ten and seven. He grossed $339 a week, including overtime, and netted $270. This was $50 less than he would receive on the dole, even after the benefit cuts.[69] Employer Capital Coast Health ran up legal fees of $443,000 during its 1994–1995 negotiating disputes,[70] close to what Harris could expect to make in his working life.

The logic of the situation was borne out by a 1991 Department of Labour survey which found little evidence that workers were using private negotiators.[71] A 1995 survey found only 3% of workers were represented by a non-union agent.[72] Employers, too, tried to save on costs by doing their own negotiating with occasional questions to accountants, other retailers, or employer organisations.[73] One director testified when her company was tried for violating the ECA that she had adapted an employment contract given her by a friend in the building industry for clerical, sales, and production workers. She had discussed its terms with her employees without the aid of the company's solicitors. The resulting document and legal troubles reflected this process.[74] Employer consultants felt the effects of these cost-saving measures. In 1996, Francis Wevers closed his consultancy as a result, he said, of an insufficient revenue stream.[75]

As Harris saw it, the only way he could get decent conditions under the ECA would be by hiring a capable bargaining representative. "Of course," he said, "it depends on who I can afford to hire, and as a family we struggle now, even cutting groceries back."[76] More employees were like Harry Harris than like Capital Coast. They could afford union representation which cost about $1.50–$4.00 a week. The alternative representatives the NZBR and NZEF had argued would come into the market just could not compete with unions,[77] especially when one adds to the outright cost the fact that employers can deduct negotiating costs as business expenses for tax purposes, something denied workers.[78]

As union numbers have declined, as employers have been given more and better tools by the ECA and court interpretations to defeat unions, the Harry Harrises of New Zealand will be denied what they know is the only way to get decent conditions—representation by a capable bargaining agent.

Notes
1. Raymond Harbridge & Anthony Honeybone, "External Legitimacy of Unions: Trends in New Zealand," 17 J. Lab. Res., 425, 433, 434–35 (1996).
2. Peter Franks, "The Employment Contracts Act and the Demise of the New Zealand Clerical Workers Union," *NZ Journal of History*, 28, 194 (1994).
3. Raymond Harbridge & Anthony Honeybone, "The Employment Contracts Act and Collective Bargaining Patterns: A Review of

the 1994/95 Year" in *Employment Contracts: Bargaining Trends & Employment Law Update 1994/95*, 9 (Raymond Harbridge & Peter Kiely, eds., 1995).
4. *NZ Dairy Workers Inc. v. Hautapu Whey Transport Ltd.* [1994] 2 ERNZ 549, 555.
5. David Barber, "Throwing Off the Cloth Cap," *National Business Review*, Sept. 13, 1991, at 30.
6. Patricia Herbert, "Workers Stick Close to Union's Petticoats," *Dominion*, June 19, 1991, at 12.
7. Nigel Haworth, "Unions in Crisis: Deregulation and Reform of the New Zealand Union Movement" in *Organized Labor in the Asia–Pacific Region: A Comparative Study of Trade Unionism in Nine Countries*, 282, 297 (Stephen Frenkel, ed., 1993).
8. Patricia Herbert, "Burying the Hatchet," *Auckland Star*, Aug. 4, 1991, at D3, D4.
9. Patricia Herbert, "Union's Radical Response to Shrinking Market," *Dominion*, Aug. 9, 1991, at 6.
10. Barber, "Throwing Off the Cloth Cap," 30.
11. Herbert, "Union's Radical Response."
12. See Hamid Azari-Rad, Anne Yeagle & Peter Philips, "The Effects of the Repeal of Utah's Prevailing Wage Law on the Labor Market in Construction" in *Restoring the Promise of American Labor Law*, 207, 209, 212–220 (Sheldon Friedman et al. eds., 1994).
13. Steve O'Neill, "Labour Market Deregulation: The New Zealand Experience," 19 (Parl. Res. Serv. Background Paper No.5 1993).
14. Rasmussen, "Chronicle," 20 N.Z. J. Ind. Rel., 342 (1995).
15. Peter Brosnan, "Labour Market Flexibility and the Quality of Work: A Case Study of the Retail Industry," 16 N.Z. J. Ind. Rel., 13, 29 (1991).
16. Janet Hector, Jon Hemming & Mary Hubble, "Industrial Relations Bargaining in the Retail Non-food Sector: 1991–1992," 18 N.Z. J. Ind. Rel., 326, 336, 340 (1993).
17. *Id.*, 29–30.
18. Rasmussen, "Chronicle," 20 N.Z. J. Ind. Rel., 346 (1995).
19. Mark Gosche, "The Impact of Enterprise Bargaining on New Zealand Workers" in *Enterprise Bargaining: Experiences From New Zealand Workplaces*, 36, 39, 40–41 (1993); "$1 an Hour Rise Recognises Extra Skills of School Caretakers," *Service Workers*, 3 (June 1996).
20. Nicola Legat, "Bargain Bin Industrial Relations," *Metro*, 104, 107 (Sept. 1995).
21. Sarah Oxenbridge, "Health Sector Collective Bargaining and the Employment Contracts Act: A Case Study of Nurses," 19 N.Z. J. Ind. Rel., 17, 26 (1994).
22. Interview with Hel Loader, Research Advocate, New Zealand Engineering Union, in Wellington (May 13, 1992).
23. Michael Pearson & Rachell Rose, "Sign or Resign: Who Wins

With Contracts?" *Management*, 57, 57 (June 1992).
24. Natalie Jackson, "Youth Unemployment and the 'Invisible Hand'— A Case for a Social Measure of Unemployment" in *Labour, Employment and Work in New Zealand 1994*, 177, 178 (Philip S. Morrison, ed., 1994).
25. Rebecca Macfie, "Employers Set Industrial Agenda," *National Business Review*, Nov. 15, 1991, at 19.
26. Richard Whatman et al., "Labour Market Adjustment Under the Employment Contracts Act," 19 N.Z. J. Ind Rel., 53, 70 (1994).
27. Raymond Harbridge, "New Zealand's Collective Employment Contracts: Update November 1992," 18 N.Z. J. Ind. Rel., 113, 121 (1993).
28. John Savage, "What Do We Know About the Economic Impacts of the ECA?" (Auckland, May 15, 1996).
29. Labour Minister Bill Birch, "Address to the N.Z. Industrial Relations Conference," 10 (Feb. 17, 1992).
30. NZEF, *Human Resources: An Introduction to Best Practice* (1992).
31. Correspondence File, *Employer*, June 1996, at 3.
32. "Skills Survey Identifies Gap," *NZ Manufacturer*, Oct. 1994, at 7.
33. Clive Gilson & Terry Wagar, *Employee Involvement and Human Resource Management in Australian, New Zealand, and Canadian Organisations* (1996)
34. NZEF, "Best Practice."
35. Roger Kerr, *Ten Myths About Training in The Next Decade of Change*, 161 (NZBR, ed., 1994).
36. Loader.
37. Roth, "Chronicle," 16 N.Z. J. Ind. Rel., 209 (1991); Barber, Barber, "Throwing Off the Cloth Cap," 30; Colin James, "Trade Halls Alive to the Sound of Labour Music," *National Business Review*, Sept. 6, 1991, at 7.
38. Herbert, "Workers Stick Close to Union's Petticoats."
39. Raymond Harbridge & Kevin Hince, *A Sourcebook of New Zealand Trade Unions and Employee Organisations*, 36 (1994).
40. "Birth of a Super Union," *Metal*, June 1996, at 1.
41. Raymond Harbridge, "Union Decline in New Zealand: Lessons from the International Experience," 9 (n.d.); Patricia Herbert, "Democracy Versus Fringe Benefits," *Dominion*, Nov. 28, 1991, at 6.
42. Mike Jaspers, "On Course for the Top," *National Business Review*, Feb. 27, 1991, at 9; Patricia Herbert, "Max Factor Behind the Birch Bill," *Dominion*, Apr. 17, 1991, at 14.
43. Loader.
44. Sue Scott, "Union Offers Contract Guide," *Evening Post*, Sept. 24, 1991, at 4.
45. "Employers Scrap Awards," *M&C Workers News*, Dec. 1991, at 6.
46. Sue Scott, "Contract Guide."
47. Roth, "Chronicle," 16 N.Z. J. Ind. Rel., 128 (1991).

48. Harbridge & Honeybone, "External Legitimacy," 434–35; Roth, "Chronicle," 16 N.Z. J. Ind. Rel., 324 (1991).
49. NZEF, *1991 Annual Report*, 9 (1991).
50. Interview with Murray French, Manager Labour Relations Services, Wellington Employers Association, in Wellington, May 14, 1992.
51. Roth, "Chronicle," 17 N.Z. J. Ind. Rel., 254, 258 (1992).
52. *Id.*; Roth, "Chronicle," 16 N.Z. J. Ind. Rel., 207 (1991); "Industry-wide Job Contracts Signed," *Dominion*, May 10, 1992, at 3.
53. Loader.
54. *Metal*, Apr./May 1992, at 1.
55. *Contract*, 1–2 (May 1994).
56. *Contract*, 2 (May 1996).
57. Interview with Suze Wilson, National Industrial Officer, NZ Engineering Printing & Manufacturing Union, in Wellington, June 16, 1996.
58. Ian McAndrew, "From Regulation to Deregulation in New Zealand Labour Relations: New Models of Bargaining Under the Employment Contracts Act 1991," 11 (Jan. 5, 1993).
59. Interview with Rick Barker, National Secretary, Service Workers Federation of Aotearoa, in Wellington, May 14, 1992; Suze Wilson.
60. Patricia Herbert, "Negotiators Flourish in the World of Contracts," *Press*, Feb. 20, 1992, at 7.
61. Michael Stutchbury, "Shake-Up on NZ Shop Floor," *Financial Review*, July 3, 1992, at 14.
62. Roger Kerr, "Bargaining Under the Employment Contracts Act," Empl. L. Bull., 97, 98 (Sept. 1995).
63. Herbert, "Negotiators Flourish."
64. Interview with Francis Wevers, Principal of Francis Wevers and Associates, Ltd., at Wellington (May 20, 1992); Herbert, "Negotiators Flourish."
65. Rebecca Macfie & Brad Tattersfield, "Govt Rules Out Actions Against Teacher Strike," *National Business Review*, Apr. 4, 1991, at 2; Herbert, "Clipping Pay on the Buses," *Dominion*, July 16, 1991, at 6; Rob Campbell, "The Employment Contracts Bill: Two Very Different Perspectives," *Examiner*, Apr. 18, 1991, at 18, 19.
66. Herbert, "Negotiators Flourish."
67. Ken Douglas, "The Employment Contracts Bill: Two Very Different Perspectives," *Examiner*, Apr. 18, 1991, at 18.
68. Barker.
69. Letter from Harry Harris to the Labour Select Committee (Feb. 8, 1991).
70. Rasmussen, "Chronicle," 20 N.Z. J. Ind. Rel., 228 (1995).
71. Macfie, "Employers Set Industrial Agenda."
72. Harbridge & Honeybone, "The Employment Contracts Act and Collective Bargaining Patterns: A Review of the 1994/95 Year," 7.

73. Hector, Henning & Hubble, 337.
74. *O'Malley v. Vision Aluminium Ltd (II)*, [1992] 2 ERNZ 660, 664–65.
75. "Loose Change," *Auckland Sunday Star-Times*, June 23, 1996, at D-1.
76. Harry Harris.
77. "A Warning: Why You Must Belong to NZNO," *Nursing NZ*, 33 (Apr. 1995); Philippa Branthwaite, "Who Gives You the Best Deal?" *NZ Nursing Journal*, 9 (July 1991).
78. Wellington Unemployed Workers Union, Submission on the Employment Contracts Act, 1, 3 (Feb. 8, 1991).

18

Who Owns the Job? Work, Unions, Society, Law, and Justice

ASKING "WHO OWNS THE JOB?" ULTIMATELY MEANS ANSWERING THE most fundamental questions about the sort of society we want to live in. To ECA proponents the answer is simple: the job is privately owned by the employer. However, if the ECA teaches anything it teaches us that jobs are owned by all of society, because they are so intertwined with the direction in which society is heading. This means that society has a right and duty to determine the nature of the job, how work is done.

If we pay attention to the lessons of the experiment known as the ECA, we are confronted with fundamental questions. How can and should work in modern society be organised? Why do or should unions exist? Can or should laws be enacted to help unions survive? How must and should labour law be drafted? The structures involved are complex in themselves and in their interactions. The discussion demands a seriousness that is equal to their complexity, even though we might prefer simple answers.

The ECA is premised on simple assumptions and easy answers, but the evidence is that these have not been adequate to the task. For example, the ECA was supposed to defuse workplace conflict by increasing and improving communication. ECA proponents relied for a while on the simple measure of strike statistics, which were low in the first few years, as proof that there was less conflict.

There are several problems with this. First, in more recent years strikes have been steadily rising. The easy answer must have missed something. Second, they picked the grossest evidence of workplace conflict, one that is not always a good indicator of its level. When workers feel too disempowered to strike, strike rates will be low, but conflict may still have negative consequences. It can be seen in high quit rates, high levels of absenteeism, less work effort expended, sabotage, and less commitment to the workplace. There have been indicators that this sort of conflict has persisted and even increased (see Chapter 10).

The increase in grievances filed[1] represents the loss of a less formal, more effective way of resolving and defusing workplace problems, with a union representative.[2] High quit rates also suggest that workers feel a lack of voice and have chosen to exit. The ECA's representation system provides incentives to file grievances. The Hotel Association's executive officer, Ian Bray, observed that, before the ECA, "most disputes were settled amicably and swiftly because there was little or no financial benefit to union delegates to prolong disputes."[3] Even if there is no financial incentive to prolong a case, unions must now show their members that they are effective and aggressive representatives and cannot risk being conciliatory.

Although ECA supporters claim that events since 1991 demonstrate that unions are unnecessary and destructive, a fair and non-ideological analysis of the facts would find the case not proven. As union density has declined, so too have conditions for many people. Disparities between those well off and those in poverty have increased rapidly. Stories of workplace mistreatment and victimisation persist. It is simply too early to conclude that unions should be discarded.

How then has the ECA performed with respect to unions? ECA supporters claim that unions have failed to thrive within a regime of freedom because unions are illegitimate. The facts do not support this claim. The second half of this book has analysed the myriad ways in which the ECA and court interpretations have undermined union effectiveness and worker choice, particularly in the crucial first three years.

Union opponents also contend that unions are illegitimate because they cannot survive without legal supports. It is fair to say that there is no evidence that unions have ever flourished for more than a relatively brief period without support from law. However, having legislative support does not mean that unions are illegitimate or weak. Law exists to help shape society according to our aspirations. Many things do not exist without the support of law—corporations, for example. However, legislators have decided that corporations serve a socially useful purpose and therefore have passed laws to create them. When legislators decide corporations are not socially useful, they can take away the statutory props and that will be the end of all corporations. In exactly this way, if we think unions are socially useful, then we should provide legislation to support them and to fashion them to perform the functions we desire.

The drafters and proponents of the ECA failed to appreciate a great deal about law.[4] They tend to think of law as statute only; however, even in the absence of statute, all things are controlled by law, including unions. When statutes are repealed, in New Zealand the common law applies. That law may be more or less favourable to unions and workers than a particular statute. Sometimes it is difficult to assess whether a law is favourable or not. For example, although many see the statutes in force before the ECA as favourable to unions, in important ways they were harmful.

However, then large numbers of unions existed and interacted with members and employers, obscuring a disturbing reality. High union density rates conveyed a false sense that unions were strong. The statistics made it easy to overlook evidence that the union movement was weak and drifting. This weakness can, in part, be attributed to labour laws which had failed to encourage unions to exercise their potential power[5] and to form strong ties with their members, and indeed prevented them from doing so. A union that does not have the support of its members is severely weakened. As Maxine Gay observed:

> [Y]ou have to go on . . . from a position of strength rather than a position of weakness. And I don't think that we did enough of our own work with our own members to have that position of strength. . . .
>
> . . . [W]e didn't know [what our members wanted]. I mean we would say, "Our members just won't tolerate this."

> We didn't know what they wouldn't tolerate because we were never willing enough to take the chance. We had no idea. We knew how many union members we had pretty much generally in the movement but we didn't know how many unionists that we had and when it came to the crunch, we were too scared to find out.[6]

Law that fosters unions' losing touch with their members is ultimately destructive of unions.[7] A challenging question, then, is whether law can be written so as to help unions be more effective. Such a law would have to encourage union activism or provide disincentives to unions which fail to represent their constituents.

Any law concerning unions must have a realistic grasp on how the employment relationship functions. The ECA is based on abstractions and is so ideologically driven that it fails to take account of or provide for common problems in work relationships. For example, in addition to failing to appreciate the ways in which conflict between employers and employees exists, the law failed to provide a reasonable way for dealing with what may be transient worker dissatisfaction within unions. Unions need to compromise and mediate diverse desires and needs in bargaining and may, as a result, make some of their members—those who do not gain by a particular compromise—unhappy. Other union actions, however, may satisfy such members so that, on balance, they are reasonably satisfied with the union. On the other hand, sometimes workers are dissatisfied with serious union malfeasance. While the previous legislation made it difficult for the latter to voice their dissatisfaction effectively, the ECA promotes exit and schism even for momentary discontent. This weakens unions and makes them ineffective at promoting member interests. The less effective they are as a result of schism, the less unions can attract new members.

Effective labour law reflects the democratic ideals of the larger society by giving workers a meaningful way to persuade others, to influence decisions, or to take power. It will foster unions which are not impervious to change, to the ferment of disparate viewpoints, and to the needs and aspirations of minorities and majorities. The ideal would be a union as a nurturing community based upon strong connections among workers and a commitment to the union's goals, a place in which members can seek meaningful access to procedural and substantive workplace justice.[8]

Thus, a union must have the stability to carry forward the members' agenda. There are many ways in which a fair and workable compromise between stability and freedom can be reached and imperviousness or ineffectiveness avoided. To make the choice of representation a serious one, it must exist for sufficient time to permit the union to carry through a program and to allow its effectiveness to be gauged. Full freedom to choose a representative leads to instability and makes bargaining chaotic.

The ECA experience also underscores the importance of establishing representation on something less variable than an individual worker. Representation needs to be based on something more permanent, such as an industry or job classification, about which meaningful bargaining can occur. This will promote stability and allow the parties to focus on negotiations, agreement, and work. To provide freedom, representation could be challenged at some reasonable interval of years.

For such a system to function, the decision as to who will represent the workers must be lodged solely with the workers. For those who argue that the employer needs to protect the business from the workers, we need to return to the question of who owns the job. Workers know they have a stake in the job's continuing to exist. There does not seem to be any good reason not to have faith in the seriousness of workers to make this decision. They know only too well the results that could flow from an unwise choice and that they are likely to bear them.

To ensure that decisions as to representation are effective and meaningful, employers must not be permitted to interfere with a free decision. This system would also mean eliminating the ECA's complex and burdensome method of authorisation. A major impediment to ECA bargaining is the ephemeral nature of designating a bargaining representative. Authorising and reauthorising bargaining representatives requires enormous effort by unions just to maintain the right to exist. This shifts resources away from workers' needs.

Recognising a union must mean more than form. Unfortunately, this is one situation in which no compromise or middle ground is possible since either the employer must recognise or not recognise the worker's choice.[9] If a society believes that collective bargaining performs a valuable role, then it must support the workers' decision. The ECA teaches us that letting the employer decide a representative's legitimacy does not work because it allows an employer to act as judge in its own case. In other words, the employer is likely to see itself as gaining by not recognising the representative. Recognition is a task which must be left to a disinterested party, and the most appropriate party is a government agency which is impervious to partisan pressures and which exists to promote fair and effective worker representation.

The ECA and its proponents insist that a worker and an employer are equals when it comes to bargaining.[10] Such a position represents a failure or a refusal to see the many ways in which law and society support employers. The most effective relationships and the best agreements occur between equals. The freedom that workers need is the ability to make a free decision to form a collective entity that can meet with the employer on equal terms. Workers cannot make a free choice unless they are assured they will not suffer retaliation, coercion, or threats. This protection must extend from the initial choice of representation to bargaining and through all aspects of the relationship.

The ECA sees only the action of agreeing to a contract as having significance. However, the work relationship is a long-term one. A labour law that ignores this reality cannot be effective. It must think through the whole course of the relationship.

The ECA story also tells us that, just as worker collective power is important to counterbalance employer power, so also more is involved than a war between the employed and employers. Not all employers used their power to exploit their workforces. Not all workers were supine in the face of superior power. Workers do depend on employer viability and success. To be useful, analyses must come to grips with these complex interactions.

The ECA experience shows that many of the arguments advanced in its support have been shown to be untrue. For example, no credible evidence has been brought forward that employees or employers want or can achieve meaningfully individualised contracts. Rather than setting wages to promote specific enterprise productivity goals, wages have tended to be set relative to those paid by competitors. Employers have tried to recreate the level playing field that previously existed. They have not demonstrated a preference for having enterprise agreements with unique terms, let alone agreements individualised for each employee.

> They all talked about how relativities should be gone, but with the Employment Contracts Act, all I've heard from the employers is relativities, that they don't them want to be paying any more than their competitors down the road or anybody else.
>
> This is not only so in the hospitality sector but in the health area. Southern Cross have told our organisation that their wage cost is fifteen percent below that which is being paid by the state, and they wish to maintain that differential or advantage or improve on it.[11]

This was also the experience in area health board negotiations with the New Zealand Nurses Association.[12]

It is necessary to develop a historical perspective and to understand the forces that shaped the system that now exists before trying to change it. If those forces and needs still exist they will reshape the new system in the image of the old. When one observes employer drift toward recreating the award system, it seems possible that it grew up to meet an employer need and that it provided a meaningful structure in which bargaining could take place. The fact that other countries have similar structures suggests that these forces are not unique to New Zealand.

Labour law must promote bargaining between or among the parties. This means deciding how to handle behaviour which damages the relationship, including attempts by the parties to exit from bargaining. It also requires deciding how to handle failures to agree on contract terms. New Zealand and other countries offer wide experience on how to resolve impasses. The one outcome that is not viable is to permit a party to impose its terms on the other. Resolving impasses in this way does nothing more than provide incentives to exit bargaining and even to create impasses to so as to provide a pretext for imposing terms. This means that the law cannot allow the employer to walk away or control the process of bargaining, especially in a situation in which the employer has proved unwilling to try to seek accommodation. Any other course creates an illusory right, and history teaches that this leads to social unrest.

Finally, in fashioning labour law, we need to acknowledge that what happens in the workplace is not merely a matter between private parties. We all own the job, and we are all responsible for what the job does to the person who fills it. We must confront what it means for society as a whole when employers have, and exercise, the sort of power the ECA has given them. One New Zealand union representative observed:

> As it stands here, it's hopeless. At the end of the day, if you are not going to get a settlement, there has to be a new dimension and if the employer continues to exercise that right—and this is one thing that the employers have learned is that they have the right to veto, the right to say no and, my God have they exercised it. Take this or leave it. And that's the end of it in 99% of the cases. And if the workers disagree with it, they just simply either deal with them individually or lock them out either technically or by direct lockout and re-engage workers, if they locked them out physically, engage them behind our backs.
>
> I mean, it's impossible to bargain in these situations as an equal. It's not designed to be equal, of course. So, for some workers who are in key and strategic industries, who are organised and understand all that, they will always be able to bargain and get a settlement.
>
> For workers who are employed in industries or in places who do not have economic clout, they will always continue to do worse.
>
> So, it comes down to what we want as a society. Do we want a society that has a great spread of incomes so you have very poor or very wealthy, or do we want a society which treats

everybody with some respect and dignity. And if we want to treat everyone with some dignity, then I think the state has to intervene on behalf of those who are less powerful and the most open to exploitation, the most vulnerable in society.[13]

ECA proponents like to claim that what they see as positive impacts flow from the statute as drafted. In fact, the ECA is legislation which is so bound by ideology as to be unworkable. The ECA tries to leave to the workings of the market every difficult issue which a labour law must face. These include the level of coercion which is acceptable in reaching agreement, how impasses are to be resolved, how representation is to be achieved and what it means once achieved, what happens during the life of a contract, and how to keep the parties working together in the system.

Lack of attention to these important matters has meant that creative lawyers and their clients have taken every opportunity to push the limits in how the ECA is to be applied. In fact, in reading through court cases, one is struck by how much creative energy has been employed in trying to restructure the ECA into a system of full employer hegemony rather than treating workers as partners in the workplace.

The bad news, for those who believe in the ECA, is that this piece of legislation has virtually never existed. In fact, it has been the effort of the courts in interpreting the law and trying to reshape it into something functional that has produced the ECA most New Zealanders experience. It is no exaggeration to say that any claims about ECA successes must acknowledge the importance of court decisions in achieving those successes.

Instead of acknowledging the important role the courts have played, the NZEF and NZBR have attacked the judiciary whenever a decision is handed down that does not permit employers to have absolute control over the workforce. It is difficult to understand why they think employer hegemony equates with industrial relations and why they think this hegemony would be good for the society.

The ECA teaches us the importance of knowledge. It owes its existence to a campaign of disinformation. The ECA not only transformed New Zealand labour relations, it also formally abolished record-keeping as to union membership and changes in wages, benefits, and other terms. As a result, the data necessary to assessing the legislation have been hard to come by. It is an interesting choice to deprive oneself of knowledge and the ability to make informed decisions, but that is what the ECA's supporters wanted and got.

Even though data are important, it must be borne in mind that simply relying on numbers may fail to provide information about the things we want to know. For example, New Zealand and other countries with high union density figures have had their industrial relations system held up as models for no reason other than those figures. A deeper look at New Zealand's situation makes it clear that union density, while easy to calculate and compare as a simple percentage, failed to capture the deep malaise of most unions.[14] Since its enactment ECA supporters have advanced figures such as official unemployment or base wage rates as demonstrating that the ECA is superior legislation. As discussed, those figures have periodically been misused to create a false picture.

This issue of information suggests the need to reassess what is measured and how. If we base our actions upon what is measured and studied, then we have to be careful what information we collect.[15] If we base too much on economic figures, then we have decided that money is the meaning of life. "What is lost coming under the influence of this dragon is the flesh and blood of people whose values and aspirations are reduced to the periodic printing of a paycheck."[16] A measurement intended to help us understand phenomena in the larger world can, if we are not careful, become that larger world. There must be a way to understand the human condition more fully than what the dollar can measure.

It is not surprising that the ECA is assessed solely in economic terms. The ECA was the spawn, in great part, of American interpretations of neoclassical economic theory. These theories appeal because they appear to explain all and to be rigorous and, hence, scientific. However, their conceptual perfection fails to explain anything we need to know about the world. Missing from this abstract world-view and from discussions about the ECA have been the important issues that humans have asked through the years—issues of justice and how to lead a good life, not only as individuals but as members of our communities and as only one of many generations. Policy based on an impoverished view of human beings—a view that respects only the individual isolated from these webs of connection—must be approached with concern.

This book is an attempt to confront and understand the phenomenon of the ECA. One book alone cannot answer the perennially difficult questions about the nature of the society we wish to live in and which we want future generations to inherit. At best, it can aim to redirect our attempts to face the profound moral and ideological changes wrought in New Zealand during the past decade. Those of us who do understand the significance of these questions of morality and justice must take on the task of ensuring that these unexamined and under-appreciated values are restored to a place in the debate.

Notes
1. *Report of the Labour Committee on the Inquiry Into the Effects of the Employment Contracts Act 1991 on the New Zealand Market*, 44–48 (1993).
2. Lana Le Quesne, "Unions Fighting for Survival," *Race Gender Class*, 13, 30 (1992).
3. Anna Dunbar, "Cards Today 'Stacked Against Employer'," *Press*, Sept. 14, 1994, at 1.
4. John Hughes, "The Critical Weaknesses in Kerr's Case Against High Court Judges," *Press*, Aug. 2, 1995, at 11.
5. Katherine Van Wezel Stone, "The Legacy of Industrial Pluralism: The Tension Between Individual Employment Rights and the New Deal Collective Bargaining System," 59 U. Chi. L. Rev., 575, 584 (1992).
6. Interview with Maxine Gay, Organiser, Public Service Association, Palmerston North, May 17, 1992.
7. James Atleson, *Values and Assumptions in American Labor Law*, 119 (1983).
8. Marion Crain, "Feminizing Unions: Challenging the Gendered Structure of Wage Labor," 89 Mich. L. Rev., 1155, 1213 (1991)
9. International Labour Organisation, 292nd Report of the Committee on Freedom of Association, Case No.1698 ¶¶ 733–735 (Mar.

1994); Kidd, Speech to the Plenary Session of the International Labour Organisation, 2 (June 8, 1994).
10. Roger Kerr, "A Crucial Weakness in the Courts," *Press*, July 26, 1995, at 11.
11. Interview with Rick Barker, National Secretary, Service Workers Federation of Aotearoa, in Wellington (May 14, 1992).
12. Sarah Oxenbridge, "Health Sector Collective Bargaining and the Employment Contracts Act: A Case Study of Nurses," 19 N.Z. J. Ind. Rel., 17, 23 (1994).
13. Interview with Rick Barker, National Secretary, Service Workers Federation of Aotearoa, in Wellington (May 14, 1992).
14. Thomas Kochan, Harry Katz & Robert McKersie, *The Transformation of American Industrial Relations*, ix (1994).
15. Cf. Kerr.
16. Edmund Byrne, *Work, Inc.: A Philosophical Inquiry*, 4 (1990).

Statutory Citations

Employment Contracts Act 1991

Long title, 196, 202
s 2, 232
s 6(2), 77
ss 6-8, 45
ss 6-10, 47
s 8, 202
s 10, 267
s 12, 197-98, 219, 267, 269
s 13, 222, 269
s 14, 223
s 15, 269
s 19, 101, 231, 233, 237, 279
s 20, 197-98, 231, 233
s 21, 217, 233
s 28, 190
s 43, 255-57
s 45, 219
s 57, 202, 243-46
s 59, 219
s 62, 258
s 63, 231, 293
s 64, 258
ss 75-140, 51
s 123, 219

Labour Relations Act 1987

s 1, 33
ss 3-7, 14
s 6, 15
s 56, 222
s 57, 14, 222
s 61-66, 25 n.44, 34
s 71, 25 n.44
s 82, 44
s 83, 44
ss 132-34, 14, 16
s 147, 14, 34
s 160, 14
s 170, 15
s 196, 14

National Labor Relations Act (US)

s 7, 29 USC s 157, 44, 47
s 8(a)(3), 29 USC s 158(a)(3), 44
s 9(a), 29 USC s 159(a), 44
s 9(b), 29 USC s 159(b), 47

Cases Cited

Adams v. Alliance Textiles (NZ), Ltd, [1992] 1 ERNZ 982, 197, 198-200, 202-03, 223, 243-44
Airline Pilots v. Mt. Cook, [1992] 3 ERNZ 355, 219
Airways Corp. of N.Z. Ltd. v. NZ Air Line Pilots Assoc. IUOW, Inc. [1996] 1 ERNZ 126, 199
Beazley v. City of Auckland, [1992] 2 ERNZ 716, 254
Caledonian Cleaners & Caterers Ltd v. Hetariki, [1994] 2 ERNZ 400, 199
Capital Coast see NZ Medical Laboratories
Eketone v. Alliance Textiles (NZ) Ltd, [1993] 2 ERNZ 783 (Ct. App.), 202-03, 211 n.19
Grant v. Superstrike Bowling Centres Ltd., [1992] 1 ERNZ 727, 253
Hawtin v. Skellerup Industrial, Ltd., [1992] 2 ERNZ 500, 263, 281
Hyndman v. Air New Zealand Ltd., [1992] 1 ERNZ 820, 259-60
IHC see Paul
James v. James, [1991] 3 ERNZ 547 (Empl. Trib.)
Medo Photo Supply Corp. V. N.L.R.B., 321 U.S. 678 (1944)
Mineworkers Union of NZ Inc v. Dunollie Coal Mines Ltd, [1994] 1 ERNZ 78, 264
National Distribution Union Inc v. Foodstuffs (Auckland) Inc, [1994] 1 ERNZ 653, 222-23
NZ Air Line Pilots Assn IUOW v. Air New Zealand Ltd., [1992] 1 ERNZ 880, 219
NZ Dairy Food and Textile Workers' Union v. Cavalier Bremworth, Ltd., [1991] 2 ERNZ 519-259
NZ Dairy Workers Inc. v. Hautapu Whey Transport Ltd., [1994] 2 ERNZ 549, 270-71, 287-88
NZ Fire Service Comm'n v. Ivamy, [1996] 1 ERNZ 85, 211
NZ Meat Processors, Packers, Preservers, Freezing Works and Related Trades Industrial Union of Workers v. Richmond, Ltd., [1991] 3 ERNZ 294; [1992] 3 ERNZ 643, 207-08
NZ Medical Laboratory Workers Union Inc v. Capital Coast Health Ltd., [1994] 2 ERNZ 93-199
NZ Merchant Service Guild IUOW; New Zealand Seafarers Union v. New Zealand Rail Ltd., [1994] 1 ERNZ 482, 204
NZ Merchant Service Guild Industrial Union of Workers, Inc. v. NZ Rail, Ltd., [1991] 2 ERNZ 587, 255
NZ Nurses Union v. Argyle Hospital Ltd., [1992] 2 ERNZ 314, 344 (Empl. Trib.), 223
NZ Public Service Association v. Design Power, [1992] 1 ERNZ 669, 208-09
New Zealand Resident Doctors Association v. Otago Area Health Board, [1991] 1 ERNZ 1206, 254

Northern Distribution Union (Inc.) v. 3 Guys Ltd, [1992] 3 ERNZ 903, 194, 219, 255, 263
Northern Local Government Officers Union, Inc. v. Auckland City, [1992] 1 ERNZ 1109, 253, 254, 255
O'Malley v. Vision Aluminium Ltd (I), [1992] 2 ERNZ 368, 262
O'Malley v. Vision Aluminium Ltd (II), [1992] 2 ERNZ 660, 262
Paul v. New Zealand Society for the Intellectually Handicapped (IHC), [1992] 1 ERNZ 65, 259-62
Petricevich v. Transportation Auckland Corporation Ltd., [1992] 3 ERNZ 807, 262
Prendergast v. Associated Stevedores Ltd., [1992] 1 ERNZ 737, 219, 254-55
Prendergast v. Associated Stevedores Ltd., [1991] 2 ERNZ 728, 258-59
United Food and Chemical Workers Union of New Zealand v. Talley, [1992] 3 ERNZ 423, 263
Witehira v. Presbyterian Support Services (Northern), [1994] 1 ERNZ 578, 264

Index

Action on Benefit Cuts (Wairarapa), 140
Administrative and General Union, 76
adversarialism, 51-54, 77, 189, 295
Air New Zealand, 172, 173, 277
Amalgamated Workers Union of New
    Zealand, 225
Anderton, Jim, 270
arbitration of awards, 34, 64 see also
    award system
Association of Salaried Medical
    Specialists
  opposition to ECA, 146
Auckland Employers Association, 31, 53
Auckland Retail Grocers Association,
    220-21
Australia, 167, 175, 186, 234, 237
  award system in, 14
  influence of ECA on, 3-4, 168, 237
Australian workplace reform, 70
award system, 13-23, 48-50
  advantages of, 15, 18, 35, 48, 92, 189,
    225
  campaign against, 26-56
  criticisms of, 17, 33-35, 39-56
  disadvantages of, 15-16, 18, 20-21
  employer support for, 18, 32-33
  level playing field, 15, 48, 49

bargaining, 175-79, 186-92, 194-210 see
    also bargaining impasses,
    collective employment contracts,
    individual employment contracts
  actual, 93
  authorisations see bargaining
    representatives
  collective, 231-41
  NZBR-NZEF opposition to, 43
  concessionary 120, 122
  employer obligation to, 46, 102, 177,
    197, 309
  impact of ECA on, 118-31, 194, 231-
    41, 287-99
  individual, 41, 46, 89-90, 231-41
  lack of, 169, 172-73, 176-77, 178,
    179, 187, 191, 194, 197, 214,
    224, 235, 236, 237-38, 246, 261,
    263, 311

  procedurally complex, 209-10, 270,
    276, 308-09
  ratification forms, 205-06
  subjects of, 68-69, 176
  under LRA, 18-19, 35, 68-69
  unilateral action, 172, 195, 238, 254-
    55
  employer preference for, 254
bargaining impasses, 101, 252-64, 310-
    11 see also partial lockouts,
    sanctity of contract
  NZEF proposal on, 256
bargaining representatives, 194-210
  accountants as, 177-78, 188, 299
  authorisation of, 97-98
  bypassing, 194, 199, 200, 202
  competition among, 279-83
  consultants as, 188, 215-16, 280, 296-
    99
  direct dealing, 194, 199, 207-8
  employer choice of, 200, 215-16, 288,
    295-96, 308
  harmful to bargaining, 203-10, 238
  harmful to freedom of choice, 203,
    204, 270-23
  lawyers as, 188, 280, 296-99
  pressure on workers to change, 102,
    172-73, 176, 190, 202-3, 216,
    308
  recognition of, 97, 194, 195-96, 216-
    17, 269-70, 309
  self, 187, 296-99
  staff associations as, 281
  unions as, 178-79, 187
  unrelated to bargaining, 196, 224
  unrelated to union membership, 270
  voluntary choice of, 45-48, 63, 64,
    189, 308-09
Barker, Rick, 30-31, 66-68, 94-95, 108,
    119, 125-26, 147, 197, 238, 310,
    311-12 see also Service Workers
    Federation of Aotearoa, Service
    Workers Union of Aotearoa
Bell, Paul, 95, 117
benefits
  as causing unemployment, 107
  cuts, 89, 106-07, 163 n.59

320 WORKING FREE

standdown period, 107
The Benefits of Bargaining Reform, 93-94
"Bill Birch Bares All" poster, 143
Birch, Bill, 88-89, 90, 97, 99, 104, 129, 130, 145, 147, 152, 172, 174, 253, 274, 291
Bishop, Sandra, 75
blanket clauses, 14, 64
Bolger, Jim, 128
boycotts, 220-21
Bradford, Max, 26-27, 152, 153, 156, 293
Bradford statistic, 162-63 n.31
Bray, Ian, 305
Briefing to the Incoming Government, 88-93
  Department of Labour 1990, 89-92
  Treasury 1990, 92-93
Brook, Penelope, 41, 50, 243, 267, 272
Burdon, Philip, 155-56

Campbell, Rob, 215-16, 274, 296, 297
Canada
  interest in ECA, 3
Canterbury Manufacturers Association, 291
Carroll, Peter, 53, 273-74
Carter Holt Harvey, 273
Centre for Independent Studies, 30
Clark, Helen, 35, 81, 154-55, 273
Clarke, Graeme, 78-79, 139 *see also* Manufacturing and Construction Workers Union
Clerical Workers Union *see* New Zealand Clerical Workers Union
Cliffe, Bruce, 159, 160
collective employment contracts (CECs), 178, 186-87, 197, 208-09 *see also* individual employment contracts
  as distinguished from IECs, 231-41, 262
  individual signatures to, 98, 232, 237
  unrelated to form of bargaining, 231-41
collectivity, 267-283, 293 *see also* schism
  legal support for worker, 202, 218, 231-41, 267-70
  legal support for employer, 218, 245-46, 267-70
common law, 50-51, 99, 103 *see also* contract law, freedom of contract
communication, 179-81 *see also* labour–management cooperation
Communication and Energy Workers Union (CEWU), 282
Communist Party
  opposition to ECA, 143
Compact, 81
COMPASS (Commercial, Professional, Administrative, Secretarial Staff Union of New Zealand), 74, 75 *see also* New Zealand Clerical Workers Union
  amalgamation with Service Workers Union, 74
compulsory unionism, 25 n.44, 34, 41-45 *see also* award system
  union dependence upon, 15, 74, 156-57
  member views on, 44
contract law, 50-51, 102-4, 253, 255 *see also* common law, freedom of contract, sanctity of contract
  as promoting conflict, 103
  relational contracts, 102-3, 223-24, 253, 254, 257-58, 309
  corporations distinguished from persons, 267-70, 271, 305-6
Council of Christian Social Services, 171
Council of Trade Unions *see* New Zealand Council of Trade Unions
Countrywide Bank, 179
Court of Appeal, 199, 202-03
Cowan, M. J., 208
Customs Officers Association, 282
Cyclemakers, 178

Dairy Industry Employers Association, 287-88
Dairy Workers Union, 270-71
Dalziel, Lianne, 160-61
Dan Long Library 116
data, problems with
  differing perceptions, 180-81
  incomplete, 174, 240
  lack of data collection, 173-74, 312-13
  misuse of data, 168, 310
  opinion surveys in place of data, 168, 291
  unconventional measurements used, 168
databases
  NZEF 116
  Dan Long Library 116
  Harbridge, 174
  Teesdale-Meuli 116
  Wellington Regional Employers Association, 116-17
Deane, Rod, 28, 29, 30, 208

de Bres, Joris, 196-97, 206, 244, 269, 274, 275-76, 280-81 *see also* Public Service Association
Deeks, John, 91
Deka, 215, 216-17
democracy, 55-56, 77, 95-96, 144, 153, 274-76, 307-08
deregulation, 33-34, 52
Design Power, 208-09
direct dealing, 46-48 *see also* bargaining representative
Distribution Workers Unions
    bargaining, 121-23, 214-26, 277, 292-93
    changes in members, 188, 214-15, 282
    dependence on award structures, 121-22
    opposition to ECA, 146
    structure of, 133 n.29
Douglas, Ken, 81-82, 118, 147, 149, 273, 298
Douglas, Roger, 3, 4, 29
drugs, 179
dues, union, 25 n.44, 34, 41-45 *see also* compulsory unionism
    employer views on, 41-42
    members views on, 44
    reduced under ECA, 68
duress, 243-46

Easton, Brian, 91-92
Economic and Social Initiative (Dec. 1990), 106-7
economy, 88, 167-72
elections
    1990, 62-82, 88
    1993, 94
Electricorp, 28, 29, 131, 198, 208
employers
    not consulted on ECB, 104
    opposition to ECB, 153
    small employers, 32, 48, 49,172, 189, 190, 239
    views as to NZBR, 31-32
    views of unions, 21-22, 121-22, 230, 234, 238-39
    views of workplace, 180-81
Employers Federation *see* New Zealand Employers Federation
Employment Contracts Act (ECA)
    anti-union law, 5, 191-92
    campaign for, 26-56
    effect on economy, 155, 156, 157-58, 161, 167-72
    impact on bargaining, 175-79, 186-299
    impact on employers, 160, 167-81, 190-91
    impact on unions, 64, 153, 154, 159-60, 186-299
    impact on workers, 156-57, 158, 160-61, 170, 172-75
    international views of, 3-4, 104, 154, 201, 202
    lack of enforcement mechanisms, 160-61
    role of court, 198
    youth rates, 175
Employment Contracts Bill (ECB)
    anticipated impact on wages, 90
    Cabinet meetings on, 101, 104
    changes to, 104, 152-54
    drafting, 94-110
    employer concerns about, 120-21
    failure to consult on, 96, 104
    impact on negotiations 118-31
    introduction into Parliament 118
    debated, 96-97, 152-61
    union reactions to 117-31, 136-49
    Labour Department views on, 99-100 *see also* Stockdill, Ralph
    problems with drafting
        bargaining agent recognition, 97, 102
        bargaining impasses, 101-2
        court, 98-99, 105
        duty to bargain, 102
        for employers, 98, 106
        inconsistencies, 97-98, 98-99, 101-2, 105
        instability, 97-98, 105
        lockouts, 97
        multiple bargaining agents, 106
        representation, 97, 102, 105
        schism, 106
        second-tier bargaining, 98
        strikes, 97
        training, 106
        unmanageable, 98
    protests against *see* general strike
    Treasury views on, 89-92, 99, 100-01
Employment Court, 51, 105, 153, 197
    impact of decisions, 197, 199-200, 207-08, 209-10, 247, 252-64
    procedure, 219-20
Employment Relations Act (proposed), 64
Employment Tribunal, 51, 153
    procedure, 219-20

Engineering Union *see* New Zealand Amalgamated Engineering and Related Trades Industrial Union of Workers
enterprise bargaining, 16-17, 32-33, 34, 45-46, 48-50, 63, 116
Epstein, Richard, 41, 243

Farmers, 215, 217, 219-20, 298
Federated Farmers, 128-29
Fergusson, Lindsay, 28, 48
Finance Bill, 137
Finance, Minister of
 Douglas, Roger, 29-31
 Richardson, Ruth, 72, 88, 99, 108-9, 161, 170
Finland
 interest in the ECA, 4
FinSec, 282
Fitzgerald, Gavin, 176
flexibility, 173, 220, 225, 235-36, 239, 291
food banks, 171-72
Foodtown, 220
Freedom at Work, 41
freedom of association, 46, 195-96, 198, 203
 limited by authorisation requirement, 203, 271-80
freedom of choice, 47, 63, 64, 105, 189, 194-96, 201, 267-83
 conflict with collectivity, 218, 308 *see also* schism
 conflict between employers and workers, 195-96, 225, 254
 limited by authorisation requirement, 203, 204
freedom of contract, 34, 90, 99
 inequality of bargaining power, 195, 201, 231-32, 244, 246, 260, 267-70, 275, 299, 309, 311
freedom of market, 52, 94, 98-99, 198
 conflict with impasses, 252, 257
 worker competition for jobs, 47, 108-9, 137, 233-34, 235-36, 254, 257
Freeman, Richard, 276
French, Murray, 17, 71, 123, 177, 253

Gay, Maxine, 74-75, 76, 81, 306
Geare, Alan, 13-14, 109-10
general strike, 136-49
 CTU refusal to support, 140-49
  impact on others, 141-42, 144, 145, 148
  reasons for, 136-37, 149
 day of action (4 April), 145, 146
 Engineering Union influence, 142-44
 impact on ECA, 139, 145, 146, 147, 149, 152
 national day of activity (30 April), 147
 relation to union schism, 139-40, 148-49, 281
 union allies, 137-38, 140-41
 week of action, 146-47, 152
 week of protests announced, 141
 wildcat strikes, 146
Germany
 interest in ECA, 4
Gibbs, Alan, 28, 30
Gingrich, Newt, 4
Grocery and Supermarket Award, 122
Growth Agreement, 81, 160

Hancock Hotel, 242
Hanson, Mike, 297, 298
Harbour Workers Union, 81
 opposition to ECA, 146
Harbridge, Raymond, 174, 186, 233-34
Harris, Harry, 298-99
Harvey, Owen , 194
Haultain, Robyn, 81-82, 140-41, 199, 222, 243-44
Haworth, Nigel, 15, 53
Herbert, Patricia, 63
Hospitality Association, 246-47, 287
Hotel Association, 123, 125, 305
hotel industry, 237-38, 239-40, 242, 247
 award, 120
 union decline in, 188
Householders' Pamphlet, 145, 152
Hughes, John, 253
hunger, 171-72
hunger strike, 221
Hutton, Athol, 48, 208

ideology, 28-35, 91, 94, 99-100, 103, 243
 appropriateness for labour law, 191-92, 195, 198, 207, 223-24, 245-46, 254, 257-58, 298-99, 307, 308, 312
 embodied in ECA, 191-92, 196, 244-45, 252, 258, 274
 instrumental use of, 103-04
individual employment contracts (IECs), 42, 46, 63, 186-87, 208, 253 *see also* collective employment contracts
 as distinguished from CECs, 231-41, 262

INDEX 323

favoured by ECA, 231-32
  not individualised contracts, 236
  not required to be written, 237
  percentage on, 232
  unrelated to form of bargaining, 231-41
Industrial Conciliation and Arbitration Act, 1894 *see also* award system
  as model for labour relations, 13-23
  compared with Wagner Act, 14-15
  enactment, 13-14
interest arbitration, 34
  definition of, 133 n.33
International Labour Organisation (ILO), 203-04, 219
  conventions, 137, 154
  criticisms of ECA, 104, 154, 201, 202
International Monetary Fund (IMF), 5, 168

Japan
  as model for labour law reform, 39, 42, 46, 49, 159
  interest in ECA, 4
"Jennicide", 108
Jones, Alan, 272

K Mart, 217, 219-20
Kelly, Pat, 141
Kentucky Fried Chicken, 241
Kerr, Roger, 28, 31, 54, 167, 168, 179, 208, 291, 296
Kidd, Doug, 104
Kimble, Paul, 19, 216
Knowles, Anne, 43-44, 260, 283

labour costs, 168
Labour Court, 50-51
  opposition to, 105
Labour, Department of
  Ministerial Brief, October 1990, 92-93
  quarterly reports, 174
    disclaimer as to accuracy, 174
Labour Government (1984-1990) *see also* Rogernomics
  links to NZBR, 29-30
  links to Treasury, 30
  labour–management cooperation, 51-54, 55-56, 93, 167, 216, 291
Labour, Minister of, 34 *see also* Birch, Bill; Clark, Helen; Kidd, Doug
  criticisms of unions, 34
  criticisms of employers, 34
Labour Party
  loss of support for, 62, 81

  rift with unions, 81
Labour Notes
Labour Relations Act, 1987
  bargaining under, 189
  campaign to eliminate, 39-56, 129
  compared with other systems, 155, 156, 157-58, 159 *see also* Japan, United Kingdom, United States
  citing out employers, 16-17
  description of, 14-15, 25 n.44
  effect on industrial relations, 18, 34-35, 156
  enactment of, 26-27, 33-35
  increased scope of bargaining, 68-69
Labour Relations Bill, 33
Labour Select Committee on the ECA
  1990, 152, 153, 156
  1993, 172-73
  Majority Report, 5-6, 174-75, 176-77, 179, 190
  Minority Report, 169, 174, 176
  Options Paper
    submissions to, 153, 204, 208
Lange, David, 62
Larkins, Dolly, 76
Larkins, George, 76
level playing field, 15, 48, 49, 201, 230, 294, 310
Lion Nathan, 242
Loader, Hel, 69-70, 71-72, 124-25, 142-43, 235-36 290, 293, 294-95
Local Government Officers Association
  opposition to ECA, 146
lockouts, 204, 209 *see also* partial lockouts

McAndrew, Ian, 187
McDonald's, 67-68, 241, 274
Macfie, Rebecca, 260-61
McKenzie, C. J., 97
management consultants, 188, 296-99
Manufacturing and Construction Workers Union (MCWU), 77-79, 80
  affiliates, 76-77
  Charter
  conflict with Engineering Union, 77, 281
  loan fund, 78-79
  opposition to ECA, 138, 144
Maori, 73, 107, 282
Marks, George, 234-35
Marshall, Steve, 115, 167, 188, 189 *see also* New Zealand Employers Association

Martin, D. J., 97
Metal, 70
Metal Trades Award, 123, 293-94
Metal Trades Industry Association (Australian), 289
minimum conditions, 153-54, 156, 172
minimum wage, 48, 90, 170
 cuts, 107-08
minority workers, 65, 107, 162 n.23, 188, 189, 230
 union treatment of, 70
Moore, Mike, 62, 97, 129
Morel, Leon, 77
Morgan, Dave, 128, 139 *see also* Seafarers Union
Motor Trades Award, 123-24, 293, 294
Mulgan, Richard, 27
multi-employer contracting, 14-15, 48-50, 124, 186, 200, 242, 287-99
 advantages of, 217, 225, 287, 294
 impact on NZEF, 296
 NZEF opposed to, 287, 294
 nonunion industry agreements, 287
Myers, Douglas, 28, 30, 47, 186, 217, 242

National Government (1990–)
 economic package (1990)
 fears about ECA, 131
National Labor Relations Act (NLRA or Wagner Act), 14
 contract bar, 47
 election bar, 47
 union dues under, 44
National Party
 1990 election, 22-23, 62-63, 163 n.59
 1990 Manifesto, 62-63, 128
 claims about, 63-64, 154
National Union of Public Employees (NUPE), 281-82
Netherlands
 interest in ECA, 4
new employees clause, 220
new hires, 237
 terms, 233-34, 241-42
New World Supermarkets, 205
New Zealand Amalgamated Engineering and Related Trades Industrial Union of Workers, 68-72, 81, 200, 281, 282
 bargaining under ECB, 123-24
 bargaining under ECA, 234-37, 288-99
 communications with members, 70, 234
 critics of, 292
 foreign influences on, 68-69, 70-71
 internal reforms, 69-70
 membership, 292
 opposition to ECA, 142-44
 preparations for change, 71, 288
 stewards, 69-70, 234
New Zealand Business Roundtable, 26-28, 197
 anti-democratic views, 52-54, 56
 anti-union views, 42-44, 54-55, 168, 188, 208, 217
 campaign to eliminate LRA, 39-56
  lack of response to, 40, 41
  tone of, 39, 48-49
 criticism of Employment Court, 255-56, 312
 criticism of Labour Court, 50-51
 criticism of LRA, 26-35, 39-56
 ideology, 27-35
 links to Labour Party, 29-30
 links to National Party, 29
 links to Treasury, 89-90
 links to NZEF, 29
 quality of research, 35, 40-41, 44-45, 49-50
 views on wages, 47
New Zealand Clerical Workers Union (NZCWU), 74-77, 156
 dependence on compulsory unionism, 74
 opposition to ECA, 138
 Submission to the Labour Select Committee on the Employment Contracts Bill (Feb. 1991)
New Zealand Communist Party, 80
New Zealand Council of Trade Unions (CTU), 79-82, 206-07, 280 *see also* Ken Douglas, general strike
 analyses of ECB, 137
 not consulted on ECA, 104
 policy on union structure, 75, 79-80
 reactions to ECB, 136
 relationship with Labour Party, 80-81
 views on NZBR, 31
New Zealand Educational Institute Te Riu Roa, 72-74, 293 *see also* Noonan, Rosslyn
 Miro Maori, 72
 opposition to ECA, 147
New Zealand Employers Federation, 27, 123, 197
 anti-democratic views, 52-54, 56
 anti-union views, 42-44, 54-55, 93-94, 188, 253, 272

bargaining, 175-76, 194
campaign to eliminate LRA, 39-56
criticism of Employment Court, 255-56, 312
criticism of Labour Court, 50-51
criticism of LRA, 17, 26-35
database, 116
   inconsistency with views, 116
effects of ECA, 242-43
intolerance of dissent, 52-54
labour-management cooperation, 55-56, 93, 115
links to NZBR, 31
reaction to ECA, 115-17
restructuring, 115-17
views on Growth Agreement, 81
New Zealand Nurses Association, 200 *see also* nurses
   injunction against, 142
   negotiations, 290, 310
   opposition to ECA, 141-42, 146, 147
New Zealand Nurses Organisation, 293
New Zealand Nurses Union, 221
New Zealand Planning Council, 91
New Zealand Post Primary Teachers Association, 293
New Zealand Rail, 128-29, 204
New Zealand Trade Union Federation, 126
Nissan Way, 71
Noakes, Barry, 282
Noonan, Rosslyn, 64, 72-73 139, 205-6
   see also New Zealand Educational Institute, Te Riu Roa
no-pay jobs, 6-7, 170-71, 173, 174, 176
Northern Clerical Workers Union, 74
   restructured as COMPASS, 75
Northern Distribution Workers Federation
   opposition to ECA, 146
nurses, 179

Organisation for Economic Cooperation and Development (OECD), 5, 45, 155, 168
organising model of unionism, 66-67, 231 *see also* servicing model of unionism
Otautahi Coalition Against Benefit Cut, 138
Oxenbridge, Sarah, 226

Pacific Steel, 237, 295
Pak'n Save, 221
Palmer, Geoffrey, 62

Parliament *see also* Labour Select Committee on the ECA
debates on ECA, 96-97, 152-61
leaving decisions to courts, 252, 254, 312
partial lockouts, 101-2, 200, 208, 258-64, 298
   distinguished from breach of contract, 258-59
   effects of, 261, 264
   reversal of, 264
part-time workers, 65, 174, 215, 230
party status, 217-20
   NZEF opposition to for unions, 219
paycuts, 137, 186, 214, 239-41, 242, 288-91
Payne, Donna, 141, 200
penal rates, 170, 172-75, 215, 220, 221, 235, 239-42, 287, 290
Peoples Alliance, 138-39
perceptions
   differences in, 180-81
personal grievances, 153, 200, 239
   increases in, 177
picketing, 220-21
Piper, Sue, 130 *see also* Public Service Association
Pizza Hut, 241
polls *see also* data
   by CTU, 149, 179-80
   by NZBR, 167
   by NZEF, 5
   problems with, 168-70
poverty, 171
power, 55-56, 118, 173, 177, 179, 180, 187-88, 195, 207-8, 233-34, 245, 246, 253, 299, 309
   impact of law on, 245-46, 260, 263, 267-70, 275-76, 299, 309
Prebble, Richard, 129
Pringle, Alistair, 226
productivity, 167, 168, 235
   bargaining on, 170, 288, 290-91
   measuring, 168-69
profits, 290
Progressive Enterprises, 195
Public Service Association (PSA) 63, 270-71, 277-83
   database, 116
   negotiations under ECB, 129-31
   negotiations under ECA, 208-09, 244, 277-83
   opposition to ECA, 143, 146, 147
   schisms, 148, 280-283
   voluntary unionism, 130

Quigg, Michael, 261-62

Radio New Zealand, 131
Railway Trades Association
  opposition to ECA, 146
Reid, Robert, 76
Reserve Bank, 28, 29, 30
Restaurants Award, 67-68
retail industry
  anti-unionism in, 121-22, 176
  impact of deregulation, 122, 215
  negotiations, 121-23, 179, 214
  skills, 289-90
  union decline in, 188, 214-26
Retail Nonfood Award, 122-23
Revell, Ian, 97
Rogernomics, 29-31, 33-35
  impact of, 30-31, 62, 88
Rogers, Joel, 276
Richardson, Ruth, 72, 108-9, 175 *see also* Finance, Minister of
Rudd, Watts & Stone, 260

Salvation Army, 242
sanctity of contract, 255-57
schism, 106, 139-40, 148-49, 225, 267-83, 307 *see also* collectivity
Seafarers Union
  bargaining under ECB, 126-29
  corner system, 126-27
  NZBR / NZEF views on, 126-27
  opposition to ECA, 146
  strikes, 127-29
  target of attack, 128, 129, 133 n.44
second-tier bargaining, 98
Service Station Agreement, 123-24, 200-1, 293, 295
Service Workers Federation of Aotearoa (SWF), 65-68
  decline under ECA, 230
  negotiations under ECB, 125-26
  opposition to ECA, 138, 141, 146
Service Workers Union of Aotearoa (SWU), 65, 68, 230-47, 292
  decline under ECA, 188, 189, 246-47
servicing model of unionism, 66-67 *see also* organizing model of unionism
  resemblance to NZBR-NZEF proposals, 41-42, 45, 67, 267, 272, 283
sharemarket crash, 33, 62, 68
Shaw, Coral, 173
Sheppard, Judy, 238
Shipley, Jenny, 107, 108
Shirtcliffe, Peter, 52

skills, 289 *see also* training
standdown period, 107
Stagecoach, 172
Steele, David, 40
Stockdill, Ralph, 97, 101, 105, 194, 199, 200
Street, Maryan, 107
strikes, 179, 293, 304-5 *see also* general strike
Sutherland, Larry, 156-57
Swain, Paul, 158-59
Sweden
  interest in ECA, 4

take-it-or-leave-it contracts, 169, 172-73, 176-77, 236, 238, 311
Tearooms and Restaurants Award, 125, 242
Teesdale-Meuli, 116, 297
Telecom NZ, 273
Tennet, Elizabeth, 156, 159
Three Guys, 220
Tiwai Point, 234-37
  impact elsewhere, 237
Toogood, Christopher, 232
training, 49, 92, 106, 168, 180, 241, 288-91
trust, 167
Treasury
  Briefing to the Incoming Government (1990), 89-92
  links to NZBR/ NZEF, 88-89
  links to Labour Party, 29-31, 33-35
Trotter, Ronald, 28, 30, 45, 50
turnover, 180

Unemployed Workers League, 143
unemployment, 88, 109, 120, 170, 171, 234-35
union democracy, 77-78
union delegates, 69-70
union density, 6, 19, 22, 186, 188, 214, 230, 246, 306, 313
  court decisions affecting, 197, 199-200, 207-08, 209-10, 247, 252-64
  explanations for decline, 188-92
  laws impact on, 188, 189, 192
  union contribution to, 190, 223, 234
union membership, 44, 186-92, 270-71, 280
union organizing
  difficult to organize members, 65, 73-74, 74-75, 188-89 *see also* minorities, women

freelance, 76-77
union stewards, 69-70, 234
unions
  changes before ECA, 64-82
  competition among, 45-46, 55, 119
    see also schism
  dues, 25 n.44, 34, 41-45
  employer-created, 178, 191, 200, 215-16, 288, 295-96, 308
  employer views of, 21-22, 42-44
  member services, 77-79, 278-79
  nature of, 272
  negotiations under LRA -18-21
  not consulted on ECA, 104
  opposition to ECA see general strike
  representation under LRA, 15-23
  representation under ECA see bargaining representatives see also schism
  worker views of, 21-22, 44
United Kingdom
  as model, 47, 68, 159, 220-21
  interest in ECA, 4
United States
  as model, 39, 42, 44, 47-48, 49, 66, 68, 220-21
  interest in New Zealand, 4
unskilled workers, 65, 119, 170, 171, 189, 230, 291
Upton, Simon, 96

vermin, 171
voluntary unionism, 41-45, 63
voluntary representation 45-48

wages
  impact of LRA on, 20-21
  impact of ECA on, 6-7, 89, 107-8, 167, 169-70, 170, 173-74, 175
Wagner Act see National Labor Relations Act
Wearing, Ian, 230
Welfare, Minister of
  Shipley, Jenny, 107, 108
Wevers, Francis, 19-20, 196, 297, 299
Wellington City Transit (WCT), 172
Wellington Regional Employers Association, 17, 71, 95, 116-17, 297
Whitcoulls, 215-16
Williamson, Maurice, 157-58
Wilson, Margaret, 21
Windows on Poverty, 171
women
  union treatment of, 70, 73
  workers, 65, 162 n.23, 188-89, 230
Woolworths, 215
workers
  not consulted on ECA, 104
  views on workplace, 180
  views of unions, 21-22, 44
workplace access, 222-24
workplace reform, 77, 288, 290, 292
World Bank, 5, 28-29

youth, 188-89, 215, 224-25
  pay, 47, 107, 175, 221